# Living Hope

A Mission 119 Guide to First Peter

Hutson Smelley

Living Hope

Copyright © 2019 Hutson Smelley

All rights reserved solely by the author. No part of this book may be reproduced in any form without the permission of the author except that, for educational purposes, permission is granted to copy and distribute in a classroom or church setting an excerpt not exceeding one chapter.

Unless otherwise indicated, Bible quotations are taken from The King James Bible.

ISBN: 978-0-9861336-3-3

www.proclaimtheword.me

# Other Works by the Author

Better with Jesus: A Mission 119 Guide to Hebrews (2015)

Love, Romance and Intimacy: A Mission 119 Guide to the Song of Solomon (2016)

Chasing Jonah: A Mission 119 Guide to Jonah (2018)

Deconstructing Calvinism - Third Edition (2019)

Looking Forward, Living Now: A Mission 119 Guide to Zechariah (2020)

# Table of Contents

| | | |
|---|---|---|
| | Preface to the Mission 119 Series | 1 |
| 1 | Introductory Matters | 4 |
| 2 | The Living Hope<br>1 Peter 1:1-12 | 46 |
| 3 | The Future Salvation That Changes Us Now - 1 Peter 1:13-25 | 89 |
| 4 | Growing Through God's Enduring Word - 1 Peter 2:1-10 | 116 |
| 5 | Transformation Through Submission<br>1 Peter 2:11-17 | 138 |
| 6 | Transformation on the Job<br>1 Peter 2:18-25 | 168 |
| 7 | Transformation in the Home<br>1 Peter 3:1-7 | 186 |
| 8 | Courageous Suffering<br>1 Peter 3:8-22 | 210 |
| 9 | Out with the Old, in with the New<br>1 Peter 4:1-11 | 252 |
| 10 | Suffering and the Judgment<br>1 Peter 4:12-19 | 276 |
| 11 | The Enemies of Salvation<br>1 Peter 5:1-14 | 296 |
| | Appendix - Excursus on the Jewish Concepts of Inheritance and Rest | 326 |
| | About the Author | 345 |

# Preface to the Mission 119 Series

The psalmist declares, "Thy word is a lamp unto my feet, and a light unto my path." (Psalm 119:105) The Bible is unlike all other books, not only in its grandeur and scope, but because its words are God's Words. The Bible presents to us God's special revelation of Himself, His biased view of history past and future, the reality of who we are, and a picture of all that we can be. Woven within its pages and spilling over is God's redemptive plan for humanity, with Jesus Christ as centerpiece. We do not study the Bible merely to accumulate head knowledge, but with the earnest expectation of knowing God more and drawing nearer to Him. Each page has something for us, sometimes encouraging us, sometimes reproving us, always revealing God, and every jot and tittle a precious morsel for our souls. Against the backdrop of a world encased in darkness, it is the light of truth that pierces through all the deceptions and puts reality in clear focus.

Every generation faces challenges, and the present generation is challenged about truth and whether any absolute truths are knowable. Like all the ones before it, this generation needs to hear God's Word taught boldly, with clarity, without apology, in grace and love. And this generation needs to be reminded by those who teach that the Bible was written for everyone. God has spoken with clarity so that all believers who come to the Bible yielded to what God has for them can know its truths as they grow and mature. The aim here is to strike the proper balance between too little detail to elucidate the message and superfluous detail that obscures, so that this volume is accessible and profitable to laypersons and teachers alike who seek to understand the author's original intended meaning and the continuing relevance of that message today. With this in mind, the Mission 119 Series is designed to provide guidance for the understanding and exposition of books of the Bible with depth and a commitment to a plain sense interpretation tethered first and foremost to the context and flow of argument of the book under consideration.

A common sentiment today is that people need only "relevant" teaching from the Bible, which suggests portions of the Bible are irrelevant, and too often means they want three steps to raising teens in place of the perfections of God, five steps to a better marriage in place of how a believer matures and walks in the Spirit, how to find blessing and wealth in place of God's demand for holy living, and so forth. May I say that every word God ever spoke was relevant and remains so today. Those who would step forward as teachers of the Word of God only do people a disservice by trying to conform God's Holy Word to the world's bankrupt self-help counterfeits when what is most needful today is the plain teaching of the whole Bible as it is. Believers engaged in the Word and yielding to the Holy Spirit will find the most practical of wisdom and grace enablement for all areas of their lives as they draw near to God in the transformative experience of knowing Him more and more. May I also suggest that while some people will flee teaching that has depth and conviction, far more people in churches today are thirsty for more depth in the teaching. They want to see that the Bible is not clichés and recycled sugar sticks but truly a light from God unto their paths. In this vein, it is my prayer that this volume of the Mission 119 Series will be a useful guide for teachers of the Bible and a special blessing for students of the Word who aspire to know God more.

# Chapter 1

# Introductory Matters

First Peter is first and foremost a book of hope and victory. As we will see in the notes to follow, the prologue in 1 Peter 1:3-9 coupled with the closing summary in 1 Peter 5:10-11 provide the best interpretive compass for the encouragement and exhortation that awaits the reader of Peter's epistle. Peter knew persecution first hand and so he understood the difficulties that faced his audience. Yet his perspective on the Christian life that he sought to convey to his readers was in all circumstances tethered to that "lively hope...to an inheritance incorruptible, and undefiled, and that fadeth not away, reserved in heaven for you...unto salvation ready to be revealed in the last time." (1 Peter 1:3-5) Indeed, "[i]t is seen throughout the Epistle that his eye is firmly fixed upon the coming of Christ and the glory in store for believers."[1] Peter wanted his readers to be so consumed by this eschatologically focused "lively hope" that their experience of life would be radically reoriented in every sphere such that their

---

[1] John Peter Lange et al., *A Commentary on the Holy Scriptures: 1 Peter* (Bellingham, WA: Logos Bible Software, 2008), 6.

*Introductory Matters*

walk would both testify of God's right to rule and result in their appropriation of their share of Jesus' inheritance. Within the few pages that comprise First Peter is found a practical edge as sharp as any New Testament writing, beckoning the reader to nothing less than a lifestyle of holiness (1 Peter 1:16: "...Be ye holy; for I am holy") during his or her temporary assignment on this earth representing Jesus.

Unfortunately, the rich theological grandeur of First Peter is too often neglected. The writings of the Apostle Peter are often placed in the shadow of the Apostle Paul's epistles. Yet I hope by these notes to aid the reader's understanding of Peter's great epistle, that its beauty and relevance may be apparent, as well as its unique contribution to the New Testament corpus, and in so doing, that the reader may see that "[t]he significance of 1 Peter is out of proportion to its size."[2] Indeed, as one commentary explained: "This letter touches some of the most controversial and most promising and challenging items in contemporary Christian discourse."[3] Peter's letter "exhibits a wealth of thought, a dignity, a fervour, a humility and love, a believing hope, a readiness for the advent of Christ, in exact harmony with the individuality of the Apostle."[4] One of the older commentaries skillfully articulated the rightful place of First Peter among the New Testament writings:

---

[2] Erland Waltner and J. Daryl Charles, *1-2 Peter, Jude*, Believers Church Bible Commentary (Scottdale, PA: Herald Press, 1999), 17.
[3] Erland Waltner and J. Daryl Charles, *1-2 Peter, Jude*, Believers Church Bible Commentary (Scottdale, PA: Herald Press, 1999), 16.
[4] John Peter Lange et al., *A Commentary on the Holy Scriptures: 1 Peter* (Bellingham, WA: Logos Bible Software, 2008), 6.

To the believer it is one of the most precious parts of Holy Scripture. It is characterized by a depth of conviction, a vivid realization of the spiritual blessings, the living hope, the abiding joy, which spring from a true faith in Christ; by a firm grasp of the necessity of reality in the Christian life, of resolute self-denial and patient obedience; by a deep and true sympathy with suffering Christians; by a steadfast faith in the Lord's atonement and the power and preciousness of his example; by an earnest presentation of the duties of humility, brotherly love, endurance trustfulness, perseverance; by a calm and holy wisdom, worthy of the first of the apostles, worthy of him to whom the Lord had given the significant name of Peter, who "seemed to be a pillar" (Gal. 2:9) of the rising Church.[5]

With these preliminary thoughts in mind, we start with who Peter is.

## The Apostle Peter

The epistle of First Peter begins with the words, "Peter, an apostle of Jesus Christ...." Notwithstanding, many modern scholars dispute that the Apostle Peter wrote First Peter and I will comment on that issue momentarily and argue that there is no persuasive evidence to question Peter's authorship. But assuming the Apostle Peter that

---

[5] H. D. M. Spence-Jones, ed., *1 Peter*, The Pulpit Commentary (London; New York: Funk & Wagnalls Company, 1909), i.

we meet in the Gospels and Acts wrote the epistle, we have a good picture from the Biblical witness of who this man was. To begin with, he is referenced by three different names in the Scripture:

> Peter is known by three different names. His Hebrew name was *Simon* (*Shimon*). It means "hear" or "hearing" and is a variation of the name Simeon – one of Jacob's twelve sons who was born of Leah (Gen. 29:33). Peter's Aramaic name was *Chephus* (*Kaifa*), which means "rock." His Greek name was *Peter* (*Petros*), meaning "stone" or "pebble."[6]

Peter was originally from Bethsaida (John 1:44) on the coast of the Sea of Galilee but by the time of his participation in Jesus' earthly ministry, Peter lived in Capernaum. (Mark 1:29) Peter was the son of Jonas (Matthew 16:17; John 1:42). He and his brother Andrew were disciples of John the Baptist (John 1:42) but upon John's identification of Jesus as the Christ, they followed Jesus. (John 1:41-42) Peter was married (Matthew 8:14) but we know little about his wife. Peter was a fisherman by trade. (Luke 5:4-11) His named was changed from Simon to Cephas or Peter by Jesus. (John 1:42) Of Peter's transformation and role within the Twelve, Fronmüller wrote:

> After sundry meetings and preparations, the Lord attached him to the number of his permanent disciples. The miraculous

---

[6] Arnold G. Fruchtenbaum, *The Messianic Jewish Epistles: Hebrews, James, First Peter, Second Peter, Jude* (Tustin, CA: Ariel Ministries, 2005), 317.

blessing which is recorded in Luke 5:1, etc., and made Peter deeply conscious of his own unworthiness and of our Lord's exaltation and holiness, was the turning point in his career. His call to the Apostolate is narrated in Matt. 4:18–20; and Luke 5:10, 11. In the four catalogues enumerating the twelve apostles, he is invariably named first, Matt. 10:2; Mark 3:16; Luke 6:14; Acts 1:13. His full resignation to the Lord, and his deeper insight of his Divine Sonship, made him not only share with John and James their Master's more intimate friendship (Mark 5:37; Matt. 26:37), but also enjoy a special preference over the rest of the apostles (Matt. 16:18, 19). Every where he appears as first among the apostles, but only as first among equals, placed not *above*, but *on a level with* them. (cf. Matt. 18:18; John 20:21; Luke 8:45; 9:32; John 1:42; 21:15; Acts 1:15; 2:14; 8:14; 10:5; 15:7.) Among the other disciples he was clothed with the dignity of being their spokesman, (Matt 16:16; 26:33; 17:24,) without thereby having a claim to outward superiority, for all believers were to regard each other as brethren and members under their one head, Christ (Matt. 23:8; John 13:14).[7]

Peter was the disciple that we can relate to. On the one hand, he walked on water (Matthew 14:29), but on the

---

[7] John Peter Lange et al., *A Commentary on the Holy Scriptures: 1 Peter* (Bellingham, WA: Logos Bible Software, 2008), 3.

other, he denied Jesus three times during his trial (Matthew 26:69-75; Mark 14:66-72; Luke 22:55-62). He, along with James and John, were the only three disciples at the Mount of Transfiguration (Matthew 17:1-8), but he also fell asleep while Jesus prayed at Gethsemane before his arrest (Matthew 26:40-41; Mark 14:37-38). Peter drew his sword to defend Jesus at his arrest (John 18:10-11) but Satan sought to sift him (Luke 22:31-34) and apparently did as Peter denied Jesus. "When Mary Magdalene first reported the empty tomb, it was Peter, together with John, who went out to investigate and left the tomb in a state of perplexity (Luke 24:12; John 20:2-10)."[8] Peter deserted Jesus after his arrest but was restored in the last chapter of John's Gospel. And in the book of Acts, we see Peter's ministry flourish:

> In the first twelve chapters of the Acts of the Apostles, Peter appears as the chief organ of the Church at Jerusalem. (Acts 1:15; 2:14). He is the spokesman of the other Apostles on the day of Pentecost, and preaches a mighty sermon on repentance, which pierces the hearts of three thousand hearers like a fiery arrow. He multiplies the number of believers both by the working of miracles, and the victorious power of the Gospel. (Chap. 3:4; 5:15; 9:34, 40). He deems it joy to endure the ignominy of Christ; and suffers neither threatenings nor ill treatment to make him falter in confessing the name of Jesus. (Ch. 4:8; 5:29). He joins

---

[8] Arnold G. Fruchtenbaum, *The Messianic Jewish Epistles: Hebrews, James, First Peter, Second Peter, Jude* (Tustin, CA: Ariel Ministries, 2005), 318.

John in carrying the Gospel to Samaria (ch. 8:14), and the coast regions of the Mediterranean. (Ch. 10:23). He is the first Apostle, who, in consequence of a vision with which he was honoured, received Gentiles into communion of the Christian Church. (Ch. 10:34). He defends this measure against the reproaches of the Jewish Christians, and protects the Gentile Christians from the heavy yoke of the Mosaic Law. (Ch. 11:1, etc.; 15:7, etc.) ... After the beheading of James the Apostle, Herod Agrippa cast Peter into prison, whence he was miraculously delivered by an angel. (ch. 12:1). After a brief absence, (ch. 12:17), subsequent to the death of his enemy, he reappears at Jerusalem (ch. 15:7) and declares, with a view to settling the dispute between the Jewish and Gentile Christians, that circumcision and the observance of the ceremonial law ought not to be exacted as necessary to the justification and salvation of believers. This event falls into the year 50 A. D.[9]

The story of Peter's life and ministry becomes more uncertain after Acts 15. There is reference to Peter in 1 Corinthians 9:5, Galatians 2:11-14, and in church tradition and early Christian writings. This author's view is that Jesus' earthly ministry lasted approximately three and a half years culminating in his crucifixion in April, 33 A.D.

---

[9] John Peter Lange et al., *A Commentary on the Holy Scriptures: 1 Peter* (Bellingham, WA: Logos Bible Software, 2008), 4.

If that is accurate, then the following abbreviated timeline from Harold Hoehner is helpful in understanding the chronology of Peter's and Paul's ministries and will aid our consideration of when and from where Peter may have written his epistle:

**April, A.D. 33**
Crucifixion

**Sunday, 24 May, 33**
Pentecost (Acts 2)

**summer 33**
Peter's second sermon and brought before the Sanhedrin (Acts 3:1–4:31)

**33–34**
Death of Ananias and Sapphira (Acts 4:32–5:11)

**34–35**
Peter brought before Sanhedrin (Acts 5:12–42)

**Apr-35**
Stephen martyred (Acts 6:8–7:60)

**summer 35**
Paul's conversion (Acts 9:1–7)

**summer 35–early summer 37**
Paul in Damascus and Arabia (Acts 9:8–25; Gal. 1:16–17)

**summer 37**
Paul in Jerusalem, first visit (Acts 9:26–29)

**autumn 37**
Paul in Tarsus and Syria-Cilicia area (Acts 9:30; Gal 1:21)

**40–41**
Peter ministers to the Gentiles (Acts 10:1–11:18)

**41**
Barnabas sent to Antioch (Acts 11:19–24)

**spring 43**
Paul went to Antioch (Acts 11:25–26)

**spring 44**
Agrippa's persecution, James martyred (Acts 12:1–23)

**autumn 47**
Relief visit, Paul's second visit to Jerusalem (Acts 11:30; Gal. 2:1–10)

**autumn 47–spring 48**
Paul in Antioch (Acts 12:25–13:1)

**April 48–September 49**
First missionary journey (Acts 13–14)

**autumn 49**
Peter at Antioch (Gal 2:11–16)

**autumn 49**
Jerusalem council, Paul's third visit (Acts 15)

**winter 49/50**
Paul in Antioch (Acts 15:33–35)

**April 50–September 52**
Second missionary journey (Acts 15:36–18:22)

**winter 52/53**
Paul's stay at Antioch

**spring 53–May 57**
Third missionary journey (Acts 18:23–21:16)

**February 60–March 62**
Paul's First Roman imprisonment (Acts 28:30)

**spring 62**
James, Lord's brother, Martyred

**62**
Peter goes to Rome

**late summer 62–winter 62/63**
Paul in Macedonia (1 Tim. 1:3)

**spring 63–spring 64**
Paul in Asia Minor

**spring 64–spring 66**
Paul in Spain (Rom. 15:24, 28)

**summer 64**
Christians persecuted, Peter martyred

**early summer 66**
Paul in Crete

**summer–autumn 66**
Paul in Asia Minor (Tit. 1:5)

**autumn 67**
Paul arrested and brought to Rome (2 Tim. 1:8; 2:9)

**spring 68**
Paul's death

**2 September, 70**[10]
Destruction of Jerusalem

What is notable from the timeline is that we have large gaps where the ministry of Peter is not entirely known. In Acts 12:17, after being supernaturally freed from prison, Luke recorded that Peter went to "the house of Mary the mother of John, whose surname was Mark," and from there "he departed, and went into another place." (Acts 12:12, 17) Peter is not mentioned again until Acts 15:7, when he spoke at the Jerusalem Council, and is not mentioned again in the Acts after that. Yet there is good reason to infer that Peter engaged in an active ministry to Jews outside of Israel before ultimately losing his life as a martyr in Rome, as Fronmüller outlined:

> Since, in the subsequent account of the transactions at Jerusalem, recorded in the book of Acts, Peter ceases to be mentioned, we may conclude that his subsequent sphere of labour had called him away from there. His abode at Antioch, and the

---

[10] H. W. Hoehner, "Chronology of the New Testament," ed. D. R. W. Wood et al., *New Bible Dictionary* (Leicester, England; Downers Grove, IL: InterVarsity Press, 1996), 198–199.

incident already mentioned above, belongs to the time from A. D. 52 to 54 (Gal. 2:11–14). It is clear, from 1 Cor. 9:5, that Peter undertook various journeys for the spread of the kingdom of God. According to an ancient tradition in Origen, which originated probably in the title of his first Epistle, Peter is said to have preached the Gospel to the Jews scattered throughout Pontus, Galatia, Cappadocia, Asia Minor, and Bithynia. He appears for some time to have had his sphere of labour in the Parthian empire, since he sends salutations from his co-elected at Babylon (1 Peter 5:13), which is probably not to be understood of Rome, but of Babylon, in Chaldea. Many Jews were dispersed there, and Christianity was early diffused in those regions. According to Dionysius of Corinth, who wrote in the second half of the second century, and according to Irenæus and Eusebius, Peter and Paul are said to have been together at Rome, and to have conjointly founded the Church at that place; Eusebius narrates that the two Apostles had shared a common martyrdom there; Peter was crucified with his head downwards. The fourteenth year of the reign of Nero, from the middle of October, A. D. 67, to the middle of A. D. 68, is mentioned as the year of the Apostle's death.[11]

---

[11] John Peter Lange, Philip Schaff, et al., *A Commentary on the Holy*

## Authorship

The first verse of the epistle claims authorship by "Peter, an apostle of Jesus Christ...." (1 Peter 1:1) For centuries the issue was largely a settled matter, until critical scholars began questioning a number of issues including how an allegedly uneducated fisherman could possibly have produced the work, as Roger Raymer explains:

> Until relatively recent times the authenticity of the epistle's claim to apostolic authorship went unchallenged. Then some modern scholars noted that Peter was considered by Jewish religious leaders as "unschooled" and "ordinary" (Acts 4:13). The superb literary style and sophisticated use of vocabulary in 1 Peter seem to indicate that its author must have been a master of the Greek language. Those who deny Peter's authorship say that such an artistic piece of Greek literature could not possibly have flowed from the pen of a Galilean fisherman.[12]

In determining the likelihood Peter could and did write what we call First Peter, the place to start is with the internal evidence. Beyond the claim in 1 Peter 1:1 of Petrine authorship, there is much within the letter to validate what the first verse explicitly asserts. In particular, Peter echoed words and phrases that he heard directly from Jesus. For instance, Peter's words "whom

---

*Scriptures: 1 Peter* (Bellingham, WA: Logos Bible Software, 2008), 4.
[12] Roger M. Raymer, "1 Peter," in *The Bible Knowledge Commentary: An Exposition of the Scriptures*, ed. J. F. Walvoord and R. B. Zuck, vol. 2 (Wheaton, IL: Victor Books, 1985), 837.

having seen, ye love" (1:8) mirror Jesus' words "blessed are they that have not seen me, and yet have believed" (John 20:29). Peter said to "gird up the loins of your mind" (1:13), similar to Jesus' admonition to "let your loins be girded about, and your lights burning" (Luke 12:35). Peter referred to "the precious blood of Christ, as of a lamb without blemish and without spot" (1:19) just like John the Baptist called Jesus "the Lamb of God" (John 1:36). Jesus and Peter both used the expression "the foundation of the world." (1 Peter 1:20; Matthew 25:34) Peter exhorted his readers to "love one another" (1:22) just as he heard his Lord instruct over and over (e.g., John 13:34). Peter likened his Christian readers to living or "lively stones" (2:5) in a similar fashion to how Jesus called Peter a "rock" (Matthew 16:18), albeit using different Greek terms. And Peter quoted Psalm 118:22 and applied it to Jesus (2:7) just as Jesus quoted Psalm 118:22 and applied it to himself (Matthew 21:42). Peter used the expression "the day of visitation" (2:12) to refer to when Jesus returns, which Jesus called "the time of thy visitation" (Luke 19:44). Peter referred to his Jewish Christian readers "as sheep going astray" who had "returned unto the Shepherd and Bishop of your souls" (2:25), which parallels Jesus' reference to the Jewish "multitudes" as "scattered abroad, as sheep having no shepherd" (Matthew 9:36).

Peter also echoed words and concepts from the famous Sermon on the Mount: "not rendering evil for evil, or railing for railing" (3:9) to "resist not evil: but whosoever shall smite thee on thy right check, turn to him the other also" (Matthew 5:39), "if you suffer for righteousness' sake, happy are ye" (3:14) to "blessed are they which are persecuted for righteousness' sake" (Matthew 5:10), "let him do it as of the ability which God giveth: that God in all things may be glorified" (4:11) to "that they may see your good words, and glorify your Father which is in heaven" (Matthew 5:16), "rejoice, inasmuch as ye are partakers of Christ's sufferings; that, when his glory shall be revealed ye may be glad also with exceeding joy" (4:13) to "rejoice, and be exceeding glad: for great is your reward in heaven: for so persecuted they the prophets" (Matthew 5:12), and "casting all your care upon him; for he careth for you" (5:7) to Jesus' words, "Take not thought for your life, what ye shall eat, or what ye shall drink....for your heavenly Father knoweth that ye have need of all these things" (Matthew 6:25, 32). And finally, when Peter exhorted the elders to "feed the flock of God" (5:2) he must have recalled Jesus' words to him in the epilogue to John's Gospel, "Feed my sheep." (John 21:16)

The Pulpit Commentary on First Peter concludes: "These and other similar coincidences with the Lord's words as reported in the Gospels are so simple and unaffected, they seem to come so naturally to the writer's thoughts, that we are led at once to infer that that writer must be one who, like St. John, could declare to others that which he had heard, which he had seen with his eyes."[13] Similar parallels are present between Peter's speeches in the book of Acts and the words of First Peter. Without cataloguing all of those here, Peter's frequent appeal to the Old Testament prophets (as in Acts 2) and his use of Psalm 118:25 in Acts 4:11 stand out. But in addition to the internal evidence, there is much external evidence validating Petrine authorship. Caffin

---

[13] H. D. M. Spence-Jones, ed., *1 Peter*, The Pulpit Commentary (London; New York: Funk & Wagnalls Company, 1909), iii.

addressed the extra-Biblical case for Petrine authorship of First Peter:

> The earliest Christian writers were not accustomed to quote the books of the New Testament by name, or to reproduce the words with exactness. Hence we do not expect to find formal quotations of our Epistle in the apostolic Fathers. But in Clement of Rome there are more than fifteen references to it; some clear and certain, such as "his marvellous light;" others less marked. In Polycarp's 'Epistle to the Philippians' (and Polycarp was bishop of one of the Churches addressed by St. Peter) there are so many undoubted quotations from this Epistle that the modern assailants of its authenticity have no resource but to attack (without any sufficient grounds) the genuineness of Polycarp's epistle. Eusebius tells us that the Epistle was used by Papias. There are manifest traces of it in the 'Shepherd' of Hermas, in Justin Martyr, and Theophilus of Antioch. Irenæus, Clement of Alexandria, and Tertullian quote it expressly, often by name. Origin refers to it frequently, and says expressly that it was accepted by all as genuine. Eusebius places it among those canonical Scriptures which are universally acknowledged. It is contained in the Peschito and the Old Latin versions. The Maratorian Canon mentions only an Apocalypse of Peter, "which some will not have read in the Church." But that document is so fragmentary that little

weight can be attached to its omission of St. Peter's Epistles.[14]

While Thomas Schreiner questions whether some of the early writings like 1 Clement depended on First Peter, he similarly affirms the strong witness among the early Christian writers to Peter's authorship of First Peter:

> ...When we read Polycarp's letter to the Philippians, we have the first evidence of dependence on 1 Peter, and the date of Polycarp's letter is quite early (probably ca. A.D. 112–114). In four texts Polycarp's wording is remarkably close to what we have in 1 Peter, so there are good reasons for thinking that Polycarp used Peter as a source (cf. Phil. 8:2 and 1 Pet 2:21; Phil. 1:3 and 1 Pet 1:8; Phil. 8:1 and 1 Pet 2:22, 24; Phil. 2:1 and 1 Pet 1:13, 22). Possibly the Didache also uses 1 Peter (see Did. 1:4 and 1 Pet 2:11), though certainty here is impossible. If the latter were to be established, the authenticity of 1 Peter would be strengthened.
>
> By the end of the second century and beginning of the third century, the letter is explicitly identified as Peter's. Tertullian cites verses from Peter and explicitly identifies Peter as the author (*Scorp.* 12; cf. *Scorp.* 14; *Orat.* 20). Clement of Alexandria and Irenaeus also quote from 1 Peter and attribute the writing to Peter himself (e.g.,

---

[14] H. D. M. Spence-Jones, ed., *1 Peter*, The Pulpit Commentary (London; New York: Funk & Wagnalls Company, 1909), iv–v.

*Paed.* 1.6.44; *Strom.* 3.11.75; 4.7.46–37; and *Adv. haer.* 4.9.2; 4.16.5 respectively). First Peter is not listed in the Muratorian Canon, but the omission may be due to the destruction of part of the document, so not much can be gleaned from this. We do learn that the external evidence for 1 Peter being authentic is quite early, and no doubts were raised about its authenticity.[15]

Despite the internal and external evidence, numerous scholars dispute that Peter wrote the epistle, as Schreiner explained:

> Despite the self-claim of the book and the early tradition attesting Petrine authorship, many scholars doubt that Peter is the genuine author of the letter. Various reasons are given for denying the authenticity of 1 Peter, though scholars who dispute authenticity differ on what arguments are persuasive and the weight that should be assigned to the different arguments.[16]

For example, Reading argues that Peter's name was attached to the letter to give it credibility:

> The author's claim to be the apostle Peter has been adamantly defended as well as denied by scholarship. The standard

---

[15] Thomas R. Schreiner, *1, 2 Peter, Jude*, vol. 37, The New American Commentary (Nashville: Broadman & Holman Publishers, 2003), 22.
[16] Thomas R. Schreiner, *1, 2 Peter, Jude*, vol. 37, The New American Commentary (Nashville: Broadman & Holman Publishers, 2003), 22–23.

arguments for or against Petrine authorship are certainly ambivalent and of varying quality. But a combination of linguistic, social, and theological reasons argue strongly against Petrine authorship and in favor of pseudonymity. The author's notable command of Greek and familiar use of the Septuagint OT indicate a Hellenistic writer. Additionally, the Christian movement has undergone important transformations since the apostolic period; thus the author employs the term *adelphotes* ("brotherhood" or "family of believers"—2:17; 5:9) to describe the community, refers to its leadership as "elders," addresses explicitly the believers' relationship to the state (2:13–17), and notes that suffering as a Christian has become a common phenomenon (4:16; 5:9). Thus we conclude that the author invokes the name of Peter (employing the formulaic: "apostle of Jesus Christ"—see Titus 1:1 and the other Paulinist letters) to add authority to the document's traditional exhortations and to insure a positive response from the audience. What one finds in 1 Peter are not the reminiscences or teaching of a Palestinian eyewitness but the complex use of paraenetic materials that have undergone considerable development prior to their application to the communities' situation.[17]

---

[17] Earl Richard, *Reading 1 Peter, Jude, and 2 Peter: A Literary and Theological Commentary*, Reading the New Testament Series (Macon, GA: Smyth & Helwys Publishing, 2000), 9–10.

One of the critical arguments, and perhaps the lead argument, against Peter having written the epistle is that the style of writing and grammar is too good for an uneducated fisherman to have produced. The problem with this argument is its unsupported premise that because Peter was a fisherman he lacked education, and further, that one lacking education cannot possibly communicate well in writing. This sort of snobbery sounds like the priests in John 7:48-49. They too could not figure out how Jesus, who did not go to one of their schools, could teach "as one having authority" (Matthew 7:29). In any event, Warren Wiersbe provides an excellent response:

> Some liberals have questioned whether a common fisherman could have penned this letter, especially since Peter and John were both called "unlearned and ignorant men" (Acts 4:13). However, this phrase only means "laymen without formal schooling"; that is, they were not professional religious leaders. We must never underestimate the training Peter had for three years with the Lord Jesus, nor should we minimize the work of the Holy Spirit in his life. Peter is a perfect illustration of the truth expressed in 1 Corinthians 1:26–31.[18]

Raymer's response to this argument against Peter's authorship is also persuasive, as he notes not only that critics have overplayed their hand about Peter's supposed lack of education, but also given insufficient weight to

---

[18] Warren W. Wiersbe, *The Bible Exposition Commentary*, vol. 2 (Wheaton, IL: Victor Books, 1996), 388.

the possibility that Silvanus (Silas) acted as Peter's secretary in taking down Peter's words:

> Though Peter could be called "unschooled" and though Greek was not his native tongue, he was by no means ordinary. The Jewish leaders saw Peter as unschooled simply because he had not been trained in rabbinical tradition, not because he was illiterate. Luke also recorded (Acts 4:13) that these same leaders were astonished by Peter's confidence and the power of his Spirit-controlled personality...
>
> Any further doubts of Petrine authorship based on linguistic style may be answered by the fact that Peter apparently employed Silas as his secretary (1 Peter 5:12). Silas, though a Jerusalem Christian, was a Roman citizen (Acts 16:36–37) and may have had great facility in the Greek language. But whether or not Silas aided Peter with the grammatical Greek nuances, the epistle's content still remains Peter's personal message, stamped with his personal authority.[19]

It is beyond the scope of this introduction to catalogue all of the other arguments. The more common ones are that (1) the epistle draws its Old Testament quotations primarily from the Septuagint even though Peter's native

---

[19] Roger M. Raymer, "1 Peter," in *The Bible Knowledge Commentary: An Exposition of the Scriptures*, ed. J. F. Walvoord and R. B. Zuck, vol. 2 (Wheaton, IL: Victor Books, 1985), 837–838.

tongue was not Greek, (2) the theology of First Peter is Pauline, (3) the wording of 1 Peter 5:12 does not support that Silvanus was Peter's secretary (or amanuensis) but that Silvanus would be charged with delivering the letter, and in any event, even if he did act as secretary there is no evidence of his wherewithal to have written the epistle, (4) the letter allegedly says little about the historical Jesus, which makes little sense for a writer who walked with Jesus for over three years, and (5) the persecution referenced in the letter was from the Roman government and was empire-wide, thus pointing to the persecution in the reign of Domitian (A.D. 81-96) or some later date.[20]

The first objection assumes Peter lacked proficiency in Greek, and in any event, the Septuagint was widely used at the time and other New Testament writers quoted it. The second objection assumes a late date for First Peter in order to conclude that it borrows from Pauline theology. As argued below, there is good reason to take First Peter to be one of the earliest New Testament epistles. But even if a later date is correct, that does not mean that similar concepts in First Peter must have been drawn from Paul's writings. There is no indication that Peter quoted Paul, as he frequently quoted the LXX. And in any event, if Paul's and Peter's writings are both inspired by the Holy Spirit, one would expect some similarities in the concepts they wrote about. But it may be added that the supposed similarities to Paul's writings are frequently overstated. Even among conservatives, there is sometimes a Pauline bias in this regard. The

---

[20] Thomas R. Schreiner, *1, 2 Peter, Jude*, vol. 37, The New American Commentary (Nashville: Broadman & Holman Publishers, 2003), 22–24.

third objection has some grounding as the expression "by Silvanus" is similar to language elsewhere that suggests not a secretary but a messenger, although some scholars argue the language may encompass both ideas. But at best this objection only speaks to whether Silvanus' role might explain the quality of the writing against the objection that allegedly unlearned Peter could not have written the epistle. Even if this objection is correct, there is still substantial internal and external evidence supporting Peter's authorship. The fourth objection is contrived as it presumes certain biographical details are necessary to establish Petrine authorship, but also overlooks the force of the internal evidence outlined above. While the author did not detail Jesus' earthly ministry, he did mirror the words and teachings Peter would have heard firsthand at the feet of Jesus. The last objection has no basis in the Text. Indeed, conservative scholars widely argue that the persecution Peter's readers were facing or would soon face was from Nero, but this is supposition as there is no indication in the Text of official governmental persecution. Even where the author addressed submission to human government, no reference is made to persecution as would be expected if the persecution were governmental in origin. Taking all of the evidence together, there is substantial reason to accept Petrine authorship and little evidence of consequence against it.

## Date and Place of Writing

The date of writing of First Peter and the place of writing tend to be related. Almost all modern conservative scholars argue that Peter wrote from Rome in the early 60's, just before or at the beginning of the official persecution from Nero and just a few years before Peter was martyred in Rome. While widely accepted, there is reason to challenge this view. The key passage is 1 Peter 5:13: "The church that is at Babylon, elected together with you, saluteth you; and so doth Marcus my son." The primary options are that "Babylon" refers to the literal Babylon or to some settlement (city) close to it that identified as Babylon, or that Peter used "Babylon" figuratively to speak of Jerusalem, Rome or some other location. The argument against the literal Babylon is that the city lay in ruins and there is no evidence of any significant Christian population there.

Wiersbe, for instance, states: "Peter indicated that he wrote this letter 'at Babylon' (1 Peter 5:13) where there was an assembly of believers. There is no evidence either from church history or tradition that Peter ministered in ancient Babylon which, at that time, did have a large community of Jews."[21] And Lenski rightly notes that we have no Biblical record that Peter, Silvanus and Mark were ever together at Babylon: "This is really not a question that concerns Peter alone. We ask further: Was there ever a time during the days of the apostles when these *three* men, Peter, Silvanus, and Mark, were together in the far east, in what was once Babylon or in that territory? No commentator has succeeded in making this view plausible. Some commentators place Peter there; but what about the other two men?"[22] And again, Lenski explains: "Was he in Babylon, in the distant east?

---

[21] Warren W. Wiersbe, *The Bible Exposition Commentary*, vol. 2 (Wheaton, IL: Victor Books, 1996), 388.

[22] R. C. H. Lenski, *The Interpretation of the Epistles of St. Peter, St. John and St. Jude* (Minneapolis, MN: Augsburg Publishing House, 1966), 231.

Is the phrase used in 5:13, 'in Babylon,' literal or figurative? We need not dwell long on this point. There is no hint in tradition that Peter was ever in the distant east. The city of Babylon no longer existed. Peter might, indeed, have gone to Babylon—tradition is full of silences. It is not, however, a question about Peter alone but also about Silvanus and about Mark (5:12, 13). All three would have had to have been in Babylon."[23]

But the real problem is that in terms of the Biblical record, as already shown above, there are gaps of many years about which we know nothing with certainty of the whereabouts of Peter, Silvanus or Mark. Against the evidence of silence, we must scrutinize whether it is possible Peter could have written from the literal Babylon, and if he did, what more (if any) would he have said to indicate that he wrote from Babylon than the words we find in 1 Peter 5:13, and if he did not, would it have been reasonable for Peter to expect his audience to understand his figurative use of Babylon as the place of writing? On the question of Peter using Babylon in a figurative sense, the likelihood of Peter so doing has been fairly questioned:

> There seem, therefore, to be no sufficient grounds for importing a figurative meaning into St. Peter's words. If he was writing from Rome, it seems strange that he should make no mention of St. Paul, who, if not then present at Rome, was so closely connected with the Roman Church, and so well known to the Christians of Asia

---

[23] R. C. H. Lenski, *The Interpretation of the Epistles of St. Peter, St. John and St. Jude* (Minneapolis, MN: Augsburg Publishing House, 1966), 10.

> Minor; while the order in which the provinces are mentioned in ch. 1:1 furnishes at least some slight support to the hypothesis that the apostle was enumerating them as they would naturally occur, one after another, to a person writing from the East. It is true that we have no historical evidence of a journey to Babylon; but then we have no certain records of the apostle's history after the date of his leaving Antioch (Gal. 2:11)...[24]

The Pulpit Commentary points out that the possibility of literal Babylon should not be so readily dismissed.[25] Despite a decided majority of conservative scholars today dismissing Babylon as even a possibility, there is a solid minority that take the literal reading of 1 Peter 5:13 to be the best:

> Some expositors see in Babylon a reference to Rome, on account of its hostility to Christianity, cf. Rev. 14:8; 17:5, 18; 18:2, 10; others to Jerusalem, and others again to Babylon in Egypt, but which was only a Roman military post. We prefer, with Weiss, the exposition according to which the literal Babylon in Chaldea is meant, although we have no account of a journey of Peter to Babylon. The designation of Rome by the term Babylon seems only to

---

[24] H. D. M. Spence-Jones, ed., *1 Peter*, The Pulpit Commentary (London; New York: Funk & Wagnalls Company, 1909), x.
[25] H. D. M. Spence-Jones, ed., *1 Peter*, The Pulpit Commentary (London; New York: Funk & Wagnalls Company, 1909), 210–211.

fit a later period, and to be ill-suited to the style of the Epistle and the sending of salutations. According to Schöttgen, the Jews did not begin to call Rome Babylon until after the destruction of Jerusalem.[26]

The place of writing was *Babylon*. Some feel that the mention of *Babylon* in this epistle is a symbol for Rome, but there is no reason to ignore the literal interpretation of this word. At this point in time, Babylonia was the center of Judaism outside the Land; it is also the place where the *Babylonian Talmud* developed. And, since Peter was the Apostle to the Circumcision, it makes perfect sense that he would have traveled to *Babylon* after he left the Land. He literally wrote the letter from *Babylon*, the center of Judaism outside the Land.[27]

To these opinions, I would add that there is evidence of Jewish residents in or near Babylon before and during the life of Peter. In fact, writing of the state of affairs existing about 40 B.C., the Jewish historian Josephus recorded that "there were Jews in great numbers" in Babylon.[28] Some have questioned whether Josephus was speaking of

---

[26] John Peter Lange et al., *A Commentary on the Holy Scriptures: 1 Peter* (Bellingham, WA: Logos Bible Software, 2008), 95.

[27] Arnold G. Fruchtenbaum, *The Messianic Jewish Epistles: Hebrews, James, First Peter, Second Peter, Jude* (Tustin, CA: Ariel Ministries, 2005), 384.

[28] Flavius Josephus and William Whiston, *The Works of Josephus: Complete and Unabridged* (Peabody: Hendrickson, 1987), 398.

a city near old Babylon that was commonly called Babylon. The Jewish Encyclopedia records that there were Christians in or near Babylon in the first century and that 1 Peter 5:13 referred to such: "Christians lived in Babylon in early times; the passage 1 Peter 5:13 refers to this (compare Josephus, Ant. xv. 2, § 2). A Christian church, said to have been destroyed by Jews under Sapor II. or Bahram, was restored in 399 (Assemani, Bibl. Orientalis, iii. 2, 61)."[29] Philo (c. 20 B.C. to c. 50 A.D.) also wrote of the extensive Jewish settlements in and around Babylon: "I say nothing of the countries beyond the Euphrates, for all of them except a very small portion, and Babylon, and all the satrapies around, which have any advantages whatever of soil or climate, have Jews settled in them."[30]

In this regard, Peter's sermon at Pentecost in Acts 2 is helpful. Recall that Pentecost was one of the Biblical feasts that the Jews were required to attend. Luke specified that the people who heard Peter's sermon included "Parthians, and Medes, and Elamites, and the dwellers in Mesopotamia, and in Judaea, and Cappadocia, in Pontus, and Asia, Phrygia, and Pamphylia, in Egypt, and in the parts of Libya about Cyrene, and strangers of Rome, Jews and proselytes, Cretes and Arabians, we do hear them speak in our tongues the wonderful works of God." (Acts 2:9-11) "These would be the Israelites of the first dispersion, the descendants of those of the ten tribes who were deported by the Assyrians, and of whom

---

[29] Isidore Singer, ed., *The Jewish Encyclopedia: A Descriptive Record of the History, Religion, Literature, and Customs of the Jewish People from the Earliest Times to the Present Day, 12 Volumes* (New York; London: Funk & Wagnalls, 1901–1906), 401.

[30] Charles Duke Yonge with Philo of Alexandria, *The Works of Philo: Complete and Unabridged* (Peabody, MA: Hendrickson, 1995), 783.

the Afghans are perhaps a remnant, and of the first Babylonian captivity. Mesopotamia and Babylon were at this time in possession of the Parthians. Babylon was a great Jewish colony, the seat of 'the princes of the Captivity,' and of one of the great rabbinical schools."[31] As Polhill similarly explains, all of these places had extensive Jewish communities:

> The territories Luke listed all had extensive Jewish communities. Parthia, Medea, Elam, Mesopotamia had large groups of Jews from the time of the exile on. There was a large Jewish contingent in North Africa, Philo noting that two of the five wards of Alexandria were comprised of Jews. Acts witnesses to the Jewish representation in Phrygia and Asia, and their presence in Pontus and Cappadocia is amply evidenced. The Jewish population in Rome is well-known. The single exception to the resident Jews at Pentecost may be the Romans, who are described as "visitors" in verse 10b. The verse division at v. 11 is somewhat disconcerting. The phrase "both Jews and converts to Judaism" probably refers to Roman Jews and Gentiles who converted to Judaism by embracing circumcision and the Jewish law, as well as by providing for a sacrifice in the temple. The reference to Cretans and Arabians comes at the end of the list,

---

[31] H. D. M. Spence-Jones, ed., *Acts of the Apostles*, vol. 1, The Pulpit Commentary (London; New York: Funk & Wagnalls Company, 1909), 50.

almost as an afterthought. There were Jewish communities on Crete as well as in Arabia, which most likely refers to the Nabatean kingdom that extended the length of the Arabian peninsula from the Red Sea to the Euphrates. Perhaps the mention of these two locales was Luke's way of rounding off his list—not only mainlanders but islanders and desert dwellers as well. In all he gave a rather representative picture of the Jewish Diaspora and its presence at Pentecost.[32]

Thus, the "three thousand" that "were added" that day (Acts 2:41) consisted primarily of Jewish people who would return to their Jewish communities within this dispersion and take their Christianity with them. Indeed, Jerusalem would continue after Acts 2 to draw in Jews from the dispersion, and as they were evangelized through the ministry of Peter and others, what were previously only Jewish settlements of the dispersion began to include pockets of Christians and probably local churches formed among the dispersion. It makes sense that Peter would travel to minister to these Jewish Christians of the dispersion, and write to them.

Accordingly, because there were unquestionably Christian Jews in or near Babylon during Peter's ministry, and because there is no textual indication that Peter used the word "Babylon" for Rome, it is entirely possible that Peter wrote from Babylon or a nearby city where Jews had settled. The gaps in the timeline of Peter's life

---

[32] John B. Polhill, *Acts*, vol. 26, The New American Commentary (Nashville: Broadman & Holman Publishers, 1992), 103–104.

provide ample time in which he could have made the journey, and as his ministry was focused on Jews, it would have made sense for him to travel to such places. However, we must keep in mind that Peter was accompanied by Silvanus and Mark (or Marcus) when he wrote the epistle. As many have pointed out, there is no evidence outside of 1 Peter 5 that places Mark, Peter and Silvanus together in Babylon. Of course, the silence does not establish that it never happened, but we know that Silvanus accompanied Paul on his second missionary journey, limiting the possibilities for when Mark, Peter and Silvanus could have been together at Babylon. For this reason, while acknowledging the possibility the book was authored in Babylon, a more likely possibility is that it was authored from Antioch.

As already indicated, there is little to commend taking Peter's reference to Babylon to mean Rome, a supposition based on an improbable interpretation of the figurative use of Babylon in Revelation 17 and 18. But it is possible Peter used the term figuratively to express the idea of being in exile. With the martyrdom of Stephen and mounting persecution from the non-believing Jews, we know Peter left Jerusalem temporarily, and indeed, Galatians 2:11-16 places Peter in Antioch in approximately A.D. 49, just prior to the Jerusalem Council of Acts 15. The persecution in Jerusalem caused a Jewish Christian exile: "Now they which were scattered abroad upon the persecution that arose about Stephen travelled as far as Phenice, and Cyprus, and Antioch, preaching the word to none but unto the Jews only." (Acts 11:19) And indeed, Antioch rapidly became a critical church at this early juncture, the believers there were first called Christians (Acts 11:26), and Barnabas and Paul ministered there for a year (Acts 11:26).

Shortly after, Peter would be imprisoned in Jerusalem, but supernaturally freed, from which he immediately went to the home in Jerusalem of John Mark's mother (and presumably also the home of John Mark). After greeting the believers at her home, Peter "departed, and went into another place." (Acts 12:17) Since Herod's soldiers would soon discover Peter missing and search the city for him, it is likely Peter left Jerusalem and the most natural place to have gone would have been the blossoming church in Antioch. It is also very possible that Mark accompanied Peter when he left Mark's mother's home. At this time, in about A.D. 44, Peter might have penned his first epistle. Having personally experienced persecution both from Herod Agrippa and non-believing Jews in Jerusalem, Peter could at that time have either been aware or at least anticipated that similar persecution (especially from non-believing Jews) would occur against believing Jews of the dispersion. While Silvanus is not first mentioned in Acts until Acts 15:22, he was at that time a prominent believer already and it is certainly possible, given the developments in Antioch, that he also could have visited Antioch at the same time. If the epistle was written at this time, the recipients might well have not been familiar with the church at Antioch, and Peter may also have wanted to identify himself with their own situation of living in exile, so that he could use Babylon not in a negative way but as a euphemism for being in exile, to wit, writing from the relatively new church in Antioch where many believers from Jerusalem had fled.

Another possibility also exists, whereby Peter may have similarly written from Antioch in around A.D. 49 or 50. We read in Acts 15:22 that the church in Jerusalem sent

Paul and Barnabas to Antioch with Judas Barsabas and Silvanus (Silas) carrying letters (Acts 15:23) explaining the wisdom of the Council. Notably, Judas and Silvanus had "hazarded their lives for the name of our Lord Jesus Christ," a reference to the non-believing Jewish persecution. We read that Silvanus stayed in Antioch after the letter was publicly read (Acts 15:34) and that John Mark was also in Antioch at this time (Acts 15:37). Note here that there is debate about whether the text of Acts 15:34 is an addition, but regardless, Acts 15:40 confirms Silvanus was in Antioch, and then left with Paul on his Second Missionary Journey. And Acts 15:36 makes it clear that Paul tarried in Antioch for some time before leaving with Silvanus. Thus, shortly after the Jerusalem Council, Peter could have returned to Antioch and written First Peter at that time, while he, John Mark and Silvanus were together. This possibility would put First Peter being written in about A.D. 49 or 50. If 1 Peter 5:12 means that the letter was carried by Silvanus, it would fit with Silvanus taking the letter from Antioch as he accompanied Paul on the Second Missionary Journey. It also fits with the fact that Paul originally purposed to go into the very regions Peter wrote to, but remember that as they came to Mysia and planned to go to Bithynia, the Holy Spirit "suffered them not." (Acts 16:7) That may be, at least in part, because Peter's letter would minister to the Jewish believers there, and at that point Silvanus could have handed off the epistle to someone to deliver.

That Peter wrote the epistle from Antioch, or some other location outside of but not far from Jerusalem in the mid to late 40's is preferable. It is compatible with the record in Acts and makes sense of Peter writing to a predominantly Jewish audience as argued below, an audience who became believers at or as a result of Peter's message in Acts 2 or his continuing ministry in Jerusalem. Were the book written in the 60's as is commonly maintained, it more likely Peter would have explicitly affirmed his writing from Rome, which by that time was the location of a prominent church. It is also likely that by that time Peter would have referenced official persecution and unlikely that he would have identified his audience as Jewish since by that later date Christianity had already proliferated among Gentiles.

## **Audience**

First Peter opens with a greeting from the apostle "to the strangers scattered throughout Pontus, Galatia, Cappadocia, Asia, and Bithynia." (1 Peter 1:1) The word "scattered" is the Greek *diaspora,* which according to Strong's means the "dispersion, i.e. (especially and concretely) the (converted) Israelite resident in Gentile countries...." Accordingly, the better view, as Fruchtenbaum explains, is that the term *diaspora* was a term of art referring to Jews living outside of Israel.

To Peter's explicit reference to the diaspora, it may be added in support of a Jewish audience that Peter was the apostle to the Jews and that his frequent allusions to and quotations of the Old Testament are thoroughly Jewish, as Lange explains:

> That the Epistle is entirely permeated by views taken from the Old Testament; it contains numerous Old Testament figures and *termini technici,* allusions to the religious institutions and the history of the Old Covenant. Compare ch. 1:10–12; 3:5, 6;

3:20. Peter frequently intertwines quotations from the Old Testament into his language, without designating them as such, and mostly in connections where it is of essential importance that they should be recognized as Scripture (ch. 1:24; 2:7, 9, 10, and other passages). No portion of the New Testament is so thoroughly interwoven with quotations from and allusions to the Old Testament. (It contains, in 105 verses, twenty-three quotations, while the Epistle to the Ephesians has only seven, and that to the Galatians, only thirteen). [33]

Notwithstanding, and in my opinion, largely due to a Pauline bias in the scholarly literature that insists Peter borrowed from Paul and thus the epistle must have been written at a late date to churches that by that time were largely Gentile, modern scholars typically argue that Peter wrote to Gentiles:

> The congregations to which Peter writes were Gentile congregations that had a minority of Jews in their membership.[34]

> The First Letter of Peter is written primarily for Gentile Christians living in the Roman provinces of Pontus, Galatia, Cappadocia, Asia, and Bithynia (1:1).[35]

---

[33] John Peter Lange et al., *A Commentary on the Holy Scriptures: 1 Peter* (Bellingham, WA: Logos Bible Software, 2008), 7-8.

[34] R. C. H. Lenski, *The Interpretation of the Epistles of St. Peter, St. John and St. Jude* (Minneapolis, MN: Augsburg Publishing House, 1966), 13.

[35] Daniel C. Arichea and Eugene Albert Nida, *A Handbook on the First*

Indeed, understanding Peter's audience as predominantly Gentile is a more recent phenomenon:

> The ancient fathers, with the exception of Augustine and Cassiodorus, thought that the [*eklektois*] related to Jewish Christians. This opinion was prevalent until modern times: several commentators added only the modification that those Churches contained also Gentile Christians, who were, however, in the minority.[36]

The primary textual argument for a predominantly Gentile audience is that Peter speaks of their past conduct in a manner inconsistent with how non-believing Jews would have lived. Typical of this argument is Schreiner's explanation:

> Today, however, most scholars agree that the readers were mainly Gentiles. The evidence in support of this conclusion is quite compelling. To say that they lived in "ignorance" (*agnoia*) suggests an idolatrous and pagan past (1:14). Even more telling is the claim that they had been "redeemed from the empty way of life handed down to you from your forefathers" (1:18). Peter would scarcely say that Jewish forefathers lived vainly, since the Jews were God's elect people (cf. also 2:10, 25). The Gentile

---

*Letter from Peter*, UBS Handbook Series (New York: United Bible Societies, 1980), viii.

[36] John Peter Lange et al., *A Commentary on the Holy Scriptures: 1 Peter* (Bellingham, WA: Logos Bible Software, 2008), 7.

> origin of the readers seems clear from 4:3-4: "For you have spent enough time in the past doing what pagans choose to do—living in debauchery, lust, drunkenness, orgies, carousing and detestable idolatry. They think it strange that you do not plunge with them into the same flood of dissipation, and they heap abuse on you." It is difficult to believe that Peter would characterize Jews as indulging in such blatant sins, whereas the vices were typical of the Jewish conception of Gentiles.[37]

Schreiner's argument overstates his case. His point seems to be that non-believing Jews would not live like Gentiles or be ignorant of the Scriptures. Schreiner appeals to 1 Peter 1:14 that speaks to them previously living "according to the former lusts in your ignorance" and the "vain conversation received by traditions from your fathers" and says this means they are not Jewish. But Peter's comments reflect what he would have heard Jesus say many times in his earthly ministry. Jesus frequently rebuffed Pharisaic Judaism, which was rooted in traditions and not the Scriptures. This is evident in the Sermon on the Mount, where Jesus rebuked their hypocrisy and exhorted his disciples to live according to the true morality of the Law. And in Matthew 9, Jesus ate with publicans and prostitutes and commented that "they that be whole need not a physician, but they that are sick...for I am not come to call the righteous, but sinners to repentance." (Matthew 9:12-13) And just a few words

---

[37] Thomas R. Schreiner, *1, 2 Peter, Jude*, vol. 37, The New American Commentary (Nashville: Broadman & Holman Publishers, 2003), 38-39.

later, he explained that he did not come to fix Pharisaic Judaism, but to replace it: "No man putteth a piece of new cloth unto an old garment...Neither to men put new wine into old bottles...but they put new wine into new bottles, and both are preserved." (Matthew 9:16-17)

Jesus blasted that Jewish generation for their religious hypocrisy (Matthew 11:18-19) and pronounced judgment on specific cities that rejected him (Matthew 11:21-24). Jesus also frequently accused his audience of being ignorant of the Law or not keeping the Law. (e.g., John 5:45-46, 7:19) And it is also noteworthy that James wrote to Jewish Christians and referenced their "wars and fightings," "lusts...in your members," killing, inappropriate prayer, spiritual apostasy, "friendship with the world," and said they were "sinners" and "double minded." (James 4:1-8) There is simply no basis for the argument that Peter could not write to Jewish believers and exhort them as he did.

Schreiner also, as many modern commentators, takes 1 Peter 4:3-4 as a clear identification of the audience as Gentile, but it hardly makes sense that Peter would criticize Gentiles for having lived as Gentiles before they came to faith in Jesus. Accordingly, there is no internal reason in First Peter to reject Peter's express identification of his audience as Jewish. And if the early date of writing argued for above is correct, the regions Peter wrote to had not been ministered to by Paul but likely developed primarily from Jews who had experienced the apostles' ministry in Jerusalem when they traveled there, as in Acts 2.

## Outline and Purpose of First Peter

Peter's Jewish audience would have been keenly interested in the coming Kingdom, as we see throughout the Gospels. Jesus said, "If you continue in my word, then are ye my disciples indeed; and ye shall know the truth, and the truth shall make you free." (John 8:1-32) Peter wanted his audience to live as true disciples, experiencing their freedom by living out the Word. But more than just an exhortation to right living, Peter wanted his audience to understand the relationship between how Christians live out their daily lives to their experience in the coming Kingdom. Peter's understanding of this aspect of the sanctification process, based on Jesus' teaching, is that if we live as true disciples we will partake in Jesus' inheritance in the world to come, which is the basis for our having during this mortal life what Peter refers to as a living hope. We choose how to invest each moment with a view either to present earthly treasures or future rewards or inheritance in the world to come. Our choices make a difference for time and eternity.

Accordingly, First Peter was written to Jewish Christians in the diaspora to explain the living hope they have as believers, freed from sin's dominion to live out their lives day-by-day and moment-by-moment on the basis of God's Word such that they are presently appropriating their inheritance in the world to come—i.e., the salvation of their soul-lives—which will be revealed to them when the Lord returns. Within this context, Peter exhorted his audience to personal holiness, humility and fervent love for one another, with further specific and practical instruction for various spheres of life. Peter anticipated

## Introductory Matters

that his readers would face trials including persecution, likely both from Gentiles that lived around them and non-believing Jewish people. Suffering for the right reasons and with the right attitude is a prominent theme in the epistle, again under the umbrella of experiencing the salvation of the soul-life.

With an emphasis on the practical process of the salvation of the soul-life, the epistle may be outlined as follows[38]:

I. GREETING (1:1-2)

    a. Author: The Apostle Peter (1:1)

    b. Audience: Jewish believers scattered abroad (1:1-2)

II. PROLOGUE (1:3-12)

    a. Born again unto a living hope (1:3)

    b. For a heavenly inheritance (1:4)

    c. For the salvation of our soul-lives (1:5-9)

    d. We are privileged recipients of this salvation witnessed by the prophets (1:10-12)

III. THE PLAN OF SALVATION (OF THE SOUL-LIFE) (1:13-4:19)

    a. That it would transform our character (1:13-2:10)

        i. That we would be holy (1:13-17)

---

[38] Portions of this outline are drawn from or adapted from the outlines in the notes provided by Dr. David Anderson in his course on this epistle as The Grace School of Theology.

- ii. Motivated by Jesus' death and resurrection (1:18-21)
- iii. With enduring love for the brethren (1:22-25)
- iv. As we grow through God's enduring Word (2:1-3)
- v. Into the household of the Son (2:4-10)

b. That it would transform our conduct through submission (2:11-3:7)

- i. Our conduct in the world (2:11-17)
- ii. Our conduct on the job (2:18-25)
- iii. Our conduct in the home (3:1-7)

c. That it would transform our conduct through suffering (3:8-4:19)

- i. Suffering without fear (3:8-22)
    1. With the right attitude (3:8-15a)
    2. With a good testimony to non-believers (3:15b-17)
    3. With a commitment to God (3:18-22)
- ii. Finished with the former lifestyle (4:1-6)
- iii. Loving and ministering to the brethren (4:7-11)
- iv. Suffering for being a Christian (4:12-19)
    1. With rejoicing (4:12-14)
    2. In view of the coming judgment (4:15-19)

IV. ENEMIES OF OUR SALVATION (5:1-11)

    a. Lead with humility (5:1-4)

    b. Clothe yourself with humility (5:5-7)

    c. Resist your adversary the devil (5:8-9)

    d. God will bind the wounds of suffering (5:10-11)

V. POST-SCRIPT (5:12-14)

    a. Stand in God's grace (5:12)

    b. Written from Babylon (5:13)

    c. Love and peace (5:14)

# Chapter 2

# The Living Hope
1 Peter 1:1-12

In some sense, the Bible confirms the conventional wisdom that "you cannot take it with you when you die." But some have tried. In certain ancient cultures, people were buried with food and treasures to aid their journey in the next world. I read an article several years ago about a man who had his favorite car modified to hold his casket, and when he died, he was buried with (really, in) his car. Yet we do not see the hearse pulling a trailer with the deceased's earthly possessions. Indeed, the Bible says that "to be absent from the body" is "to be present with the Lord." (2 Corinthians 5:8) All that we can see and touch is left behind. But what about our experience of life? If being a Christian frees us from the power of sin over our lives so that our experience of life may now be oriented to God, then in what sense, if any, does our experience of this "newness of life" (Romans 6:4) affect our experience when we go to be with the Lord? In other words, to what extent can our lives on earth be preserved, in the sense of continuing significance, in the world to come?

*The Living Hope*

The Bible affirms that how we live out our Christian lives affects our experience in the world to come. While conventional wisdom says you only go around once so live it up now, the Bible says we should live a life rich toward God and, if we do, we will be rewarded in the Kingdom. We have been set "free indeed" (John 8:36) and as we live moment-by-moment we are free to make decisions either according to God's Word or our fleshly lusts. To the extent that we live our lives on the basis of faith responses we are experiencing the freedom we have, and at the same time those faith responses "lay up... treasures in heaven, where neither moth nor rust doth corrupt, and where thieves do not break through nor steal." (Matthew 6:20) So while we cannot take earthly riches and fleshly experiences with us, we can live out our freedom in such a way that heavenly treasures are applied to our account. In that way, our experience of this life will have continuing significance in the world to come. The Apostle Peter called this our living hope and urged believers to be transformed in their faith with confidence that no matter the trials they may face in this world, a life lived for God would result in their full realization of their inheritance in the world to come.

## Outline

I.  GREETING (1:1-2)

    a. Author: The Apostle Peter (1:1)

    b. Audience: Jewish believers scattered abroad (1:1-2)

II. PROLOGUE (1:3-12)

    a. Born again unto a living hope (1:3)

b. For a heavenly inheritance (1:4)

c. For the salvation of our soul-lives (1:5-9)

d. We are privileged recipients of this salvation witnessed by the prophets (1:10-12)

## Scripture and Comments

> <u>1 Peter 1:1</u> Peter, an apostle of Jesus Christ, to the strangers scattered throughout Pontus, Galatia, Cappadocia, Asia, and Bithynia, <u>2</u> Elect according to the foreknowledge of God the Father, through sanctification of the Spirit, unto obedience and sprinkling of the blood of Jesus Christ: Grace unto you, and peace, be multiplied.

These two verses comprise Peter's formal greeting by identifying the author and audience and stating a blessing. In the prior chapter of this guide, the technical details concerning both Petrine authorship and his predominantly Jewish Christian audience were covered in some measure of detail and the bases for these conclusions will not be repeated here. The author is identified as **Peter, an apostle of Jesus Christ**. The term **apostle** is the Greek *apostolos*, which Strong's defines as "a delegate; specially, an ambassador of the Gospel; officially a commissioner of Christ...." But the term can be used in a technical and non-technical sense. By technical, I mean to refer to one of "the twelve" as in Matthew 10:2: "Now the names of the twelve apostles are these; The first, Simon, who is called Peter...." Sometimes the word is used in a non-technical sense of an ambassador of the

Gospel (e.g., Galatians 1:19), but not a specially commissioned **apostle**. But unquestionably, the text here speaks of **Peter** as **an apostle of Jesus Christ** in the technical sense, and we understand him to be one of the twelve apostles Jesus personally selected during his earthly ministry. In Acts 1, when Matthias was selected to replace the traitor Judas Iscariot, Peter described how an **apostle** in the technical sense had to have been a witness of Jesus' earthly ministry from his baptism to his ascension. (Acts 1:21-22) And we understand from the Gospels that Peter not only was a witness of these things, but even within the twelve, Peter was among that most intimate circle of Jesus' disciples that included Peter, James and John (the brothers, the "sons of thunder").

Peter wrote **to the strangers scattered through Pontus, Galatia, Cappadocia, Asia, and Bithynia**. The term **strangers** is the Greek *parepidemos*, which according to Strong's means "an alien alongside, i.e., a resident foreigner:--pilgrim, stranger." The term **scattered** is the Greek *diaspora*, which means the dispersion, specifically of Jewish people among the Gentile nations. Thus, Peter's audience was Jewish Christians in **Pontus, Galatia, Cappodocia, Asia and Bithynia**. These were Roman provinces in Asia Minor. While Paul would eventually minister in some of these provinces, he likely did not go to the northern regions of Galatia, and indeed, in Acts 16, Paul intended to go into Bithynia (and that would naturally lead to Pontus) but the Holy Spirit turned him to Macedonia instead. So Peter's audience unquestionably included people Paul did not minister to, and if First Peter was written relatively early and its audience included primarily Jewish Christians, many who were originally evangelized during their pilgrimages to

Jerusalem (remember, Jewish men were required to travel to Jerusalem three times a year for the feasts, Deuteronomy 16:16), we can understand why Peter wrote his epistle as an encyclical letter to be shared among these Jewish believers over a large geographic area rather than any specific local church. For such was a significant part of the fruit of Peter's public ministry in Jerusalem, as Acts 2 amply demonstrates. While it is possible Peter journeyed to these areas at some point in his ministry, it is not necessary that he did so. This audience knew of Peter either from personally hearing his teaching in Jerusalem or being evangelized from those who did.

Peter added to his identification of his audience as those of the diaspora that they were **elect according to the foreknowledge of God the Father**. Because of Peter's use of the word **elect** and its association with Calvinism, this verse has been the subject of debate. While it is beyond the scope of this book to address in detail the issue of election, it is important that we accurately exegete the verse at hand. Many non-Calvinists suggest that God foreknew those would place faith in Christ and elected or chose them in eternity past based on His foreknowledge. Many (perhaps most) Calvinists equate foreknowledge to foreordination or predestination, and so for them, this verse teaches that God decreed in eternity past those He would save (or justify). The Greek adjective translated **elect** is *eklektos* (and here it is the plural, *eklektois*), which some incorrectly assume means something about picking people for justification. A word study will help to better grasp what this word is all about so that this verse may be correctly understood.

A place to start is with the leading Greek lexicon (often referred to as BDAG for short), which defines *eklektos* as "pertaining to being selected," but with secondary meanings "pertaining to being especially distinguished" (referencing as an example the "elect angels" or "distinguished angels" of 1 Timothy 5: 21) and "pertaining to being considered best in the course of a selection, choice, excellent." For the latter definition, BDAG cites numerous examples in the Bible and other Greek literature. Context must drive our determination of which usage applies in a particular verse. The meaning of "choice" or "distinguished" or "excellent" is common and best fits most of the New Testament usages.

We may begin with the occurrences of *eklektos* in the Septuagint (the Greek translation of the Old Testament), Apocrypha, and Pseudepigrapha. To list some of the examples, the term *eklektos* is used as follows: "choice" sepulchres (Genesis 23:6), "well favoured" animals (Genesis 41:2, 4, 18, 20), "rank" corn (Genesis 41:7), "chosen [i.e., the best] chariots" (Exodus 14:7), "pure myrrh" (Exodus 30:23), "young men" (Numbers 11:28; 2 Kings 8:12; Isaiah 40:30; Lamentations 1:15, 5:13-14), "choice vows" (Deuteronomy 12:11), "chosen [i.e., the best] men" (Judges 20:15, 34; 1 Samuel 24:2, 26:2; Judith 2:15; 1 Maccabees 9:5, 15:26; Psalm 78:31), "pure" (2 Samuel 22:27; Psalm 18:26), "fat oxen" and "fatted fowl" (1 Kings 4:23), "choice fir trees" (2 Kings 19:23), "choice... men" (1 Chronicles 7:40), "great stones" (Ezra 5:8), "choice sheep" (Nehemiah 5:18), "best horseman" (1 Maccabees 4:1), "dainties" or food delicacies (Psalm 141:4), "choice silver" (Proverbs 8:19), tried or refined "hearts" (Proverbs 17:3), "excellent... cedars" (Song of Solomon 5:15), "choice" child (Song of Solomon 6:9), "best myrrh" (Sirach 46:1), "plenteous" meat (Habakkuk 1:16), the "pleasant land" (Zechariah 7:14; Jeremiah 3:10), "choicest valleys" (Isaiah

22:7), "precious cornerstone" (Isaiah 28:16), "polished shaft" (Isaiah 49:2), "pleasant stones" (Isaiah 54:12), "valiant men" (Jeremiah 46:15), "pleasant vessel" (Jeremiah 25:34), "precious clothes" (Ezekiel 27:20), "costly stones" (Enoch 8:1), and "choice portions" (Testament of Levi 14:5). All of these usages support the meaning of being choice, distinguished or excellent.

Moreover, the writings of Philo are also informative on the usage of *eklektos* in the general period when the New Testament was written. The patriarch Abraham is referred to as the "great father of sounds" in Cherubim 7 (with "great" translating *eklektos*), and the "elect father of sounds" in several places. The name is explained: "The word 'elect' belongs to the mind of the wise man, for whatever is most excellent is found in him." (Names 69) And in another place: "And by the addition of the word elect his goodness is intimated. For the evil disposition is a random and confused one, but that which is elect is good, having been selected from all others by reason of its excellence." (Abraham 83) Once again, *eklektos* is not about being selected for anything, but being excellent.

As these examples demonstrate, the adjective *eklektos* is commonly used with a derived meaning of choice, distinguished, the very best in quality, or excellent. To this we may add that Jesus was often referred to as the chosen (or elect) one even though he did not need to be selected for salvation. In Luke 23:35, we read: "And the people stood beholding. And the rulers also with them derided him, saying, He saved others; let him save himself, if he be Christ, the chosen of God." The point is that Jesus is the choice or excellent one of Isaiah 42:1, the Messiah. This is consistent with what we read in 1 Peter

2:4, 6 where Jesus is the "chosen of God" and "elect, precious": "To whom coming, as unto a living stone, disallowed indeed of men, but chosen of God, and precious... Wherefore also it is contained in the scripture, Behold, I lay in Sion a chief corner stone, elect, precious: and he that believeth on him shall not be confounded." The meaning of "choice, distinguished or excellent" also makes the best sense of the wedding parable in Matthew 22:1-14, where Jesus explained that believers are "chosen" (*eklektos*) in the sense of being excellent after their accepting the calling or invitation of God. Based upon this usage, the New Testament references to Christians as "elect" or "chosen" make perfect sense as a positional truth, i.e., an attribute we have by virtue of our identification with Jesus by faith. Just as Paul referred to Christians as "saints" (literally, holy ones), the references to Christians as choice, distinguished or excellent fits our position in Christ because it is true of Christ.

Returning to the verse at hand, there is no verb about anyone being picked for anything. The adjective **elect** does not occur in verse 2, but in the first verse immediately before **strangers**. While in Greek the words of the sentence do not require the standard ordering of our English sentences, it helps to see that in the literal word ordering of the first verse, Peter wrote **to the [elect] strangers scattered...Bithynia according to the foreknowledge of God....** The preposition **according to** (Greek *kata*) does not denote purpose, but has the sense of being in harmony with **the foreknowledge of God**. It is not that people were "elected" based on God's **foreknowledge** that they would in their lives trust Christ, but that their excellence in Christ was foreknown of God.

For the Calvinistic view of "election" these verses should say that God selected people prior to creation for salvation. Instead, Peter wrote that the means by which his audience became **elect** was **through** or by **sanctification of the Spirit**. The word **sanctification** (Greek *hagiasmo*) is a noun and means a setting aside or holiness. The point then is that the basis of their being **elect** is that they were set aside by the Holy **Spirit**, and that happens when a person places faith in Christ in response to the gospel. (Romans 15:16; 1 Corinthians 1:2, 6:11) Thus, in Peter's thinking, believers become **elect** or distinguished or excellent by their being set aside by the Holy **Spirit** when they are born again. And indeed, what Peter added further confirmed this view, when he wrote **unto obedience and sprinkling of the blood of Jesus Christ**. The word **unto** is the common Greek preposition *eis* and is the first of several uses by Peter of "to" or "unto" to mean something like "with a view to" or "for the purpose of." Here, Peter wrote that his readers were set aside by the **Spirit** for the purpose of **obedience and sprinkling of the blood of Jesus Christ**.

Some commentators argue that the **obedience** in view is **obedience** to the gospel, but the text does not say that. Peter used the same term again in 1:14 to indicate obedience to God's Word, and in particular, the command to be holy. Thus, it is better to understand **obedience** to mean the believer's adherence to the God's Word, which Peter later indicated was the means of spiritual growth. (1 Peter 2:2) The meaning of the **sprinkling of the blood** has been highly debated. Without being dogmatic, I take it as a reference to the **sprinkling** in connection with an affirmation of covenant faithfulness. In Exodus 24:7-8, we read:

> Exodus 24:7 And he took the book of the covenant, and read in the audience of the people: and they said, All that the LORD hath said will we do, and be obedient. 8 And Moses took the blood, and sprinkled *it* on the people, and said, Behold the blood of the covenant, which the LORD hath made with you concerning all these words.

But the blood in Exodus 24 was animal blood, not the blood of **Jesus**. Peter's audience was brought into covenant not by animal blood, but the very **blood of Jesus Christ**. (see Hebrews 9:18-23) And the reference to the **sprinkling** coupled with **obedience** suggests their commitment of faithfulness to that New Covenant. This interpretation is consistent with the focus on sanctification throughout the epistle and Peter's later references to his readers as "an holy priesthood" and "a royal priesthood," both expressions that make sense in view of the New Covenant inaugurated with Jesus' **blood**.

To his Jewish Christian readers, Peter offered a traditional greeting: **Grace unto you, and peace, be multiplied**.

> 3 Blessed *be* the God and Father of our Lord Jesus Christ, which according to his abundant mercy hath begotten us again unto a lively hope by the resurrection of Jesus Christ from the dead,

Following his greeting (vv. 1-2), in what formed the prologue to the book (vv. 3-9), Peter set out the primary subject matter of his epistle, namely their **lively hope**. He began his introduction of this significant concept by praising God, writing **blessed *be* the God and Father of our Lord Jesus Christ**. The *be* is in italics in the KJV because there is no verb in the Greek text, but the sense of **blessed *be*** is worthy of praise and honor. We frequently read "blessed" in verses like the Beatitudes, "Blessed *are* the poor in spirit: for theirs is the kingdom of God." (Matthew 5:3) In such verses, the "blessed" is the Greek *makarios*, which Strong's says means "supremely blest; by extension, fortunate, well off:--blessed, happy." But the **blessed** in 1 Peter 1:3 is the Greek *eulogetos*, meaning "adorable:--blessed." The verbal form of the term means to bless or praise. For the new birth that brought them **a lively hope, God** is worthy of all praise.

We should not casually pass over Peter's reference to **God** as the **Father of our Lord Jesus Christ**. Jesus frequently spoke of **God** as his **Father**, which the Jewish people understood made **Jesus** to be equal with God, and which the unbelieving Jewish people considered blasphemy. Recall when **Jesus** healed the paralytic in John 5 on the Sabbath: "therefore did the Jews persecute Jesus, and sought to slay him, because he had done these things on the sabbath day." (John 5:16) Jesus responded to their hardness of heart and accusation of violating Sabbath law: "My Father worketh hitherto, and I work." (John 5:17) Because of this, "the Jews sought the more to kill him, because he not only had broken the sabbath, but said also that God was his Father, making himself equal with God." (John 5:18) Occasionally, I find someone who argues that Jesus never claimed to be God and that being God's son is something altogether different, but we have to stand in first century Jewish sandals when we listen to Jesus' conversations with a first century Jewish audience and understand his words as they would. Indeed, Jesus repeatedly claimed to be God, as he did in John 5, and the Jewish people of his time understood that plainly, and some of them plotted to kill Jesus for it. Peter did not run from this reality, but reminded his audience up front of the deity of **Jesus** as the son of **God**. But also this **Jesus** is **Lord** and **Christ**; the word **Lord** translates the Greek *kurios* meaning "supreme in authority" and, in itself, affirms the deity of **Jesus** from the perspective of his authority. And the reference to **Christ**, a transliteration of the Greek *khristos*, means "anointed, i.e., the Messiah" according to Strong's. Thus, in these few words, Peter proclaimed the deity of **Jesus** as son and as **Lord**, and his role as Messiah.

The reason for giving **God** adoration and praise is that **according to his abundant mercy** He **hath begotten us again**. The phrase **begotten...again** is the Greek *anagennaō* and is used only twice in the New Testament, here and in 1 Peter 1:23. The words translated "born again" in John 3:3 are different. Peter unmistakably spoke of a new birth, sourced in God's great **mercy** (not human effort), and it was God alone that provided this new birth. The word **mercy** is the Greek *eleos* meaning (according to Strong's) "compassion (human or divine, especially active):-- (+ tender) mercy." Paul employed the same term when he wrote: "But God, who is rich in **mercy**, for his great love wherewith he loved us, even when we were dead in sins, hath quickened us together with Christ, (by grace ye are saved;) And hath raised us up together, and made us sit together in heavenly places in Christ Jesus." (Ephesians 2:4-6) And again: "Not by works of righteousness which we have done, but according to his **mercy** he saved us, by the washing of regeneration, and renewing of the Holy Ghost." (Titus 3:5)

Much could be said from other places in the Bible about God's mercy and our justification, but we will see in what follows that Peter focused not so much on how or why this new birth was accomplished but on the purpose for which **God** gave us this new birth. In short, Peter spoke to the issue of how believers should live in light of the new birth. We must bear in mind, as noted in the prefatory material in the first chapter, that Peter's target audience was composed primarily of Jewish believers, and so his central concern in this epistle was not the gospel and how to "get saved" from sin's penalty, for he affirmed plainly that they were already born again. Rather, it was the purpose and implications of their having been granted the new birth that Peter intended to unravel for his audience, and by application, for us as well. Peter answered the question, "What next?" His focus was on their sanctification. You have been born again and made a child of God, but what comes next? Shall you wait for the day when you are given a harp, a halo and a cloud to rest upon? Or is the reality of the Christian life something far more sobering and spectacular that we are to engage immediately after becoming Christians.

Peter explained first that his readers were born again **unto a lively** or living **hope by the resurrection of Jesus Christ from the dead**. The preposition **unto** is again the familiar *eis* and is flexible but frequently indicates purpose, so that something is "unto" or "to" in purpose, i.e., with a view to or for the purpose that. That sense will become apparent in this prologue. Peter said they were given a new birth "with a view to" something or "for the purpose that" something. We need to understand what that "something" is. And he began by saying the something is a **lively** or living **hope**.

The Bible never guarantees, and indeed denies, that the Christian life will be an easy one. From the earliest times, there was persecution and even martyrdom. Jesus told his disciples, "If the world hate you, you know that it hated me before it hated you." (John 15:18) And aside from persecution, Christians face trials just like everyone else. God does not prevent all trials, but instead uses them to grow us. (e.g., James 1:2-4) Notwithstanding the difficulties and sorrows we may face, the Bible does say a great deal about this concept of **hope**, which Peter will build out. But we do enough for the moment to observe that it is not an empty or uncertain **hope**, like "I am hoping for good weather" or "I hope the fish are biting today." Rather, our **hope** is rooted in the veracity of God and the certainty that what God says is true. Indeed, as someone has said, reality ever conforms to the Word of God. "[L]et God be true, but every man a liar." (Romans 3:4) The concept of **hope**, then, is an unwavering conviction that impacts how we live. We see this illustrated by Abraham's hope in the veracity of God's promise to him that he would be a father of nations: "Who against hope believed in hope, that he might become the father of many nations, according to that which was spoken, So shall thy seed be." (Romans 4:18)

Peter said the new birth was with a view to a **lively** or living **hope**. So we must seek to understand in what way this **hope** is **lively** or living? The opposite would be a dead **hope**, in other words, a **hope** that is useless, i.e., a hope that does not make a practical difference in our lives. This living **hope** is intended to change us now. It is helpful to consider how the author of Hebrews linked the faith that fuels the Christian life to a **hope** rooted in the Word of God: "Now faith is the substance of things hoped for, the evidence of things not seen." (Hebrews 11:1) The eleventh chapter of Hebrews reviews many examples of Christian endurance—believers whose lives in the present were reoriented around God's Word about the future so that they endured in faithfulness. These examples include Enoch, Noah, Abraham, Moses and others. They all experienced changed lives because of their firm conviction about the veracity of God's Word to them. Although God's Word to them primarily concerned future blessings or future events, their lives changed in the present because they believed God and reoriented their lives around this trust in what God told them. Their hope changed them, and this is the **lively hope** that Peter said is a purpose of the new birth. But **hope**, like faith, requires content, which we will address momentarily.

We are not merely saved from sin's penalty, but our new birth is with a view to our being transformed by a **lively hope** that is made possible **by the resurrection of Jesus Christ from the dead. Jesus** rose victorious over sin and death. Because he lives, we also live. This is the substitutionary life of Christ. Paul had much to say about this **resurrection** life. Indeed, Paul said we are to "reign in life by one, Jesus Christ." (Romans 5:17) And then in the next chapter of Romans he built on this idea, teaching that just as Christ was resurrected, we should walk in newness of life:

> Romans 6:3 Know ye not, that so many of us as were baptized into Jesus Christ were baptized into his death? 4 Therefore we are buried with him by baptism into death: that like as Christ was raised up from the dead by the glory of the Father, even so we

> also should walk in newness of life. 5 For if we have been planted together in the likeness of his death, we shall be also *in the likeness* of *his* resurrection.

This living **hope** Peter explained is an aspect of the "newness of life" and "reign[ing] in life" that Paul taught. We need to understand that what Peter had to say is central to the Christian life. The next verse addressed the content of this **lively hope** that is to transform us.

> 4 To an inheritance incorruptible, and undefiled, and that fadeth not away, reserved in heaven for you,

Peter explained that the new birth is with a view to our having a living hope, which in turn is with a view **to an inheritance incorruptible, and undefiled, and that fadeth not away**. Thus, it is the **inheritance** that defines the specific content of the hope Peter made the subject of his epistle. But what is this **inheritance**? Remembering that Peter's audience was composed of Jewish believers, this term **inheritance** carried a special meaning to them. Upon hearing the term, they would immediately think of the **inheritance** God promised to national Israel in the Old Testament as He freed them from bondage in Egypt and guided them to the Promise Land, i.e., their inheritance in their time. At this juncture, I note that the issue of **inheritance** and the related issue of the "salvation of the soul" that Peter will address in the next verse are central to 1 Peter. Thus, an excursus on the Old Testament concept of **inheritance** and **rest** and how the writer of Hebrews applied that to the New Testament concept of rewards at the bema is contained in the Appendix.

Peter made a spiritual application of the familiar Jewish concept of **inheritance**, just as the writer to Hebrews did with the concept of "rest" (inheritance) in the Promise Land. (Hebrews 4) To get hold of the New Testament concept of **inheritance** we need to also understand the notion of heirship, because only heirs receive of the **inheritance**. The Jewish people in the Old Testament understood the concept of heirship, and in particular, that the firstborn son received a double portion of the inheritance from his father. (Deuteronomy 21:17) In the New Testament, we learn that upon his resurrection, Jesus was declared Son, in fulfillment of Psalm 2. (Psalm 2:7-8; Acts 13:33) This declaration of Jesus as Son was a legal declaration (Hebrews 1:5) that Jesus "hath [been] appointed heir of <u>**all things**</u>." (Hebrews 1:2) In Paul's writings, Christians are said to be "in Christ," and indeed, in Christ "we have obtained an inheritance." (Ephesians 1:11) We are qualified to inherit because we are heirs through Jesus Christ: "Wherefore thou art no more a servant, but a son; and if a son, then an heir of God through Christ." (Galatians 4:7) And not just heirs, but joint-heirs in Jesus' inheritance of all things: "And if children, then heirs; heirs of God, and joint-heirs with Christ; if so be that we suffer with *him*, that we may be also glorified together." (Romans 8:17)

Peter did not quantify exactly what is included in the **inheritance**, but he explained it is heavenly and permanent. The **inheritance** is **incorruptible, and undefiled, and that fadeth not away**. The meaning of **incorruptible** is that it is not subject to decay with the passage of time. The **inheritance** is also **undefiled**, meaning it is not soiled in any way. Not only that, it **fadeth not away**, meaning it is eternal in its duration.

Reading these words, it is apparent that Peter had in mind Jesus' words in Matthew 6:19-21 where, in the Sermon on the Mount, Jesus talked about this issue of inheritance in terms of laying up treasure in heaven, i.e., investing our lives in the things of God and, by so doing, laying up in heaven our inheritance:

> <u>Matthew 6:19</u> Lay not up for yourselves treasures upon earth, where moth and rust doth corrupt, and where thieves break through and steal: <u>20</u> But lay up for yourselves treasures in heaven, where neither moth nor rust doth corrupt, and where thieves do not break through nor steal: <u>21</u> For where your treasure is, there will your heart be also.

Recall that the Sermon on the Mount was directed at Jesus' disciples. (Matthew 5:1-2) He sought to teach them in practical terms about experiential righteousness as contrasted to the empty legalism of so many Jewish religious leaders at that time. Jesus taught them to invest their lives in the things of God and not the accumulation of worldly wealth. I must hasten to add at this point that Jesus was not prohibiting the exercise of diligence and wisdom in financial planning, such as maintaining a savings account or 401K. For Solomon taught that we can learn wisdom from the ant because even ants have the sense to store up food for winter. (Proverbs 6:6 ff.) But clearly, Jesus taught his disciples to be rich toward God.

Since our lives do not consist of our possessions, we should not invest our lives to the acquisition of things that have only temporal value, but instead lay up treasures in heaven. The **inheritance** Peter referred to is the very same "treasures in heaven" Jesus taught about. We will put more meat on the bones in the notes that follow, but we note that this issue of laying up treasure is not limited to financial giving. Rather, it is about obedience to God's Word and the investment of one's life to the things of God, for time and eternity, and that takes many forms. It may be various avenues of service in the local church and generally ministering to those in our respective spheres of influence. But it is broader than that, and in my view would include matters like pouring yourself into the Biblical rearing of your children and caring for elderly parents.

Peter added that this **inheritance... [is] reserved in heaven for you**. The term **reserved** is in the Greek perfect tense, indicating past completed action with continuing consequences. We may have little treasure on earth, but the **inheritance** of the Son that we will share in is safely **reserved in heaven**. But does this mean that the Christian life results in "participation ribbons" for every believer? In other words, can we live any way we please and then all share equally in this **inheritance** in the world to come? The short answer is a resounding "NO." Or as Paul might say, "God forbid...." (Romans 6:1-2) The treasure is **reserved in heaven** yet Jesus plainly taught to "lay up for yourselves treasure in heaven," by which he spoke to the issue of appropriating the treasure to our account by our faithful living. We will build out more details about how this **inheritance** is personally appropriated as we continue through Peter's prologue.

> 5 Who are kept by the power of God through faith unto salvation ready to be revealed in the last time....9 Receiving the end of your faith, *even* the salvation of *your* souls.

Just as the inheritance is kept in heaven, so also are the heirs **kept by the power of God through faith unto salvation ready to be revealed in the last time.** The word **kept** translates the Greek *phroureō* which means, according to Strong's, "to be a watcher in advance, i.e. to mount guard as a sentinel (post spies at gates); figuratively, to hem in, protect...." In other words, it has the sense of being guarded or protected. A common interpretation is that Peter here taught "eternal security," that is, that a justified or regenerate person cannot lose their justification. While this author agrees the Bible teaches eternal security, what Peter addressed in this context is something different.

To understand better the sense in which believers **are kept** or guarded / protected **by the power of God through faith** we note first that this protection is **unto** (with a view to or for the purpose of) the **salvation ready to be revealed in the last time.** This is a **salvation** in the future, i.e., **in the last time**, and not justification, and as will be further discussed below, this **salvation** relates directly to faithfully living in obedience and is called the **salvation** of the soul. The source of this protection is the **power of God** but the means of that protection is **through** his readers' **faith.** Thus, it seems best to understand that Peter was speaking of God's ongoing provision for His people while they lived by **faith** in obedience to God's Word so that they would receive this future **salvation**. It is clear from verse 6 that Peter anticipated their going through trials, and so he was not saying his readers were being **kept** from trials or the like. Rather, this verse speaks of their being **kept** through the trials, that is, strengthened and enabled by God to endure in **faith unto** the **salvation ready to be revealed in the last time.** The opposite of this would be their falling back in the face of adversity and trials. This understanding is confirmed by 1 Peter 4:19, which in the context of suffering and trials, states: "Wherefore let them that suffer according to the will of God commit the keeping of their souls *to him* in well doing, as unto a faithful Creator."

In verse 9, Peter further identified this **salvation** as the **salvation of your souls** that he anticipated his audience **receiving**. The Greek verb translated **receiving** is *komizō*, which has the sense of receiving a wage or something earned. Since we do not earn our salvation from sin's penalty, justification is not the **salvation** in view. But what is this **salvation of** the soul? For some, any reference to **salvation** brings to mind **salvation** from sin's penalty. But the word translates the Greek *soteria*, a very flexible term that means a rescue or deliverance. When we encounter this term, or the word *sozō* (to save), we must ask what we are being rescued or delivered from, and what we are being delivered to.

We find varied examples including rescue or deliverance from the penalty of sin (Acts 16:31; Ephesians 2:5-8); from a sickness (Matthew 9:21; Mark 5:34; Acts 14:9); from sleep (John 11:12); temporal deliverance from a perverse generation (Acts 2:40); from bondage in Egypt (Acts 7:25); from drowning (Acts 27:20, 31); from dying (Matthew 8:25); from death on the cross (Matthew 27:42); of the soul (1 Peter 1:9). For this reason, to merely assume when we find the words save, saved or **salvation** that deliverance from the penalty of sin is at issue is misguided. As already indicated, the **salvation** Peter had in mind was not the rescue from sin's penalty that occurred at the moment they believed the gospel and trusted Christ as their sin bearer. Instead, there is a future aspect to this **salvation** and it will be received as one receives a wage. At this point, we would benefit from briefly looking at this concept of the **salvation** of the soul in the larger New Testament context.

## Excursus on the Salvation of the Soul

In 2 Corinthians 5:10, Paul taught about a future judgment of believers, sometimes referred to as the bema judgment: "For we must all appear before the judgment seat of Christ; that every one may receive the things *done* in *his* body, according to that he hath done, whether *it be* good or bad." Paul referenced believers appearing before the judgment seat (bema) of Christ to be recompensed based on their works. Note that Paul's use of "receive" is the same Greek verb we find in 1 Peter 1:9. In 1 Corinthians 3:11-15, Paul elaborated on this future judgment for believers:

> 1 Corinthians 3:11 For other foundation can no man lay than that is laid, which is Jesus Christ. 12 Now if any man build upon this foundation gold, silver, precious stones, wood, hay, stubble; 13 Every man's work shall be made manifest: for the day shall declare it, because it shall be revealed by fire; and the fire shall try every man's work of what sort it is. 14 If any man's work abide which he hath built thereupon, he shall receive a reward. 15 If any man's work shall be burned, he shall suffer loss: but he himself shall be saved; yet so as by fire.

The stuff of our lives is pictured as being tested by fire, and either it burns away like wood, hay and stubble, or it survives into eternity with eternal consequence and value. This judgment is not about heaven and hell, nor about whether they have trusted Christ for the forgiveness of sins, but about faithfulness, which will determine whether rewards are received. This is clear because Paul contemplates a hypothetical man whose life has nothing of eternal value to show for it (it all burns up), but he "shall be saved; yet so as by fire."

This teaching on rewards (or inheritance) for faithful endurance was taught not only by Paul, but Jesus taught on the subject. On the heels of Peter's great confession in Matthew 16:16 ("Thou art the Christ, the Son of the living God"), Jesus addressed rewards for faithful endurance:

> Matthew 16:24 Then said Jesus unto his disciples, If any *man* will come after me, let him deny himself, and take up his cross, and follow me. 25 For whosoever will save his life shall lose it: and whosoever will lose his life for my sake shall find it. 26 For what is a man profited, if he shall gain the whole world, and lose his own soul? or what shall a man give in exchange for his soul? 27 For the Son of man shall come in the glory of his Father with his angels; and then he shall reward every man according to his works.

The Bible teaches that justification is by faith alone in Christ alone, but to be a faithful disciple will cost us. Throughout this passage, the Greek term *psuche* is translated as "life" or "soul." Although some take the

English word "soul" to mean spirit it almost never carries that meaning in our Bibles. The term "soul" almost always refers to the conscious experience of our lives. Dr. Harry Leafe defined the "soul" as the temporal experience of human life. It is not merely being alive, but that which we do and experience. We see plainly in the scripture that our experience of life can be restful, physical bliss (Luke 12:19) as well as "exceeding sorrowful, even unto death." (Matthew 26:38) Broadly speaking, our soul consists of our thoughts (1 Corinthians 4:3-5), words (Matthew 12:36-37) and actions (Romans 2:6), all of which will be judged.

To his audience Jesus said, "If any man will come after me...." He was not speaking figuratively, but of literally pursuing after him in his earthly ministry as a disciple, as Peter did. The disciple must deny himself, subjecting his will to Jesus' will, his plans to Jesus' plans, etc. When Jesus spoke in verse 25 of "save" and "lose," he spoke to his believing apostles (except Judas Iscariot), and the point Jesus made is that a disciple chooses between (life no. 1) the life Jesus has for him or her and (life no. 2) the life they might otherwise pursue to serve their own self-interest. You cannot have both, Jesus explained, and indeed "whosoever will save his life [no. (2)] shall lose it [no. (1)]." And in contrast, "whosoever will lose his life [no. (2)] for my sake shall find it [shall save no. (1)]." One life can be saved or delivered into eternity, being rewarded and having continuing significance and eternal value, while the other will last no longer than our short time sojourning here.

The point Jesus made in Matthew 16 is that a man that chooses to invest his life in pursuing earthly treasures, even to the point (hyperbolically) of gaining the whole world, will profit nothing from it in the world to come. In the world to come, when "the Son of man shall come in the glory of his Father with his angels... he shall reward every man according to his works." Jesus frequently taught about rewards. (e.g., Matthew 5:12, 6:1, 10:42, 19:21; Mark 9:41, 10:21; Luke 6:23, 12:33-34, 18:22) Jesus' Parable of the Pounds (Luke 19:11-27) illustrates the doctrine. There, a nobleman was to journey to a far country to receive a kingdom, then return. For that interim period of his absence he left his ten servants with ten pounds, and then "when he was returned, having received the kingdom, then he commanded these servants to be called unto him, to whom he had given the money, that he might know how much every man gained by trading." (Luke 19:15) The first had gained ten pounds, to which the king said, "Well, thou good servant: because thou hast been faithful in a very little, have thou authority over ten cities." (Luke 19:17) Each servant was rewarded in accordance with how that servant used their allotted money, but one servant only returned the pound without any gain. (Luke 19:20) To that servant, the master said, "Take from him the pound, and give it to him that hath ten pounds...For I say unto you, That unto every one which hath shall be given; and from him that hath not, even that he hath shall be taken away from him." (Luke 19:24-26) This pictures a loss of rewards, not salvation, as Luke 19:27 makes clear: "But those mine enemies, which would not that I should reign over them, bring hither, and slay them before me."

We will either be rich toward the world, and then at the bema judgment as Paul described it, all will be burned away and our only reward will be smoke, or we will be rich toward God. In that case, we will lay up treasure in heaven and thus reap an inheritance in the future. Jesus well understood our tendency to invest in things of the world rather than of God when he warned in Luke 12:15: "Take heed, and beware of covetousness: for a man's life consisteth not in the abundance of the things which he possesseth." He then told the parable of the rich fool who, in the face of material blessings, invested in bigger barns so he could gain more and more. Hear the fool's thinking: "And I will say to my soul, Soul, thou hast much goods laid up for many years; take thine ease, eat, drink, *and* be merry." (Luke 12:19) In contrast to his perspective, we must heed God's rebuke: "But God said unto him, *Thou* fool, this night thy soul shall be required of thee: then whose shall those things be, which thou hast provided?" (Luke 12:20) And then Jesus' commentary, which ties the parable back to his teaching in Matthew 6:19-21 about laying up treasure in heaven: "So *is* he that layeth up treasure for himself, and is not rich toward God." (Luke 12:21)

## Scripture and Comments

Putting the pieces together, Jesus taught about the salvation of the soul-life in Matthew 16, and so it is no surprise to find that Peter taught this doctrine in 1 Peter 1:9. Jesus' half-brother James taught the same doctrine in James 1:21 ("save your souls") and the writer of Hebrews addressed the issue in Hebrews 10:39 ("the saving of the soul"). These concepts of saving the soul, laying up treasures in heaven, and our inheritance are all tied together. Dr. Harry Leafe summarized these verses in his book *Running to Win*:

It is difficult for grace-oriented believers to think in terms of earning anything from God. Certainly, salvation from the penalty of sin is a free gift of God's grace. However, Peter now tells us that we attain (Gr. *komizō*) as the goal of our faith "the salvation of our souls" (v. 9). Clearly, the salvation of verse 5 is the same as verse 9, "a salvation ready to be revealed in the last time." Recall...that *komizō* means "to receive something that is due, or to get for oneself by earning."

The point is clear. Our share in the inheritance is determined by that portion of our soul-life that is saved or delivered into eternity. And *that* salvation is demonstrated by our good works or, as Peter put it, the *proven character* of faith. We receive inheritance on the basis of our *demonstrated* faith (good works). And that is what "salvation of the soul" is all about![1]

Conventional wisdom is that "you cannot take it with you" when this mortal life ends. But there is a sense in which we can. How we invest our lives will determine whether, at the bema, we are rewarded. When we invest our lives so that we are "rich toward God," the outcome at the bema will be that that aspect of our lives will translate into rewards or inheritance. And in that sense, our experience of life, our soul-life, is saved or delivered

---

[1] Leafe, G. Harry, *Running to Win*, Second Edition (Biblical Studies Press 2004), 18.

into eternity as we exchange our experience of life for our inheritance, the treasure in heaven that we appropriated over a lifetime of faithfulness. Verses 6-7 will build on this understanding of the salvation of the soul.

> 6 Wherein ye greatly rejoice, though now for a season, if need be, ye are in heaviness through manifold temptations:

Peter said that we **greatly rejoice** in the inheritance that will be revealed in the last time, but **now for a season, if need be, ye are in heaviness through manifold temptations**. The **if** is what is known in Greek grammar as a first class condition and has the notion of "since." It assumes the reality of what is said. While they have reason to **rejoice**, they also must suffer for a short time in **manifold** or various **temptations** or trials. The word **temptations** here is not about being tempted to sin, but enduring trials, and can include persecution as well as the normal trials of life (e.g., illness, financial struggles). The question is why is it necessary that they suffer, which is answered in the next verse.

> 7 That the trial of your faith, being much more precious than of gold that perisheth, though it be tried with fire, might be found unto praise and honour and glory at the appearing of Jesus Christ:

Peter next explained the significance of trials in the life of a believer. The noun **trial** is the Greek *dokimion,* which Strong's defines as "a testing; by implication, trustworthiness:--trial, trying." The word can refer either to the test or to the genuineness or proven character of that which is tested, depending on the context in which it is used, and the term could be used, for example, of testing coins for genuineness and testing pottery against defects. The related verbal form of this word, *dokimazō*, means to test with a view to approval. Certainly, Peter was not saying that trials are more valuable than **gold**. Rather, it is the results or responses to those trials as our faith is **tried with fire** and proven that is more valuable. We understand that **gold** is earthly treasure with transient value, while our good works is heavenly treasure with permanent value.

Peter's metaphor is that the quality of precious metals (like **gold**) is **tried with fire** to remove the impurities (the dross) and purify the product to make it more valuable. So also the trials of life prove and refine our **faith**, as we exhibit **faith** responses to the trials, and the product of that testing—our **faith** responses—is **much more precious** or valuable **than of gold that perisheth**. Peter was not talking about determining whether someone is a "true believer," or separating real **faith** from fake **faith**, but instead, that the trials will show what we really believe. Our **faith** responses made on the basis of the Word of God will inherently take the form of thoughts, words and actions. In different ways, every day of our life presents new challenges, some small and others large. As believers engaged in God's training program we are to handle the challenges on the basis of God's Word and His wisdom. Dr. Leafe summarized the role of trials in the salvation of our soul-lives:

> The trials Peter has in mind are designed by our heavenly Father to prove the character of our faith (not destroy it!). To be sure, trials also demonstrate lack of

faith. But the issue here is the *proven character* (Gr. *dokimion*) of our faith, said to be "more valuable than gold – gold that is tested by fire, even though it is passing away." The clear implication is that gold, in this analogy, has only temporary value, while the *proven character* of faith has eternal value. This is further expressed in the outcome – such proven faith results in "praise and glory and honor when Jesus Christ is revealed."

\*     \*     \*

Clearly, then, the trials we experience in life are designed to test our faith, and of necessity, the testing involves our thoughts, words and actions. This being the case, will we then evaluate our circumstances on the basis of God's Word – a biblical worldview – or on some other basis, whatever that might be? Will the intent of our words be to minister and to build up those around us? Will the purpose of our actions be to demonstrate our faith in Christ? If these responses issue from faith in God and His Word, then they become what Peter calls the *proven character* of our faith. And that proven faith will be demonstrated and rewarded "when Jesus Christ is revealed," an event of great importance....[2]

---

[2] Leafe, pp. 15-17.

Recall earlier that Peter said our inheritance is reserved in heaven and we are to live by faith with a view toward a salvation to be revealed in the last time. Consistent with that, our **faith** responses will translate **unto praise and honour and glory** (part of our rewards) when Jesus returns, and that is why it is more valuable than **gold**. The word **praise** means commendation, as Jesus may say, "Well done, thou good and faithful servant." (Matthew 25:21) The word **honor** means exaltation, and may have to do with our place of authority in the world to come. Again, think of Jesus' words, "Well done, good and faithful servant; though hast been faithful over a few things, I will make thee ruler over many things: enter thou into the joy of the lord." (Matthew 25:23) Finally, the word **glory** means reputation, and here it is the recognition of a race run well, a life that was rich toward God rather than earthly pursuits.

Before leaving this verse, we must comment that it is especially the **trials** that reveal and grow our faith. We see elsewhere (e.g., James 1:2-4; Hebrews 12:1-11) that God uses the challenges and trials of life to grow us. It seems that when everything is going smoothly, our faith is not tested as strenuously, nor do we have the same opportunity for growth by applying the Word of God to real life issues. And so Peter focused on how the **trials** fit into God's training program for us and give us opportunity to lay up treasures in heaven, that is, to appropriate our inheritance in real time as we live by **faith**. But there are a couple of caveats. First, many Christians face trials because they are obnoxious, which is not a spirit gift! They perceive the response of others to their bad attitude and bad behavior as related to their being a Christian, but such is not persecution. Second, some Christians face trials but do not do so on the basis of God's Word. Either because they do not know God's Word, or because they choose to set aside God's Word, they face the trials on the basis of self-sufficiency and worldly wisdom, and the results show. There is no laying up treasure in heaven when the result of the testing does not reflect proven character. Moreover, sometimes when you fail the test, you get to take it again.

> <u>8</u> Whom having not seen, ye love; in whom, though now ye see *him* not, yet believing, ye rejoice with joy unspeakable and full of glory:

In reference to the return of Christ and echoing Christ's words in John 20:29, Peter remarked that while they had not **seen** him, they **love** him. The **love** they have is volitional love (Greek *agapaō*), a love that necessarily exhibits itself in action. Jesus used the same term in John 14:21 when he said: "He that hath my commandments, and keepeth them, he it is that loveth me: and he that loveth me shall be loved of my Father, and I will love him, and will manifest myself to him." Though his readers had not physically **seen** Jesus, their faith motivated their **love** for him, seen in how they lived, and especially how they lived during the trials they faced.

Thus, Peter said, **though now** they **see him not, yet believing** (moved by faith in what Jesus said), they **rejoice with joy unspeakable** (i.e., indescribable, beyond words) **and full of glory**. In a life full of trials, these Christians **rejoice** in Jesus Christ because of their firm conviction of his imminent return and the revealing of their inheritance in Christ as they enter the Kingdom. It bears saying here that a great many Christians fail to experience this **joy** in a real, tangible sense. These are not just words on a page. God expects us to experience a persistent and overwhelming **joy** rooted in our conviction of things future, things associated with the return of Christ, and especially receiving his approval and commendation as we receive of our inheritance. It is no exaggeration to say that many Christians are not even aware of this inheritance, or if they are, they do not care. We do well to get our myopic focus away from things of the world and toward the things of God, for therein is the key to **joy**.

> 9 Receiving the end of your faith, *even* the salvation of *your* souls.

The rejoicing of verse 8 does not happen in a vacuum. As already seen in Peter's prologue to this point, the rejoicing is rooted in love for the Saviour and a focus on his return and his rewarding the saints with the inheritance that is reserved in heaven for them. But more than that, the rejoicing is accompanied by an understanding that how we live now presently affects our future. Peter said that as their faith was being tested, and the assumption is that they were meeting the trials with proper faith responses, they were presently **receiving** or appropriating **the end** or final outcome **of** their **faith** lived out, **even the salvation of** their **souls**. As they lived, facing life on the basis of **faith**, specifically trusting the content of God's Word and applying God's Word moment by moment to the challenges of life in this fallen world, they were, to use Jesus' words from the Sermon on the Mount, laying up treasure in heaven.

They chose in each moment to live by faith or by the flesh, and thus chose to invest that moment with God and exchange it for heavenly treasures. To say it a different way, they were presently appropriating (**receiving**) the inheritance that would be revealed to them at the return of Christ. And insofar as they appropriated that inheritance during this lifetime, they were presently **receiving the end** or product or outcome of their **faith** life, namely the exchange of their present soul-lives (the temporal experience of life, i.e., the substance of their lives—thoughts, words, actions) for an eternal inheritance. Peter did not delineate the precise nature of this inheritance, but it is critical we understand that we are sharing in Jesus' inheritance, and he inherited everything. (Hebrews 1:2) Jesus will exercise complete dominion in the world to come, and we will share in that.

This makes how we live serious business. While we are saved by grace, the idea that how we live now does not have consequences for time and eternity is absurd. One of those consequences is whether we will be rewarded at the return of Christ or just fill the room with smoke as the substance of our lives, all earthly pursuits, burns up. In that event, our **souls** will not be exchanged at the bema for rewards, yet as Paul explained in 1 Corinthians 3, that person is still saved, though as by fire.

Do not miss what Peter was saying in the big picture. God is working through our lives, including especially in the trials, to produce faith responses as we live on the basis of the Word of God, and God rewards us in the process. As Peter indicated in 1 Peter 2:2, it is by the Word of God that we grow. But what does this mean for the Christian that refuses to engage the Word of God as a daily life practice? What of the Christian that will squander their life away on worldly pursuits and largely ignore the Word of God? It means they will meet the challenges of life on the basis of their self-sufficiency, falling back on worldly wisdom, and will make a mess of things. But worse than that, they will be embarrassed at the bema when nothing in their mortal life translated into something permanent in eternity.

> 10 Of which salvation the prophets have enquired and searched diligently, who prophesied of the grace *that should come* unto you: 11 Searching what, or what manner of time the Spirit of Christ which was in them did signify, when it testified beforehand the sufferings of Christ, and the glory that should follow. 12 Unto whom it was revealed, that not unto themselves, but unto us they did minister the things, which are now reported unto you by them that have preached the gospel unto you with the Holy Ghost sent down from heaven; which things the angels desire to look into.

In reference to the future **salvation** of the soul, or **salvation** of the soul-life, that Peter introduced in vv. 3-9 as the content of the living hope, Peter would have his audience (and by application, us) understand the significance of this blessing. In God's unfolding progressive revelation, He did not reveal in one moment everything He would ultimately include in the completed cannon that we now refer to as the Bible. We sometimes forget there was a time when there were people of faith, like in the time of Abraham and Job, but there was not yet any written special revelation, i.e., no Bible or even one book of the Bible available to them. The process of

God's Word being recorded in written form would begin during the life of Moses, but even then, the people of God did not have a complete Bible. Based on the testimony of Scripture, Moses wrote the Torah or Pentateuch (i.e., the first five books of the Bible). But other books, like the historical narratives we have in Joshua, Judges, and Samuel, would come in the centuries that followed. Following the implementation of the monarchy over Israel, over the course of several centuries, some of God's prophets had a writing ministry, such as Jeremiah and Hosea. But even with the writing prophets, God's written special revelation was continuing to unfold. There would also be a time with no new writing prophets (the so-called silent years), following Malachi and before the New Testament writers. Even with the New Testament writings, God's additional revelation did not all occur at once, nor even in the order presented in our New Testaments.

God continued in the first century A.D. the process of progressive written revelation, revealing new truths and further building upon and clarifying truths that were the subject of prior writings. And we would be remiss if we failed to note that all of these writings did not constitute the best revelation of God. Rather, the ultimate revelation of God was "Son revelation" as the god-man Jesus Christ lived on this planet and carried out his ministry, which in turn was foundational to the apostolic writings. (Hebrews 1:1-2) As an example of God's progressive revelation, we observe that while God had revealed much about the end times in the Old Testament writings, additional revelation would come in the Gospels and New Testament epistles, culminating in the book of Revelation.

With the progressive nature of God's revelation in mind, we can understand what Peter was expressing in these verses. Based on the incomplete revelation the Old Testament **prophets** had, this **salvation** of the soul was the subject of their intense study. Peter says **the prophets enquired and searched diligently.** They were eager to comprehend God's plan for bringing about this **salvation**, but as Peter explained, his audience (and us also) have more revelation and therefore a more complete understanding. These **prophets** of old...**prophesied of the grace that should come unto you.** Peter would have his audience understand how privileged they were to be witnesses to that which the **prophets** of old could only see in the distant future. The **grace** in view is God's provision in Jesus Christ, which includes the new birth but Peter's special focus is on the substance of their living hope. Thus he explained the content of this **grace** in verse 13 as "the grace that is to be brought unto you at the revelation of Jesus Christ," referring to the salvation of the soul that was Peters' overarching focus throughout his epistle. Indeed, as Peter closed his epistle he exclaimed: "I have written briefly, exhorting, and testifying that this is the true grace of God wherein ye stand."

Peter continued by explaining how the Old Testament **prophets** probed or **searched what, or what manner of time the Spirit of Christ which was in them did signify.** We note here that Peter referred to the **Spirit of Christ**, just as Paul did. (Romans 8:9; Philippians 1:19) Unquestionably this refers to the Holy Spirit, and Peter emphasized this name for the Holy Spirit as he referenced the moving of the Holy Spirit in the Old Testament prophets to prophecy of Jesus. The **prophets** sought to understand the timing and circumstances **the Spirit of**

**Christ which was in them did signify** when the Holy Spirit **testified beforehand the sufferings of Christ, and the glory that should follow.** In other words, the Holy Spirit **testified** through these **prophets**, but they struggled to fit all the pieces together. They grappled with understanding the timing and circumstances of how the Messiah or **Christ** would suffer, and by implication, die, but after the suffering there would be a **glory** to **follow**. And so they had many pieces, and the challenge was like assembling a jigsaw puzzle without having the complete picture to compare. But now we understand that Jesus' suffering (death) brought us the **grace** of the new birth and our sharing in the **glory** to **follow** insofar as we will share in the inheritance as joint-heirs with the Son of God. The **glory to follow** is the exaltation of Christ to the right hand of God the Father, his legal declaration as Son and heir of all things, and his imminent return to implement his Kingdom. (Psalm 2:7-8; Ephesians 1:20-22; Hebrews 1:2-4)

Indeed, we read from various writers in the Old Testament that the Christ would be betrayed for thirty pieces of silver (Zechariah 11:12; Matthew 26:14-15); betrayed by a friend (Psalm 55:12-14; Matthew 26:49-50); the money would be cast to the potter (Zechariah 11:13; Matthew 27:5-7); he would be forsaken by his associates (Zechariah 13:7; Matthew 26:56); accused by false witnesses (Psalm 35:11; Matthew 26:59-60); spit upon (Isaiah 50:6; Matthew 27:30); silent before his accusers (Isaiah 53:7; Matthew 27:12-14); wounded and bruised (Isaiah 53:5; Matthew 27:26, 29); his hands and feet pierced (Psalm 22:16; Luke 23:33); executed with criminals (Isaiah 53:12; Mark 15:27-28); he would pray for his persecutors (Isaiah 53:12; Luke 23:34); be ridiculed (Psalm 22:8; Matthew 27:41-43); his garments parted and lots cast

(Psalm 22:18; John 19:23-24); his forsaken cry (Psalm 22:1; Matthew 27:46); given vinegar (Psalm 69:21; John 19:28-29); abandoned by his friends (Psalm 38:11; Luke 23:49); no bones broken (Psalm 34:20; John 19:33, 36); pierced in his side (Zechariah 12:10; John 19:34-37); the land would go dark (Amos 8:9; Matthew 27:45); and the Christ would be buried in a wealthy man's tomb (Isaiah 53:9; Matthew 27:57-60).[3] But the prophecies also told of his resurrection (Psalm 16:8-10, 30:3, 41:10, 118:17; Hosea 6:2), his return (Psalm 50:3-6; Isaiah 9:6-7, 66:18; Daniel 7:13-14; Zechariah 12:10, 14:4-8), and his everlasting kingdom (1 Chronicles 17:11-14; Psalm 72:8; Isaiah 9:7; Daniel 7:14; Psalm 2;6-8, 110:1-3, 45:6-7).[4]

Peter's point was that while the **prophets** struggled with all the puzzle pieces and longed to understand the entire picture, their prophecies were not for their direct benefit in the sense that the events would occur in the future. In fact, **it was revealed** to them that their prophecies concerning the **Christ**, his **sufferings** and **the glory that should follow**, were not primarily for **themselves** and their generation **but unto us they did minister the things, which are now reported unto you**. Peter's audience should have been encouraged by the fact that they were privileged to see how the pieces fit together and experienced the prophesied blessing. More specifically, Peter's audience received additional revelation in God's unfolding progressive revelation to enable their understanding.

The **prophets...ministered the things** (i.e., concerning **the grace that should come unto you**), and in the first century

---

[3] J. Hampton Keathley, III, *Messianic Prophecies*, available at https://bible.org/article/messianic-prophecies (last verified 7.14.18).
[4] *Ibid.*

those **things** were **reported unto** Peter's audience **by them that have preached the gospel unto you with the Holy Ghost sent down from heaven**. Indeed, the prophetic mystery had come full circle as the **Spirit of Christ** preached through the **prophets** of old and centuries later, in Peter's day, worked through those that brought the **gospel** to his readers. The term **gospel** means good news and should not, in this context, be limited to the facts of the death, burial and resurrection of the **Christ**. Rather, the good news includes both the **sufferings of Christ, and the glory that should follow**. Peter noted that this good news was **preached** to his audience **with the Holy Ghost sent down from heaven**. This not only views the continuing ministry of the **Holy** Spirit through the **prophets** of old and now through the apostles and other ministers of the **gospel**, but also that the **Holy** Spirit was **sent down from heaven**. This likely refers to Pentecost and the new aspects of the ministry of the **Holy** Spirit in Peter's time and ours. Jesus promised that following his earthly ministry he would send the **Holy** Spirit, the Comforter, to us, and "he shall testify of me." (John 15:26; see also John 14:16, 26, 16:7)

As already noted, the **glory that should follow** pertains to Jesus' exaltation and his imminent return and implementation of his Kingdom. We will see in the immediate context that verse 13 refers to "the revelation of Jesus Christ." The salvation of the soul and the inheritance that Peter focused on will be revealed in connection with the return of Jesus Christ and that is subsumed within **the glory that should follow**. Finally, further demonstrating how privileged they (and we) were to have an understanding of these matters, Peter added the comment, **which things the angels desire to look into**.

Peter's point seems to be that like the Old Testament **prophets**, the **angels** also do not know exactly how God's plan all fits together. They too watch eagerly as the pieces come together and are revealed by God progressively. Peter would address later in his epistle that his readers were experiencing persecution, likely both because they were Jewish and because they were Christians. Understanding the privilege they enjoyed in being recipients of that which was foretold but neither the **prophets** nor the **angels** fully understood would be an encouragement to Peter's readers.

Christians today have a completed cannon—even Peter did not have that. To have access to the completed cannon and the freedom to read and teach from it is a tremendous privilege we should never take for granted. And in particular, we have a more complete revelation of the **grace** prophesied in the Old Testament. That being the case, how should we respond? Peter turned to that question next, and in a few words, it should be a spiritual game changer. But even now, there is yet more to be revealed when Christ returns, and it is likely impossible for us to achieve anything near a complete comprehension of the coming **glory that should follow**. We have nothing to relate it to, and perhaps that is one reason far too many take it lightly.

## Closing

Life is like a book and every day God turns the page. We do not know what tomorrow's page of our story will bring, but we have an opportunity each day as Christians to face that day's challenges and decisions, big and small, on the basis of the Word of God—to truly live by faith. We can live in this world as pilgrims and sojourners (1 Peter 2:11) with a future and heavenly focus, appropriating our inheritance and looking forward with great joy to the return of Christ. Or we can live in this world as citizens of it, having no serious commitment to studying and meditating on the Word and no serious commitment to any local church. That flesh-based living has a big price tag. Peter wanted his audience, and by application, us, to experience joy and live rich toward God in a world that is going to throw us curve balls. With the right focus, we can face tomorrow's page of our story with maturity: "God, what do you have for me today?" We can see life in a different framework altogether from how non-believers view life. Each day is more opportunity to make our soul-lives count for time and eternity.

## Application Points

- **MAIN PRINCIPLE:** Christians are born again with a view to experiencing a living hope that changes and grows us as we take joy in God's promised future blessings, facing life's challenges on the basis of faith in His Word and thereby appropriating to our account during this present time our share in Jesus' inheritance reserved in heaven for us, which is to be revealed to us when Jesus Christ returns, which Peter calls the salvation of our soul-lives.

- Hope means certainty, and the content of our living hope is the coming salvation of our soul-lives when the Lord returns.

## Discussion Questions

1. Does it really matter if we live a Christian life that results in receiving a share in the inheritance?

2. Is there any practical importance of understanding what God says about end times matters like the return of Jesus Christ?

3. What is faith in the context of someone who is already a believer?

4. Where does real joy come from?

5. What is the salvation of the soul and where in the Bible is this concept specifically addressed?

# Chapter 3

# The Future Salvation That Changes Us Now
1 Peter 1:13-25

Paul wrote to the church in Colossae: "For this cause we also, since the day we heard it, do not cease to pray for you, and to desire that ye might be filled with the knowledge of his will in all wisdom and spiritual understanding; That ye might walk worthy of the Lord unto all pleasing, being fruitful in every good work, and increasing in the knowledge of God." (Colossians 1:9-10) Notice key aspects of the transformation Paul prayed for in his audience—that they would have knowledge of God's will, wisdom and spiritual understanding, and that these would lead to fruitfulness and more knowledge of God. Both occurrences of "knowledge" in these verses are the Greek *epignosis*, which means a full knowledge based on experience. Experiential knowledge is learned progressively in life. And note also Paul's statement in Colossians 1:28: "Whom we preach, warning every man, and teaching every man in all wisdom; that we may present every man perfect in Christ Jesus." God uses His Word to develop a "perfect" or mature believer in Jesus Christ.

This transformation will not be a mere outward conformity to some standard of conduct, but a radical inner transformation of our thinking so that our outward conduct follows our new mind. Paul captured this idea when he exhorted the members of the church in Rome: "And be not conformed to this world: but be ye transformed by the renewing of your mind, that you may prove what is that good, and acceptable, and perfect, will of God." (Romans 12:2) Our learning God's Word is critical to this process. Paul explained, "Let the word of Christ dwell in you richly in all wisdom...." (Colossians 3:16) This is not just reading the Word, or attaining a level of academic knowledge of the words on a page, nor even committing it to memory, but to let the Word "dwell" or inhabit us "richly," that is, abundantly. The Word saturates our mind as the world's philosophies are jettisoned and replaced with God's thinking. And as the Proverbs remind us, "For as he thinketh in his heart, so is he...." (Proverbs 23:7) Our creed always directs our conduct.

And if that is the case, then what we believe matters greatly because what we believe will guide our decisions and responses to life. What Peter had to say in his prologue to his great epistle about the future salvation of our soul-lives was intended to fill our minds with wonder, fuel our rejoicing at the coming of the Lord, and change us at this present moment. To catch hold of the notion that how we live our Christian lives matters for time and eternity is a game changer. A life of faith is a life that is reoriented around what God says, and especially what God says about the future. Peter sought to explain to his readers how their living hope should change their thinking, their living before God, and their living toward fellow believers. This is all a part of what is referred to as sanctification, and the main body of Peter's epistle that we begin to address below focused on what we might refer to as the plan of salvation of the soul-life.

### Outline

III. THE PLAN OF SALVATION (OF THE SOUL-LIFE) (1:13-4:19)

    a. That it would transform our character (1:13-2:10)

        i. That we would be holy (1:13-17)

        ii. Motivated by Jesus' death and resurrection (1:18-21)

        iii. With enduring love for the brethren (1:22-25)

### Scripture and Comments

In the prologue, Peter introduced the living hope that all born again believers have, and explained that the content of that hope is an inheritance reserved in heaven to be revealed when Christ returns. Peter explained that those who live by faith appropriate their share in the inheritance, and in that way presently receive the end or outcome of a life well lived, the salvation of their soul-lives. Now Peter would have his audience understand that this future salvation should produce right thinking, holy living, and fervent love for one another in the family of God. In other words, it should transform our character.

> 1 Peter 1:13 Wherefore gird up the loins of your mind, be sober, and hope to the end for the grace that is to be brought unto you at the revelation of Jesus Christ.

Peter launched this new section of his epistle with a **wherefore** (or "therefore"). A "therefore" is always there for a reason, and indeed, it looks back to preceding materials and draws an important conclusion or application. In this context, Peter said **wherefore** in reference to the living hope with a view to the salvation of our souls that he introduced in vv. 3-9 and explained as a fulfillment of prophecy in vv. 10-12. The doctrine about the salvation of our souls puts life in a starkly different paradigm than worldly thinking does. The world says, "eat, drink and be merry." You have one candle to burn, you only go around once, and so look out for number one and live it up while you can. But God says our lives have significance beyond the grave and there are tremendous implications to how we live now. Who we are does not end with our last mortal breath, but instead, how we live now directly relates to our experience in the world to come. The living hope should change us, and here Peter explained how. We need to overhaul our thinking and our doing.

Since there is this relationship between how we live now and our inheritance, Peter exhorted his audience to **gird up the loins of your mind, be sober**. In the ancient world, people wore long robes and would tuck their robes into their belts before engaging in strenuous physical activities. Peter used that common experience as a metaphor for our minds (not the physical organ we call a brain, but the spiritual seat of our thinking, often referred to in Scripture as heart). Our minds, like the long, flowing garments Peter's readers wore, can be a distracting obstacle. We have undisciplined thinking. We not only lose focus, but we think on the wrong things, and think incorrectly rather than seeing things as God does. Just as in physical activities, we need to **gird up** our minds, pulling in the robes of misguided and distracting thinking. Such thinking may be a preoccupation with pursuing worldly pleasures, accumulating wealth, or getting caught up in destructive philosophies like Darwinism. Peter said we have to take control of our thinking so that bad thinking does not inhibit our walk with God as flowing robes inhibit vigorous activity. We need prepared minds for what God has for us. The tucking in of our thoughts prepares us to focus on how we should live in light of this great salvation of the soul.

We should note at this point that Satan is scheming to take control of our thinking, knowing our conduct will follow our creed. Peter addressed Satan in 1 Peter 5:8-9 in relation to the very issue of our thinking and referred to him as our "adversary the devil" and "a roaring lion, walking about, seeking whom he may devour." This is sometimes referred to as spiritual warfare. Paul explained that our weapons in this struggle are not physical or fleshly because what we are fighting against is not physical or fleshly:

> <u>2 Corinthians 10:3</u> For though we walk in the flesh, we do not war after the flesh: 4 (For the weapons of our warfare *are* not carnal, but mighty through God to the pulling down of strong holds;) 5 Casting down imaginations, and every high thing that exalteth itself against the knowledge

of God, and bringing into captivity every thought to the obedience of Christ; 6 And having in a readiness to revenge all disobedience, when your obedience is fulfilled.

Paul zeroed in on where the fight is—between the ears, in our minds / hearts. The danger we face is ideas and philosophies ("imaginations") that are exalted "against the knowledge of God." The best antidote to bad thinking is truth. Thus, when Paul addressed the nature of our "weapons" in what we refer to as the "armor of God," Paul exhorted us to "stand therefore, having your loins girt about with truth." (Ephesians 6:14) Peter similarly instructed that we prepare our minds for vigorous activity.

Peter also added, **be sober**. This means to be alert and ready and apply clear thinking to life. Jesus' words in this regard are apropos here:

> Luke 12:32 Fear not, little flock; for it is your Father's good pleasure to give you the kingdom. 33 Sell that ye have, and give alms; provide yourselves bags which wax not old, a treasure in the heavens that faileth not, where no thief approacheth, neither moth corrupteth. 34 For where your treasure is, there will your heart be also. 35 Let your loins be girded about, and *your* lights burning; 36 And ye yourselves like unto men that wait for their lord, when he will return from the wedding; that when he cometh and knocketh, they may open unto him immediately. 37 Blessed *are*

> those servants, whom the lord when he cometh shall find watching: verily I say unto you, that he shall gird himself, and make them to sit down to meat, and will come forth and serve them.

Jesus said that in view of the coming kingdom, his disciples should lay up treasure in heaven. Jesus observed that there is a critical role in the matter of laying up treasure in heaven regarding how we think. If you lay up treasure on earth, that action shows your thinking is focused on earthly things. But if you lay up treasure in heaven, that action shows your thinking is focused on heavenly things. In light of the importance of where our heart's focus is, Jesus said, "let your loins be girded about and your lights burning." The metaphor Peter employed in verse 13 was what he heard Jesus teach years earlier. Jesus essentially said, have your minds prepared and live in a state of preparation for his return. Those who do this will be blessed when Jesus returns.

To the girding up of our thoughts and being alert, Peter added that we should **hope to the end for the grace that is to be brought unto you at the revelation of Jesus Christ**, which of course mirrors what Jesus said in Luke 12:32-37. Peter stated earlier that we have a living hope, and now Peter said to focus and maintain that **hope** completely on the **grace** to be given us when Jesus returns. The **grace** here is the same as the future "grace that should come unto you" of verse 10 and "the glory that should follow" of verse 11. This **grace** is "the glory" of the salvation of the soul Peter expounded, and thus relates again to the inheritance of verse 4 and the "salvation ready to be revealed in the last time" of verse 5.

Peter said their **hope** should be oriented on these things. Remember, the notion of **hope** is not contingent, but based on the firm conviction that what God has said will come to pass, and thus **hope** is certain and rooted in specific content.

This, of course, is not natural for us. What comes from our flesh is to set our hope on the things of the flesh, especially those things that promise immediate gratification. But that gives us an experience of death rather than the rejoicing Peter said we should have based on this salvation to be revealed. Paul addressed this issue in Romans:

> <u>Romans 8:5</u> For they that are after the flesh do mind the things of the flesh; but they that are after the Spirit the things of the Spirit. <u>6</u> For to be carnally minded *is* death; but to be spiritually minded *is* life and peace.

Paul said that if we cater to the flesh then our "mind" or thinking will be on the "things of the flesh." Likewise, if we are living for the things of God our thinking will reflect that as well. Carnal thinking brings about an experience of death, and spiritual thinking an experience of "life and peace." So to put it back in the words of Peter, where is your **hope**? Is it bound up with possessions, affluence, and personal relationships? Is your **hope** in the creation or the Creator? Peter said the same thing Jesus said—lay up treasures in heaven, be rich toward God, be about the business of appropriating the inheritance reserved for us as those qualified as joint-heirs with Jesus. This **hope** changes everything.

**14** As obedient children, not fashioning yourselves according to the former lusts in your ignorance:

Peter continued building on his **wherefore** and exhorted his audience **as obedient children** of God **not** to **fashion[] yourselves according to the former lusts in your ignorance**. This grows out of his exhortation in the prior verses. Peter just told them to have prepared minds fixed on the "hope" that looks to the "grace" to be revealed to them when Jesus returns. In other words, "be heavenly minded!" How we think is critical to the Christian walk, and we will either live on the basis of God's Word day-by-day and moment-by-moment in how we assess life, process new information and make decisions, or we will fall back on our own thinking. How nice it would be if, as Christians, we could learn God's Word and delete the old stuff the way we would delete a computer file, but it is not so easy. Paul warned of the same danger that Peter did here: "And be not conformed to this world: but be ye transformed by the renewing of your mind, that ye may prove what *is* that good, and acceptable, and perfect, will of God." (Romans 12:2) Paul said we are to be about the business of rebuilding our minds brick by brick on the basis of God's Word and not to be pushed into the world's mold. The reality is that whatever controls our minds controls our lives and if our minds are filled only with the world's thinking, we will not glorify God with our lives. So Peter said to his audience, do not fashion your lives **according to the former lusts**, meaning the worldly way of thinking they had before they became Christians, **in** their **ignorance**. Peter assumed our conduct will follow our thinking.

As an aside, those who maintain that Peter wrote to Gentiles center on verses like this one, generally arguing that unsaved Jews would not have lived according **to the former lusts in** their **ignorance**. The argument assumes a level of knowledge of God and piety among unsaved persons just because they were Jewish. But this flies in the face of much of the Old Testament. One could hardly get through the book of Judges without realizing that despite God's tremendous revelation to Israel, they frequently lived in idolatry and willful ignorance. (see Judges 21:25) The book of James was also directed toward Jewish Christians and included strong language about their behavior even as Christians. (e.g., James 4:1-10) That Peter addressed a Jewish audience is again confirmed in the next verse by his appeal to Leviticus for a call to personal holiness.

> <u>15</u> But as he which hath called you is holy, so be ye holy in all manner of conversation;
> <u>16</u> Because it is written, BE YE HOLY; FOR I AM HOLY.

The conjunction **but** set off a contrast. And in contrast to living on the basis of our "former lusts," we should be **holy**. For **as** God **which hath called you is holy**, Peter exhorted, **so be ye holy in all manner of conversation**. The notion of being **called** refers to being the recipients of the gospel message referred to in v. 12. Paul similarly taught: "Whereunto he **called** you by our **gospel**, to the obtaining of the glory of our Lord Jesus Christ." (2 Thessalonians 2:14) The word **conversation** means behavior and so includes our thoughts, words and actions, the very substance of our soul-lives that will either lay up treasure on earth or in heaven. Thus, having introduced the concepts of our inheritance and the salvation of the soul whereby we exchange our life for the inheritance, Peter told his audience to prepare their minds and focus their hope on this salvation, not on their former lusts.

This right thinking should be followed by right conduct, and the model is God's holiness. That is a high bar! Paul said essentially the same thing to the Colossians about right thinking and right conduct:

> Colossians 3:1 If ye then be risen with Christ, seek those things which are above, where Christ sitteth on the right hand of God. 2 Set your affection on things above, not on things on the earth. 3 For ye are dead, and your life is hid with Christ in God. 4 When Christ, *who is* our life, shall appear, then shall ye also appear with him in glory. 5 Mortify therefore your members which are upon the earth; fornication, uncleanness, inordinate affection, evil concupiscence, and covetousness, which is idolatry: 6 For which things' sake the wrath of God cometh on the children of disobedience: 7 In the which ye also walked some time, when ye lived in them. 8 But now ye also put off all these; anger, wrath, malice, blasphemy, filthy communication out of your mouth. 9 Lie not one to another, seeing that ye have put off the old man with his deeds; 10 And have put on the new *man*, which is renewed in knowledge after the image of him that created him: 11 Where there is

> neither Greek nor Jew, circumcision nor uncircumcision, Barbarian, Scythian, bond *nor* free: but Christ *is* all, and in all.

Note Paul's exhortation to "set your affection" (Peter says set your **hope**) "on things above" looking to Christ's return, but do not do the things you formerly did as unbelievers. Rather, "put on the new man...which is renewed in knowledge after the image of him [i.e., God] that created him." This mirrors Peter's exhortation to think on the things of God and model our behavior after God's own holiness. Indeed, **because it is written** (e.g., in Leviticus 20:26), **Be ye holy; for I am holy**.

The notion of **holy** means separated, a cut above. We read this word throughout the Bible but we struggle to comprehend it because we are so deep in worldliness that the extreme opposite is difficult for us to fathom. We get glimpses of God's holiness in the Scriptures, and as we come to appreciate better what holiness is, we become more acquainted with our own lack of holiness, our own sin. Make no mistake on this point. Peter was not just making a plea for clean living. He was exhorting his audience to life on an entirely different plain and on an entirely different set of motivations. This is life with one foot in heaven's door and a controlled mind focused on heavenly things. Some have said, "[so and so] is too heavenly minded to be any earthly good." But in truth, no one was ever too heavenly minded. What the Bible affirms is that some are too earthly minded to be any heavenly good.

> **17** And if ye call on the Father, who without respect of persons judgeth according to every man's work, pass the time of your sojourning *here* in fear:

Peter said **if** using a Greek first class condition; it assumes the reality of what is said, and thus could be understood as "since." Thus Peter said, since **ye call on** or pray to God **the Father, who without respect of persons judgeth according to every man's work, pass the time of your sojourning here in fear**. The term translated **call on** carries the meaning of calling out for help; Peter assumed his audience's prayerful dependence on God. Peter reminded his audience that God will exercise judgment over the works of all persons, Christian or not. As already noted, the judgment of Christians is not with a view to their eternal destiny, but relates to their inheritance. But that our works will be judged makes life serious business so that we should **pass the time of** our **sojourning here in fear**.

Peter characterized the Christian life as a temporary time of **sojourning**. We must keep in our hearts that we are not in our permanent home, as it were, but are temporary residents. According to Hebrews, our citizenship is in the heavenly city. (Hebrews 12:22, 13:14) But we are to live in **fear**. It seems that **fear** is more than reverence, and entails a healthy recognition that as God's children we are obligated and accountable to Him. Thus, Paul wrote to the Philippians, in reference to their sanctification process: "Wherefore, my beloved, as ye have always obeyed, not as in my presence only, but now much more in my absence, work out your own salvation with <u>**fear and trembling**</u>." (Philippians 2:12) Paul's coupling of **fear** with trembling as we "work out" (not for) our "salvation" suggests a sense of accountability, not just respect. When we stand before the Lord, we will not be able to "lawyer up" or present character witnesses. Everything will be manifest. We will have proven character (good works) to show for our lives or we will not, and that will have consequences.

Thus, it is difficult to reconcile a believer claiming to **fear** God who does not also eschew evil. (see Job 1:1, describing Job as "perfect and upright, and one that feared God, and eschewed evil.") It is easy to express our confessional theology, but what is our experiential theology? What is our theology that other people see? It should be a life in **fear** of God—a life that eschews evil because we recognize God's authority over us. We are on temporary assignment and need to represent God well before a world that is watching. And the **fear** coupled with our understanding that we are on temporary assignment should motivate us to pursue holiness with all diligence. In grade school, most of us had a healthy understanding that at the end of the term we would get a report card that had to be signed by a parent or guardian, an experience that could result in rewards or repercussions. We could goof off in school for the whole term but eventually there would be a reckoning. And so we went to school and did our work with a healthy "fear." The same is usually true in the workplace, where at some point our diligence (or lack thereof) in carrying out our duties to our employer will be evaluated by the boss.

Someone may say they are not concerned about an inheritance. It is good enough if they "get in." And besides, laboring for an inheritance must be a self-interested motive. Peter says, "when the report card is issued you are going to care." What follows in the next several verses is in furtherance of our experiencing the holiness Peter commanded in verses 15-16.

> **18** Forasmuch as ye know that ye were not redeemed with corruptible things, *as* silver and gold, from your vain conversation *received* by tradition from your fathers;

> **19** But with the precious blood of Christ, as of a lamb without blemish and without spot:

Peter already explained that in light of our salvation we should live differently and, indeed, seek to exhibit holiness and not fall back on our former lusts, i.e., being driven by fleshly thinking and cravings. Peter said we should live this way because we **know** that we **were not redeemed with corruptible things, as silver and gold…but with the precious blood of Christ, as of a lamb without blemish and without spot**. The word **redeemed** is the Greek *leutroō* and means to ransom. We were ransomed away from sin and death by the **precious blood of Christ**. Using the language descriptive of a Passover lamb, Peter referenced Jesus as **a lamb without blemish and without spot**. (see Exodus 12:5) Jesus was the sinless one and only his **blood** had sufficient value to ransom us, and that value was far beyond any **silver and gold**.

Of course, the Passover lamb accomplished God passing over the people despite their sin, but John the Baptizer said of Jesus, "Behold the lamb of God, which **taketh away** the sin of the world." (John 1:29) Passing over and taking away are not the same. The writer to the Hebrews said:

> Hebrews 9:12 Neither by the blood of goats and calves, but by his own blood he entered in once into the holy place, having obtained eternal redemption *for us*. **13** For if the blood of bulls and of goats, and the ashes of an heifer sprinkling the unclean, sanctifieth to the purifying of the flesh: **14** How much more shall the blood of Christ, who through the eternal Spirit offered himself without spot to God, purge

your conscience from dead works to serve the living God?

We have been freed from sin to serve to the living God. No greater price could possibly have been paid on our behalf than what Jesus paid for you and me. Shame on us if we count Jesus' sacrifice a small thing and squander the opportunity we have to serve righteousness. Peter wrote that his readers were **redeemed** or ransomed away from their **vain** or empty **conversation received by tradition from** our **fathers**. Peter used the word **conversation** speaking of behavior or a way of life, which was inherited from those before them.

Peter's readers were, before coming to Christ, very much a religious people, but not godly. They were like so many today who have a "form of godliness" (see 2 Timothy 3:5), who in their lives acknowledge God in some way, post religious things on social media, and perhaps check in at church once in a while to make sure God is still there. But their religion is empty or **vain**. We frequently see in the Gospels Jesus' criticism of the emptiness of Pharisaic Judaism, and that was the **tradition from** their **fathers** that, unfortunately, infected the masses. So empty was this religion that Jesus could heal someone and all the religious folks cared about was that the miraculous healing purportedly violated a Sabbath rule found nowhere in the Pentateuch, but from their oral tradition. (e.g., John 9) The Bible has no kind words for empty religion. And people who truly fear God refuse empty religion. We must remember that Jesus paid the price to give us the opportunity to live right. We have all the resources we need for a faithful Christian life, and we need to live in light of what we know.

**20** Who verily was foreordained before the foundation of the world, but was manifest in these last times for you,

The **who** in verse 20 is Jesus. Peter explained that Jesus **verily was foreordained before the foundation of the world**. The word **foreordained** is the Greek *proginoskō* and means, according to Strong's, "to know beforehand, i.e., foresee:--foreknow (ordain), know (before)." Before **the foundation of the world**, in other words, before the creation event of Genesis 1, the Godhead foreknew the future work of Christ to ransom us. By implication, God created with the knowledge that giving humanity volition would result in humanity's rebellion and the awful consequences of the Fall. (Genesis 3) Yet God still created humanity, already having a redemptive plan. As John recorded in the Apocalypse, Jesus was "the Lamb slain from the foundation of the world." (Revelation 13:8) And Jesus **was manifest** or revealed **in these last times for** us, i.e., for our benefit, a reference to his earthly ministry and especially the finished work on our behalf at the cross of Calvary.

Regarding Peter's reference to **these last times**, Peter clearly considered Jesus' earthly ministry to occur in the **last times**. The Greek here is literally "at the last of the times." Recall this was what the prophets were looking forward to. (1 Peter 1:10-11) Peter's reference does not mean Jesus' earthly ministry was the end of time, but that it was that pivotal event that was the culmination of so much of what had come before and of that which had been **foreordained**. But as Peter already explained, Jesus is not done, and will return.

**21** Who by him do believe in God, that raised him up from the dead, and gave him glory; that your faith and hope might be in God.

Peter's audience, and by application all Christians, **by him**, that is, by Jesus, **do believe** or trust **in God**. Faith always must have content. It will not do to say the empty words, "you just need to have faith." To have faith is to **believe**, and one cannot **believe** nothing. Belief must have discreet content. Faith must reside in something or someone, and Peter said here, the faith in view is **in God** who **raised** Jesus **up from the dead, and gave him glory** so **that** our **faith** / trust **and hope** (confident expectation) **might be in God**. The **hope** here is the same as the lively or living hope of verse 3 that Peter there explained was "a lively hope by the resurrection of Jesus Christ from the dead." Jesus was victorious over sin and death and by his resurrection became heir of all things, which is the basis for our "inheritance incorruptible, and undefiled, and that fadeth not away, reserved in heaven." (1 Peter 1:4) The **glory** given to Jesus is the same "glory that should follow" in verse 11, speaking of his exaltation to the right hand of the Father, his becoming heir of all things, and his imminent return to implement his Kingdom.

Here, Peter made the same point, but viewing verses 20-21 together, we see the larger plan of God both to ransom sinners by Jesus Christ, as well as give **him glory**. We now have **faith and hope...in God** as we live for and look forward to sharing in that **glory** when our future salvation (of the soul) is revealed. While **faith** is believing or trusting, **hope** is the presently realized confidence that God can and will do what He said He would. And this

**faith and hope** should be a basis for rejoicing (1:8) as well as an impetus to a radically changed life. Our shared **faith and hope** should also affect how we interact with our brothers and sisters in the family of God. Indeed, putting together vv. 1:13-21, Peter said that if our **faith and hope** is fixed on the return of Christ and the great "salvation ready to be revealed in the last time" (1:5), the natural result should be our becoming an obedient (1:14) and holy (1:15-16) child of God. Peter spoke not of academic or ivory tower theology, but authentic truth that speaks to us on an imminently practical level.

> 22 Seeing ye have purified your souls in obeying the truth through the Spirit unto unfeigned love of the brethren, *see that ye* love one another with a pure heart fervently:

The new birth has implications. Peter wrote, **seeing ye have purified your souls in obeying the truth**, which parallels the expression "being born again" in the next verse. The phrase **have purified** is in the perfect tense (just as "being born again" in the next verse is in the perfect tense), indicating past completed action with continuing consequences, to wit, that the purification occurred in the past and its effects were continuing. The word **purified** is the Greek verb *hagnizō* and means (per Strong's) "to make clean, i.e., (figuratively) sanctify (ceremonially or morally):--purify (self)." The term is usually used in connection with ritual cleansing. (See e.g., John 11:55; Acts 21:26) Here, the cleansing came with obedience to **the truth** on the basis of blood of Christ. (1 Peter 1:19) Peter's point is that their **souls**—again the meaning is not spirit but the temporal experience of life (thoughts, words, actions)—were morally **purified** or cleansed **through the Spirit**. Their lives were previously characterized as consisting of "vain conversation received by tradition from your fathers" (1 Peter 1:18), but now they have been morally cleansed for a new way of living. This reflects what we may call a "positional" truth, reflecting who and what we are in Christ. The expectation is that positional truth will become experienced truth as we live and grow in obedience to God's Word. The new birth and positional purification came **in** or by **obeying the truth**, which in context of verses 19-21 is a reference to their believing the **truth** of the gospel.

This work of the Holy **Spirit** was with a view to (or had as one goal) Peter's readers having **unfeigned** or sincere and unhypocritical **love of the brethren**. The expression **love of the brethren** is the Greek *philadelphia*, from which we get the name of the city Philadelphia. The verb for **love** here is *phileō* **love** and not *agapaō* love, the *phileō* **love** indicating affection and an emotional bond whereas *agapaō* is the verb for **love** indicating a volitional choice to do in another's best interest. Peter said the new birth and our moral purification is with a view to our having **unfeigned** affection for **the brethren**, meaning our brothers and sisters in Christ. This association makes sense as a purified morality ought to produce healthy and loving relationships. Moreover, the new birth brings us into the family, and our response to others ought to reflect the family relationship. Peter's words here presume the development of relationships with other believers so that *phileō* **love** may flourish.

Then Peter issued the command, **love one another with a pure heart fervently**. In so doing, Peter changed words—

for he cannot command affection or emotional bonding (*phileō*), but he did command *agapaō* or volitional love for **one another** in the family earnestly or **fervently** from **a pure heart**. In other words, consistency and motives matter. Too many people "love" with an agenda. They love to forward their own self-interests, seeing others as targets for manipulation, and apart from having something to gain, there would be no love. But we see this love illustrated in the Parable of the Good Samaritan who showed compassion on the injured man when he had nothing to gain for himself. (Luke 10:30-37) We would be remiss if we did not take notice that God repeats this command to **love one another** in John 13:34-35, 15:12, 17, Romans 12:10, 13:8, 1 Thessalonians 3:12, 1 John 3:23, 4:7, 4:12, and 2 John 5. We ought to take this issue quite seriously. But one may ask, what if I do not like so and so? Jesus said in Matthew 5:44 to "love your enemies," so surely we can volitionally love **the brethren** even if some of them are a challenge. It helps if we remember that we also are not always easy to **love**.

> <u>23</u> Being born again, not of corruptible seed, but of incorruptible, by the word of God, which liveth and abideth for ever.

Continuing the thought that his audience should "love one another with a pure heart fervently," Peter provided a framework for understanding the nature and strength of this love. He reminded them they have been **born again**, that is, given a new birth, **not of corruptible** or perishable **seed, but of incorruptible** seed. The phrase **born again** is the same Greek term as in 1:3 and these are the only two occurrences of this term in the New Testament. The verb is in the Greek perfect tense, indicating past completed action with continuing consequences. What verse 3 made clear was that it is "the God and Father" that "hath begotten us again" or given us the new birth. Also, the term **corruptible** translates the same Greek term Peter used in verse 4 ("an inheritance incorruptible") to mean that it cannot decay with time. The **seed** likely references our regenerated spirit. As Paul wrote to Titus: "Not by works of righteousness which we have done, but according to his mercy he saved us, by the washing of regeneration, and renewing of the Holy Ghost." (Titus 3:5) Similarly, Peter said in 1 Peter 3:4 that a woman's beauty should first be in "the hidden man of the heart, in that which is not <u>corruptible</u>." Putting the parallels of verses 22 and 23 together, the new birth purified our soul-lives (v. 22), setting us apart for a new way of living, and gave us an **incorruptible seed** or inner man (spirit) enabling us to live out the new life we have in Christ. Believers are new creatures prepared for good works. (2 Corinthians 5:17; Ephesians 2:10; Galatians 6:15)

Peter's point was that a natural consequence of **being born again**, given a purified soul and **incorruptible seed**, should be our fervent love for one another. We should be reminded of Paul's words to the Galatians, "But the fruit of the Spirit is love...." (Galatians 5:22) Without question, we have the ability to love fervently. We who are in the family should express that relationship in love. But more than that, the new birth that enables this love came to us **by the word of God, which liveth and abideth for ever**. The specific **word** in view is no doubt the gospel message, in parallel with the "truth" of verse 22, which Peter confirmed in verse 25. But here Peter made a bold statement about the **word** of God in general, namely that it **liveth and abideth for ever**. That the **word** is alive was elaborated on by the author of Hebrews:

> Hebrews 4:12 For the word of God *is* quick, and powerful, and sharper than any twoedged sword, piercing even to the dividing asunder of soul and spirit, and of the joints and marrow, and *is* a discerner of the thoughts and intents of the heart.

In this verse, the author of Hebrews made one of the most powerful statements in the whole of the Bible about the effectiveness of God's Word, which he described as quick, and powerful, and sharper than any two-edged sword. This is reminiscent of God's Words through Isaiah, "So shall my word be that goeth forth out of my mouth: it shall not return unto me void, but it shall accomplish that which I please, and it shall prosper in the thing whereto I send it." God's Word is viewed as a living organism (quick or living) that is powerful, meaning it has the ability to accomplish God's purposes. To be sure, God's Word always accomplishes His purposes. In the most fundamental of examples, God said in Genesis 1:3, "Let there be light: and there was light."

When we speak of the Bible, we are talking about the written record of God's Word, and that record through the ministry of the Holy Spirit will be quick and powerful in our lives. So for example, in Colossians 3:16, Paul wrote: "Let the word of Christ dwell in you richly in all wisdom, teaching and admonishing one another in psalms and hymns and spiritual songs, singing with grace in your hearts to the Lord." Paul captured the same idea in Ephesians, encouraging them to "be filled with the Spirit," and the point was to be influenced or controlled by the Spirit who uses the Word of God to affect change in us. (see also Ephesians 4: 20 ff.)

The **word of God** has the ability, analogous to a two-edged sword, to cut even to the dividing asunder of soul and spirit, and of the joints and marrow. Of course, the best of swords can cut exceedingly fine in the physical realm but God's Word is like such a sword in spiritual matters. And thus the "word of God... is a discerner of the thoughts and intents of the heart." The term discerner is the Greek *kritikos* from which we get the English term "critique." It looks beyond the merely physical and examines and reveals our internal heart motivations. So also here in First Peter, we are reminded that the **word** is alive, and that means it has the power to change us from the inside out. And there is no plan B.

God by His Spirit will change us through the ministry of His **word** but we have to participate. We have to put our heads in the Book as a daily life practice, taking it and applying it to life. But note that Peter added that the **word** also **abideth for ever**. His point is that the **word** that was used to bring about our new birth is both living and enduring. The natural inference is that the new birth and its results should likewise be active and enduring, and in the immediate context, our fervent love for one another that is an outgrowth of our new birth ought to be active and enduring, being rooted in an active and enduring **word of God**.

> **24** FOR ALL FLESH *IS* AS GRASS, AND ALL THE GLORY OF MAN AS THE FLOWER OF GRASS. THE GRASS WITHERETH, AND THE FLOWER THEREOF FALLETH AWAY: **25** BUT THE WORD OF THE LORD ENDURETH FOR EVER. And this is the word which by the gospel is preached unto you.

Consistent with Peter having a primarily Jewish audience in mind, he provided Old Testament support for his statement in verse 23 that God's **word** is alive and enduring. Specifically, Peter quoted from Isaiah 40:6, 8, but we should see the fuller context from which Peter selected his words:

> Isaiah 40:3 The voice of him that crieth in the wilderness, Prepare ye the way of the LORD, make straight in the desert a highway for our God. 4 Every valley shall be exalted, and every mountain and hill shall be made low: and the crooked shall be made straight, and the rough places plain: 5 And the glory of the LORD shall be revealed, and all flesh shall see *it* together: for the mouth of the LORD hath spoken *it*. 6 The voice said, Cry. And he said, What shall I cry? **All flesh *is* grass, and all the goodliness thereof *is* as the flower of the field:** 7 The grass withereth, the flower fadeth: because the spirit of the LORD bloweth upon it: surely the people *is* grass. 8 **The grass withereth, the flower fadeth: but the word of our God shall stand for ever.**

We should recognize the words of Isaiah 40:3-4 as those fulfilled in John the Baptizer. (See e.g., Matthew 3:3; John 1:23) But in the same context of Isaiah, we read, "the glory of the LORD shall be revealed...for the mouth of the LORD hath spoken it." This was, of course, fulfilled in the One whom John the Baptizer announced, but this occurred centuries after Isaiah's writing. That is why God through Isaiah added the assurance that His word endures. And Peter, having been an eyewitness to the fulfillment of Isaiah 40:3-4 (see John 1) could surely affirm from his experience that God's word endures. So Peter said, **for all flesh** or living things (including people) are temporary **as** or like **grass, and all the glory of man** temporary like **the flower of grass,** which **withereth, and the flower thereof falleth away.** Just as **grass** is here today and gone tomorrow, so is mortal life and the **glory** or fame **of man, but** in contrast to man's short life (James said in James 4:14 our mortal lives are but a vapor) **the word of the Lord endureth for ever.**

Now, making application of Isaiah's words, Peter said, **and this is the word,** meaning the same living, enduring **word** of God, **which by the gospel is preached unto you.** The **gospel** message they heard and received is the very **word of the Lord** and as such, lives and endures forever. Accordingly, its natural results, meaning that which it naturally stimulates, including love for the brethren, ought also to endure. God's **word** makes no place for transient, on and off again love, nor hypocritical or empty love. Love is the natural product of our relationship with Jesus Christ, and since this is an abiding relationship, the outflowing love for the brethren should abide.

## <u>Closing</u>

Several years ago I watched a video taken on a foreign mission field where there had previously been no Bible in the native language. The missionary work there had reaped a harvest but these new converts' only source of God's Word was hearing it orally read to them by the missionaries. The video was made the very day a small plane landed in a remote village bringing a shipment of new printed Bibles in their native tongue. The scene was one of sheer exuberance as these new Christians cried tears of joy as they placed their hands around these new Bibles. And I thought to myself how we esteem it a small thing that in the United States we have such easy access to the printed Word of God. Where does it rank among all the other things vying for our time? Do we experience joy in reading it? Here is the reality—our attitude concerning the Word of God will directly impact our obedience to the Word of God. If we want the radically changed life the Bible talks about, we must have a heart that takes joy in God's Word and sees it as living and enduring, a solid foundation for our living hope.

## Application Points

**MAIN PRINCIPLE:** Christians are the privileged recipients the promised salvation of the soul, and that should spur us to a spiritual alertness concerning the grace that awaits us when Christ returns, practical holiness in our daily lives, and a fervent love for our fellow Christians.

## Discussion Questions

1. In practical terms, what does it mean to "gird up the loins of your mind"?
2. What is the content of the "hope" Peter wants us to experience?
3. In practical terms, how does a life of holiness look different than a life that does not exhibit holiness?
4. What are specific ways in which we can show love to our brothers and sisters in Christ?
5. What does it mean that the "word of the Lord" is living? Why does it matter?

# Chapter 4

# Growing Through God's Enduring Word

1 Peter 2:1-10

When January rolls around each year, many of us embrace New Year's resolutions. Sometime they stick. Often they stick for about a week. Many a Christian has made a resolution to get serious about reading the Word of God. "I am going to read the entire Bible this year!" Some make it through Genesis, and then some of them get through Exodus, but few survive the arduous journey through Leviticus (of course the weakness is ours alone and not Leviticus). For most of us the bare resolution to do better about our Bible study can be compared to this resolution: "This year I am giving up bacon!" Or if that does not hit close enough to home: "This year I am giving up watching sports!" Or for our friends in Texas: "This year I am giving up Blue Bell ice cream!" Many a pastor exhorts the congregation each Sunday to read their Bibles. So why doesn't it take? Why won't we JUST READ IT?

The temptation is to try to earnestly study God's Word on the basis of nothing more than personal discipline. And I suspect there are some folks out there that can keep it up for extended periods, dutifully spending 15 or 30 or 60 minutes a day in Bible study. However, there is a big difference between doing our duty and doing the desire of our hearts. There is a big difference between studying the Bible because we feel bound to do so and having such a deep and compelling desire to engage God's Word that neither people nor circumstances can keep us from it. Peter will tell us: "As newborn babes, desire the sincere milk of the word, that ye may grow thereby." (1 Peter 2:2) Peter did not exhort us to read the Word, but to "desire...the word." What we are after is not another resolution, but a passion and yearning for God's Word that will energize and motivate us to consistent study and meditation upon the things of God and His Word, so that we could join in the disciples' exclamation, "Did not our heart burn within us, while he talked with us by the way, and while he opened to us the scriptures?" (Luke 24:32) And may I say that God would not command us to "desire...the word" if it were not possible for us to do exactly that!

## Outline

III. THE PLAN OF SALVATION (OF THE SOUL-LIFE) (1:13-4:19)

    a. That it would transform our character (1:13-2:10)

        i. That we would be holy (1:13-17)

        ii. Motivated by Jesus' death and resurrection (1:18-21)

iii. With enduring love for the brethren (1:22-25)

iv. As we grow through God's enduring Word (2:1-3)

v. Into the household of the Son (2:4-10)

## **Scripture and Comments**

In 1 Peter 2, Peter continued building on his command to holiness and his introduction of the living and enduring Word of God. Peter would have his audience understand the importance of setting aside those things contrary to holiness and contrary to love of the brethren, the importance of the Word of God to spiritual growth, the training program from God's perspective (Jesus is the corner stone and we are living stones), and what God is making of us in Christ (e.g., a royal priesthood, holy nation).

> 1 Peter 2:1 Wherefore laying aside all malice, and all guile, and hypocrisies, and envies, and all evil speakings, 2 As newborn babes, desire the sincere milk of the word, that ye may grow thereby: 3 If so be YE HAVE TASTED THAT THE LORD *IS* GRACIOUS.

This is a tremendous **wherefore** in the unfolding of what Peter wrote. The natural conclusion from what Peter said about our new birth, the inheritance reserved for us, our calling to holiness, the living and enduring nature of God's Word, and the purpose that we fervently love one another, is that we will change and grow. That process requires an affirmative decision to lay **aside all malice, and all guile, and hypocrisies, and envies, and all evil**

**speakings**. These things go with the person we were before knowing Christ, not the new person that we are. And they are all contrary to loving the family. The word **malice** is the Greek *kakia* and means ill will toward others, which is just the opposite of Peter's command that we fervently love the brethren. The word **guile** is the Greek *dolos* and means deceit or deviousness in dealing with others that covers a hidden agenda. The word **hypocrisies** is the Greek *hypocriseis* and is living behind a mask or professing one thing while living another. The word **envies** is the Greek *phthanos* and occurs when we have an evil eye toward someone who has a position, power, or possession we want; this heart attitude fits in the glove of self-promotion. Finally, **evil speakings** is the Greek *katalalias* and means verbally running others down.

There is an unmistakable focus on words here, and no doubt that is because our words tend to reveal where we are spiritually, and they are also our favorite assault weapons. James referenced the issue of our speech in all five chapters of his epistle, and urged his readers to "be swift to hear, slow to speak, slow to wrath." (James 1:19) If we are to engage in God's training program for us, we must be willing to set **aside all** of these weapons of assault and deception. Notice that Peter did not say "some" but **all**. But surely we can keep some of this in the vault for those people that really deserve it? The fact is that if we are unwilling in our hearts to set **aside all** of these, then we are deciding up front that God will not be allowed to really change us.

In contrast to these abuses of words that stunt or prevent spiritual growth, Peter told his readers to listen to God's **word**. Indeed, with the strong craving **newborn babes** have for **milk**, we are to **desire the sincere** spiritual **milk of the word** of God. The verb **desire** is the Greek *epipotheō*, which means to intensely desire or crave something. Much could be said about this issue of craving God's **word**. As noted in the introduction above, the temptation is to try to earnestly study God's Word on the basis of nothing more than personal discipline. But there is a big difference between studying the Bible because we feel bound to do so and having such a deep and compelling **desire** to engage God's Word that neither people nor circumstances can keep us from it.

Recall the words that introduce the Psalter: "But his delight is in the law of the LORD; and in his law doth he meditate day and night." (Psalm 1:2) Here again we find that the spiritual life is not plodding through God's Word because we were told we must, but growing through God's Word because it is our delight, so much so that it consumes our thought life. Perhaps no place in the Bible better captures the enthralling satisfaction of God's Word than Psalm 119. Here are just a few of the Psalmist's expressions of joy in God's Word:

> Psalm 119:16 I will delight myself in thy statutes: I will not forget thy word... 35 Make me to go in the path of thy commandments; for therein do I delight... 47 And I will delight myself in thy commandments, which I have loved.

There is good reason to delight in God's Word. "The law of the LORD is perfect, converting the soul: the testimony of the LORD is sure, making wise the simple." (Psalm 19:7) As Peter said, we are to **desire...the word, that** we **may grow thereby**. There are a great many people that tacitly assume there is a path to spiritual growth that does not involve engaging God's Word as a routine life practice. Many even spend a great deal of time reading books about God's Word (like this one), yet are not engaged in meditating on their Bibles. The **word** is like **milk** to the infant—no milk, no growth. And those that do not **grow** will not routinely lay up treasures in heaven so that they are experiencing the living hope with a view to the salvation of the soul.

And so we must ask, what is our attitude toward the Word of God? God chose to reveal himself to us primarily through His Word, and it is by an experiential knowledge of that **word** that we grow in Christlikeness and ultimately become equipped to rule and reign with Jesus Christ in the world to come. The "experiential" piece of the equation is critical; head knowledge is not enough. God's university is not about a diploma on the wall but holiness expressed in real life by living out **the word** in the power of the Spirit. As James wrote, "be ye doers of the word, and not hearers only, deceiving your own selves." (James 1:22) People deceive themselves into believing they will experience the salvation of the soul and earn their portion of the inheritance by knowing without doing. (cf. James 1:21-22) James said it is the "engrafted word, which is able to save your souls" just before his well-known warning about being hearers and not doers. This should be a sobering message for us all. The inheritance that is the promise that forms the basis of our living hope depends on our growing on the **word**.

Peter added, **if so be ye have tasted that the Lord is gracious**. He was quoting Psalm 34:8: "O taste and see that the LORD *is* good: blessed *is* the man *that* trusteth in him." Peter's **if** is a first class condition and assumes that his readers had, in fact, **tasted that the Lord is gracious**. He assumed they were believers. Peter's quote is fitting because he likened God's **word** to **milk**, i.e., food, and here used the word **tasted** figuratively for experiencing. Peter's point was that their prior experience of the Lord's goodness should form the appetite in them for more of the good things of God, which should manifest itself in a deep-seated **desire** for His **word**.

> 4 To whom coming, *as unto* a living stone, disallowed indeed of men, but chosen of God, *and* precious, 5 Ye also, as lively stones, are built up a spiritual house, an holy priesthood, to offer up spiritual sacrifices, acceptable to God by Jesus Christ.

Having pointed to his readers' need to take in God's Word in order to grow spiritually, Peter turned to explaining in metaphors that growth process and God's personal role and the uniqueness of God's work in the life of each believer. In reference to Jesus, Peter wrote, **to whom coming, as unto a living stone, disallowed indeed of men, but chosen of God, and precious**. Jesus is a **living stone**, a *lithos*, the type of **stone** fit to be worked or shaped in a construction project. But the **living stone** was rejected by **men**, and in contrast, was God's **chosen...and precious**. The word **chosen** is the Greek adjective *eklektos* that was examined in some detail in the notes for 1 Peter 1:2. It was shown there that the term indicates being excellent, of the finest quality or most highly valued. This fits Peter's pairing of *eklektos* with **precious** (Greek *entimos*), which Strong's defines as "dear, more honourable, precious, in reputation." The word **precious** has the sense of being priceless. Jesus is the most excellent, most valuable, and priceless One of God the Father, yet rejected **of men**. The use of *eklektos* is used the same way elsewhere of believers and means the same thing there. In any event, Jesus' rejection is evident in the Gospels where many believed but many others did not, even explaining away the miracles as being done in the power of Satan. (e.g., John 8:48, 10:20)

Just as Jesus is a **living stone**, Peter wrote that Christians are **also, as lively stones** being shaped and worked by God in His construction project. Back then, the builder had to work the **stones**, which come in all shapes, to fit them in just the right place with mortar to build the walls of a structure. Each stone has its place not properly occupied by another stone. So also we **are** being uniquely and individually **built up** into **a spiritual house**. We are metaphorically **living stones** and obviously not literal **stones**. As **living stones** (*lithos*), God is working and shaping us in what He is building, **a spiritual house**. There is a tendency among modern readers to see **house** but read "Church." But Peter nowhere mentions the word "church" in this epistle. Instead, Peter identifies this **spiritual house** with **an holy priesthood, to offer up spiritual sacrifices, acceptable to God by Jesus Christ**. Peter's point was that God is building a new humanity for whom Jesus Christ is the chief corner stone (see verse 6). The writer of Hebrews similarly wrote to his Jewish Christian audience that Christians comprise the "house" of Jesus:

> <u>Hebrews 3:1</u> Wherefore, holy brethren, partakers of the heavenly calling, consider the Apostle and High Priest of our profession, Christ Jesus; <u>2</u> Who was faithful to him that appointed him, as also

> Moses *was faithful* in all his house. 3 For this *man* was counted worthy of more glory than Moses, inasmuch as he who hath builded the house hath more honour than the house. 4 For every house is builded by some *man*; but he that built all things *is* God. 5 And Moses verily *was* faithful in all his house, as a servant, for a testimony of those things which were to be spoken after; <u>6</u> But **Christ as a son over his own house; whose house are we**, if we hold fast the confidence and the rejoicing of the hope firm unto the end.

The direction of Peter's argument makes perfect sense as Peter will segue next to those Jewish people that reject Christ. Pharisaic theology in the first century taught that all Jewish people enter the kingdom. We see this attitude reflected in Matthew 3:9: "And think not to say within yourselves, We have Abraham to *our* father: for I say unto you, that God is able of these stones to raise up children unto Abraham." But in fact, only those who identify by faith with the Son become a part of the Son's house, which is the **spiritual house** God was building, and Peter wanted his readers, in the midst of their struggles, to see their privileged position. In contrast to God's physical house (the Temple) that was likely still standing in Jerusalem when Peter wrote, and was tended by Levitical priests, this **spiritual house** is **an holy priesthood**. That means we are priests. Paul commented on this in 2 Corinthians 3:6: "Who also hath made us able ministers of the new testament [or covenant]; not of the letter, but of the spirit: for the letter killeth, but the spirit giveth life."

We are a **holy priesthood**, but unlike the Levitical priests that offered up animal (and other) physical sacrifices, we are **to offer up spiritual sacrifices, acceptable to God by Jesus Christ**. Of course, it makes sense that we should **offer up...sacrifices**, since that is what priests do. But what are these **spiritual sacrifices**? Bearing in mind that we are **living stones** being worked by God, these **spiritual sacrifices** are tied up with our giving of ourselves to the things of God. (see Romans 12:1) Indeed, the writer of Hebrews explained that we have "boldness to enter into the holiest by the blood of Jesus" but our sacrifices include endurance in the faith (Hebrews 10:23), provoking our fellow believers to "love and to good works" (Hebrews 10:24), and not forsaking church attendance but instead exhorting the brethren (Hebrews 10:25). More broadly speaking, the **spiritual sacrifices** in view are the very faith responses to life on the basis of God's Word that were introduced in Peter's prologue. Whereas under the Old (or Mosaic) Covenant, physical sacrifices were required, these **spiritual sacrifices** are **acceptable to God by Jesus Christ**. The reason, of course, is that **Jesus** made the one and final blood sacrifice that could address our sin problem, which is precisely what the writer of Hebrews addressed in Hebrews 10. Now, Jesus is our High Priest (e.g., Hebrews 5:10) under whom we serve as an **holy priesthood** of believers under the New Covenant. As Revelation 1:6 states: "And hath made us kings and priests unto God and his Father; to him be the glory and dominion for ever and ever. Amen."

> <u>6</u> Wherefore also it is contained in the scripture, BEHOLD, I LAY IN SION A CHIEF CORNER STONE, ELECT, PRECIOUS: AND HE THAT BELIEVETH ON HIM SHALL NOT BE CONFOUNDED.

Peter referred to **the scripture** anticipating his readers' familiarity with the quoted passage. This further bolsters the conclusion that he wrote to Jewish Christians. In any event, Peter quoted Isaiah 28:16, which reads: "Therefore thus saith the Lord GOD, Behold, I lay in Zion for a foundation a stone, a tried [*eklektos*, here meaning approved] stone, a precious corner *stone*, a sure foundation: he that believeth shall not make haste." It is interesting that where Isaiah said "a tried stone," meaning an approved stone, we have in 1 Peter 2:6 the word **elect**, which is again the adjective *eklektos* previously considered in some detail. And so here, **elect** carries the meaning of approved indicating excellence of quality, which I argued was the essential meaning in Peter's prior usages of the term. The New Testament does teach a doctrine of election, but it involves election in terms of people in Christ being approved or excellent, as Christ is approved and excellent, and has nothing to do with being picked for justification.

Remember, Peter said God is building a spiritual house. This was in view back in Isaiah 28, where God said through the prophet that this great project is a work of God ("I lay in Zion") and would be initiated with the setting down of the "precious corner stone" as "a sure foundation." This denotes the building of the spiritual house of which Jesus is the **chief corner stone**. Recall that in Hebrews, Jesus is the sole High Priest of the priesthood after the order of Melchizedek. (e.g., Hebrews 5:1-10) Since Peter's prior verse referenced the priesthood, the notion in verse 6 that Jesus is the **chief corner stone** is consistent with his place as High Priest. Further, Jesus is the **elect** (approved, excellent) and **precious** (priceless) One of the Father, and as a result, **he**

**that believeth on** Jesus **shall not be confounded** or put to shame. This is a double negative for emphasis. Those that trust Jesus will be approved of God.

> 7 Unto you therefore which believe *he is* precious: but unto them which be disobedient, THE STONE WHICH THE BUILDERS DISALLOWED, THE SAME IS MADE THE HEAD OF THE CORNER,

Just as Jesus is priceless to the Father, so also he is **precious** to Christians—those **which believe** on him. Those who do not believe on him are **disobedient**, and Peter quoted from Psalm 118 to show that their lack of belief fulfills prophecy. Psalm 118:22 reads: "The stone *which* the builders refused is become the head *stone* of the corner." The **builders** refers to the Jewish leadership, but despite their rejection of **the stone**, God made **the same...the head of the corner**, i.e., the corner stone. God is using Jesus as the centerpiece of His redemptive work as He builds the "spiritual house" of verse 5. It is notable that Psalm 118:22 is also quoted in Matthew 21:42, Luke 20:17, and Acts 4:11. Jesus personally applied Psalm 118:22 to himself:

> Matthew 21:42 Jesus saith unto them, Did ye never read in the scriptures, The stone which the builders rejected, the same is become the head of the corner: this is the Lord's doing, and it is marvellous in our eyes? 43 Therefore say I unto you, The kingdom of God shall be taken from you, and given to a nation bringing forth the fruits thereof. 44 And whosoever shall fall on this stone shall be broken: but on

whomsoever it shall fall, it will grind him to powder.

We might ask concerning Matthew 21:43, which "nation"? Peter will answer that in verse 9. But note that in Acts 4, Peter preached Jesus to the "rulers of the people" (i.e., the builders):

> Acts 4:8 Then Peter, filled with the Holy Ghost, said unto them, Ye rulers of the people, and elders of Israel, 9 If we this day be examined of the good deed done to the impotent man, by what means he is made whole; 10 Be it known unto you all, and to all the people of Israel, that by the name of Jesus Christ of Nazareth, whom ye crucified, whom God raised from the dead, *even* by him doth this man stand here before you whole. 11 This is the stone which was set at nought of you builders, which is become the head of the corner. 12 Neither is there salvation in any other: for there is none other name under heaven given among men, whereby we must be saved.

What Peter said here would particularly resonate with his Jewish Christian audience, for those that would persecute them were like the Jews that rejected Jesus, aligning themselves with the builders whom God judged. In contrast, Peter's readers aligned themselves with the "head of the corner" that God exalted.

> 8 And A STONE OF STUMBLING, AND A ROCK OF OFFENCE, *even to them* which stumble at the word, being disobedient: whereunto also they were appointed.

Once again, Peter appealed to the Old Testament to support his argument, and in this case, to Isaiah 8:14, which in context reads:

> Isaiah 8:11 For the LORD spake thus to me with a strong hand, and instructed me that I should not walk in the way of this people, saying, 12 Say ye not, A confederacy, to all *them to* whom this people shall say, A confederacy; neither fear ye their fear, nor be afraid. 13 Sanctify the LORD of hosts himself; and *let* him *be* your fear, and *let* him *be* your dread. 14 And he shall be for a sanctuary; but for a stone of stumbling and for a rock of offence to both the houses of Israel, for a gin and for a snare to the inhabitants of Jerusalem.

This Jesus whom the builders rejected (and many after their example) was to them **a stone of stumbling, and rock of offence**. Specifically, they stumbled **at the word** about the Christ, **being disobedient** to what God said of Him. I note that the phrase **whereunto they were appointed** has engendered debate. Some argue that this verse says certain people were predestined not to believe in Jesus and are not capable of doing so. But this verse certainly does not say that unsaved people cannot believe the gospel.

The proper interpretation turns first on the meaning of the Greek term translated **appointed**, and then of course on the context in which this verse appears in Peter's epistle. The Greek term is *tithemi* (Strong number 5087), which appears in the New Testament 96 times. There is not a single instance in which it clearly has the sense of predestine, but rather, it is typically translated as put, set, laid, or make, as the context dictates. BDAG gives its primary meaning as "to put or place in a particular location." It is occasionally translated as **appointed**. (e.g., 1 Thessalonians 5:9; 2 Timothy 1:11; Hebrews 1:2) Peter used the term only three times. (1 Peter 2:6, 8; 2 Peter 2:6; translated lay, appointed, and making, respectively) In our English language, it is a simple matter to check a dictionary and find that the term appoint is typically defined along the lines of "to fix, set, or arrange." According to BDAG, the term can have the meaning of "to assign to some task or function." Neither the Greek term nor its translation here in 1 Peter 2:8 mean predestination.

With this background, let's look to the context. The term at issue, *tithemi*, was used by Peter in 2:6 (quoting Isaiah 28:16) and again in 2:8 (quoting Isaiah 8:14). In 2:6, he wrote about God appointing, placing or setting the chief corner stone, Jesus, in Sion. In other words, Jesus was placed by God in a position of honor and those who believe in Jesus are likewise exalted or honored by God ("shall not be confounded," i.e., dishonored or put to shame). To set up the contrast, Peter quoted Isaiah 8:14 in verse 8 and addressed the consequences for those that reject the Word of God. We should note here what follows in Isaiah 8:15: "And many among them shall stumble, and fall, and be broken, and be snared, and be taken." Isaiah prophesied that many people would reject the living stone, Jesus Christ. The point is that these disobedient people are confounded or put to shame or debased because of their disobedience in rejecting the Word of God about Jesus Christ. For that reason alone, they are assigned a position of dishonor and condemnation. This says nothing about anyone being unable to believe or predestined not to believe, but instead, Peter merely explained the consequence of their disobedience.

> 9 But ye *are* a chosen generation, a royal priesthood, an holy nation, a peculiar people; that ye should shew forth the praises of him who hath called you out of darkness into his marvellous light:

In contrast to the position of shame for those that reject Jesus, those who believe in him constitute **a chosen generation, a royal priesthood, an holy nation, a peculiar people**. These are corporate descriptions of those that comprise the spiritual house God is constructing with Jesus as the chief corner stone. Again, Peter appealed to expressions that would resonate with a Jewish Christian audience since these expressions allude to Old Testament descriptions of God's people:

> Exodus 19:5 Now therefore, if ye will obey my voice indeed, and keep my covenant, then ye shall be a peculiar treasure unto me above all people: for all the earth *is* mine: 6 And ye shall be unto me a **kingdom of priests, and an holy nation**. These *are* the words which thou shalt speak unto the children of Israel.

> Isaiah 43:20 The beast of the field shall honour me, the dragons and the owls: because I give waters in the wilderness, *and* rivers in the desert, to give drink to my people, **my chosen**. 21 This people have I formed for myself; they shall **shew forth my praise**.

> Deuteronomy 14:2 For thou *art* an **holy people** unto the LORD thy God, and the LORD hath chosen thee to be a **peculiar people** unto himself, above all the nations that *are* upon the earth.

The phrase **chosen generation** or race means a **chosen** humanity of whom Christ is head (remember, Jesus is the corner stone of this house). And the word **chosen** is the Greek *eklektos* previously examined, and has the same meaning here of believers in Jesus as it did of Jesus himself when Peter used it (translated "elect") to describe Jesus in verse 6. Believers are identified with the qualities of the chief corner stone. Jesus is **chosen** or elect in the sense of being excellent and approved, particularly as to faithfulness to the Father's will, and so also are believers. And someone might say to this, "I am frequently less than excellent." Peter's point here is that God sees us in our identification with the Son, and He is working in our lives to the end that we would experience the excellence and holiness that is already identified with us through the Son, to wit, that our position would become our condition.

We are also a **royal priesthood**, indicating being both priests and kings. (Revelation 1:6) Bear in mind that the **priesthood** of which Jesus is High Priest is after the order of Melchisedec. This man Melchisedec, of whom we do not know a great deal, was introduced in Genesis 14 as the "king of Salem" and "the priest of the most high God." (Genesis 14:18) While it is beyond the scope of the immediate text to pursue this issue at any length, the writer of Hebrews did exactly that. In short, Jesus is of the tribe of Judah, and so while he could not be a Levitical High Priest (they must be from the tribe of

Levi, in the lineage of Aaron), Jesus could be a High Priest of this different priesthood, that associated with Melchisedec. And because he was of the tribe of Judah, Jesus could also be a king. As believers in Jesus who are identified with Him by faith, we are identified with Jesus' **priesthood**. This is a **royal priesthood** because its members are priest-kings like Melchisedec and like Jesus. That the Christ would be a priest-king was foretold in Zechariah 6:9-15. The writer of Hebrews explained that Jesus was "made an high priest for ever after the order of Melchisedec." (Hebrews 6:20) Indeed, "now hath he obtained a more excellent ministry, by how much also he is the mediator of a better covenant, which was established on better promises." (Hebrews 8:6) The notion of being a king implies a position of authority and leadership, and it looks forward to our role in the Kingdom.

Next, Peter described his readers as **an holy nation**. Here, **holy** has the idea of being separated, and **nation** implies a community of people. Remember, Peter exhorted his readers in 1:16 to "be ye holy." And 1 Peter 2:5 already referred to believers as "an holy priesthood." What God wants for us in our experience is already who we are in Christ. But we need to grow and mature as God shapes us as living stones so that our position becomes our condition. If we are a **holy nation**, and the Scripture plainly says we are, that ought to mean something, not only individually but corporately. Christians ought to stand out profoundly distinct from the impurities and vain pursuits of the world, from the crass language and sensual overload of Hollywood's films, and from the selfish ambition of the corporate norm. We must see who we are in Christ and understand how God is shaping us and training us to be **holy**. I might add here that many teachers of the Word are always saying we are sinners. But of believers the Bible more often speaks of us through our identification with Jesus, not as sinners but as **chosen** and **holy**.

Next, Peter wrote that believers are **a peculiar people**. The word **peculiar** has to do with being owned or possessed, and the point is that we are a **people** for God's possession. Peter will say in verse 11 that we are "strangers and pilgrims" in this world. To be **chosen**, **holy**, and God's possession, identifies us corporately as those that are in the world but not of it. God is building a new humanity from living stones on this planet for something glorious. We have a living hope rooted in God's construction project. He is shaping us and growing us and will ultimately reward us with an inheritance for what He did through us. This is reason to shout! And so Peter concluded that we are God's own **that we should shew forth the praises of him who hath called** us **out of darkness into his marvelous light**. Because of what God has done for us and is doing through us, we praise His virtues. We are no longer in **darkness**, which expresses a state of blindness to truth, but are in God's **marvelous light**, where we can now see clearly. As Paul wrote: "Who hath delivered us from the power of darkness, and hath translated *us* into the kingdom of his dear Son." (Colossians 1:13) Our lives ought to reflect the reality of who we are and where we are.

> 10 Which in time past *were* NOT A PEOPLE, but *are* now the people of God: which had NOT OBTAINED MERCY, but now have obtained mercy.

Completing his explanation of the spiritual house God is building with His Son as the chief corner stone, Peter wrote of his readers that **in time past** they **were not a people, but are now the people of God**. Here Peter quoted from Hosea 1:6, 9, and 2:23:

> Hosea 1:6 And she conceived again, and bare a daughter. And *God* said unto him, Call her name Loruhamah: for I will no more have mercy upon the house of Israel; but I will utterly take them away.... 9 Then said *God*, Call his name Loammi: for ye *are* not my people, and I will not be your God....2:23 And I will sow her unto me in the earth; and I will have mercy upon her that had not obtained mercy; and I will say to *them which were* not my people, Thou *art* my people; and they shall say, *Thou art* my God.

Hosea was a prophet to Israel (meaning the Northern Kingdom) near the time of the ministries of Amos and Jonah to Israel. The nation had wholly given itself over to idolatry and so God spoke through His three prophets of turning them over to the wicked Assyrians. Yet through Hosea, God also promised a future forgiveness and restoration when Judah and Israel would again be united. (Hosea 1:10-11) Hosea looked to this future time in 2:23, quoted by Peter, when God would plant a people unto Himself in the Holy Land. Peter borrowed from these familiar prophecies, not to say that Hosea's prophecies were fulfilled in his readers, but that His readers occupy the blessed position of being God's people by virtue of their identification with Jesus, a position they did not previously have before they were born again.

## <u>Closing</u>

I was at a restaurant recently that had some large saltwater aquariums teaming with a variety of fish. The patterns of the fish—a variety of stripes, colors, and shapes—were amazing, and their diversity comes together into something more graceful and magnificent than any one or two of them alone. And I was reminded that God is the master artist. We need to be wowed again and to marvel at the beauty of what issues from God's Hand. But the beauty in nature, as striking as it is, falls short of His artistic masterpiece.

Out of a dark and fallen world, God created a new humanity on the foundation of His Son Jesus Christ. Individually, we are living stones, but corporately, with all of the stones on the canvas, we are identified with the chief corner stone and together form a spiritual house, a royal priesthood, and a holy nation, fit out and qualified as heirs in the world to come. We are the people of God, and it is imperative that we see ourselves as the master artist sees us. This is who we are and who we will continue to be in the world to come, and in our experience we ought to increasingly exhibit behavior befitting that which God made of us by being people of the Book. We are to be a people that prioritize the things of God above all else, and live our lives on the basis of His Word. And we are family, and as such we have family obligations that require attention and deliberate effort as we minister to one another. But we are still in the world and so we bear individual responsibility for how we carry ourselves while we are in the world on temporary assignment from the King, which as we will see, Peter addressed in detail in the balance of his epistle. Seeing ourselves as God does, a new people in Jesus Christ, a new and beautiful canvas from the master artist, should be a radically transformative paradigm for how we live our lives. Indeed, our lives in the present ought to be reoriented around what God says of who we are and the blessings to come.

## Application Points

**MAIN PRINCIPLE:** Christians are a new humanity together with Jesus Christ, that God describes as His own people, a chosen generation, a royal priesthood, and a holy nation, and that reality should encourage and motivate us as we grow through an experiential knowledge of His Word.

## Discussion Questions

1. What is the role of the Word of God in our growth as believers?

2. Can a Christian grow to maturity without mature knowledge of the Word of God?

3. What are the implications for us individually that we are in God's hands living stones?

4. As a "holy priesthood" and a "royal priesthood," what type of sacrifices are we to offer?

5. What are the practical implications of believers having been called "out of darkness into his marvelous light"? (It is critical we know what darkness and light are in this context!)

# Chapter 5

# Transformation Through Submission

1 Peter 2:11-17

An ambassador is a diplomatic official sent by one sovereign state to another as a resident representative. While that ambassador might enjoy diplomatic immunity, the ambassador nevertheless represents his or her nation of citizenship before the people and government where he or she resides and works. The ambassador's conduct, good or bad, reflects on the government the ambassador represents. In a similar way, First Peter teaches that we are ambassadors for the King, living in this world on temporary assignment "as strangers and pilgrims" (1 Peter 2:11). We identify with the spiritual house that God is building in Christ. And because we so identify ourselves with that nation, our conduct, good or bad, will reflect positively or negatively on the One we represent in this world. As Jesus' ambassadors, our lives are under observation by those around us, and we need to represent Jesus well. This entails specific obedience in various contexts.

There are spheres within which God has delegated authority, and in those spheres we represent Jesus Christ well by our submission to that delegated authority. In general, to obey the delegated authority is to obey God, and to disobey the delegated authority is to disobey God. One of those spheres of delegated authority that touches all of our lives is human government. Whatever we may think of the government where we live (or of the taxes it imposes), Peter said to his readers, and by application to us, that we must obey human government. This glorifies God and this is what experiencing the salvation of our souls looks like in day-to-day, practical terms. Do you want to lay up treasure in heaven? Peter said, if I may paraphrase, "obey God's delegated authority in human government."

## Outline

III. THE PLAN OF SALVATION (OF THE SOUL-LIFE) (1:13-4:19)

    a. That it would transform our character (1:13-2:10)

    b. That it would transform our conduct through submission (2:11-3:7)

        i. Our conduct in the world (2:11-17)

## Excursus on the Divine Institution of Human Government

While our primary focus in this commentary is the content and exegesis of First Peter, what Peter wrote was not in a vacuum, but was part of God's larger progressive revelation to humanity. We will be benefited in considering what Peter wrote in his epistle against the larger backdrop of God's progressive revelation about human government.

The Bible teaches that there are divinely ordained institutions that include, for example, the home or family, the church, and human government. What is helpful to understand from this excursus concerning human government is the following: (1) God raises and removes nations and rulers; (2) human government is divinely ordained; (3) believers are called upon to submit to human government except when human government takes action to prevent the believer from doing what God's Word commands or force the believer to do that which God's Word prohibits; (4) believers are called upon to honor (respect) those within positions of authority in human government; and (5) believers are called upon to pray for those in all levels of human government. Unquestionably, the single passage from the New Testament with the most content on the issue of human government is Romans 13:1-7, and so I will turn to that passage to guide this excursus.

> Romans 13:1 Let every soul be subject unto the higher powers. For there is no power but of God: the powers that be are ordained of God. 2 Whosoever therefore resisteth the power, resisteth the ordinance of God: and they that resist shall receive to themselves damnation.

The first observation we make is that **higher powers** refers to governing authorities (as the balance of the passage makes clear), and these **powers** or authorities

God **ordained**. So human government is not man's idea, but God's. And it is not merely some aspect of human government, but all **the powers that be are ordained of God**. For this reason, Paul concluded that defiance of human government is defiance of God—**whosoever therefore resisteth the power, resisteth the ordinance of God**. Moreover, since resisting human government is rebellion to God, those **that resist** or rebel against human government **shall receive to themselves damnation** or judgment. This judgment has nothing to do with our eternal destiny as believers, but temporal consequences for resisting a human government to whom God delegated authority to impose punishment. That every human government on this planet now and at all times in human history ultimately derives its authority and existence from God presupposes God's sovereignty over the affairs of humanity. And indeed, the Bible makes clear that God raises and removes nations and rulers as He wills.

Indeed, we find many examples in the Bible of God's sovereignty over all levels of human government. Consider the example of the Pharaoh that God commanded through Moses to release the Jewish people:

> <u>Romans 9:17</u> For the scripture saith unto Pharaoh, Even for this same purpose have I raised thee up, that I might shew my power in thee, and that my name might be declared throughout all the earth.

In this verse, Paul made the point that God, in order to **shew** His **Power** through **Pharaoh...raised** him **up**. This is not a reference to creating **Pharaoh**, but to sovereignly promoting a specific individual into the role as **Pharaoh**, i.e., king of Egypt, at a specific time in history for a specific purpose. Indeed, in this instance, God used this individual as a means of demonstrating his **power...that His name might be declared throughout all the earth**. If there is any question that the God of Israel succeeded during this time in history in making His **name** (i.e., reputation) known, we need only jump ahead to Rahab's profession of faith in Joshua 2:

> Joshua 2:9 And she said unto the men, I know that the LORD hath given you the land, and that your terror is fallen upon us, and that all the inhabitants of the land faint because of you. 10 For we have heard how the LORD dried up the water of the Red sea for you, when ye came out of Egypt; and what ye did unto the two kings of the Amorites, that *were* on the other side Jordan, Sihon and Og, whom ye utterly destroyed. 11 And as soon as we had heard *these things*, our hearts did melt, neither did there remain any more courage in any man, because of you: for the LORD your God, he *is* God in heaven above, and in earth beneath.

We find another powerful example in Pontius Pilate, the Roman official that tried Jesus and declared him a "just person" (Matthew 27:24) and publicly stated, "I find no fault in this man" (Luke 23:4). But when Pilate spoke privately to Jesus, he was taken aback that Jesus would not answer his interrogation, which he took as an affront to his authority:

> John 19:7 The Jews answered him, We have a law, and by our law he ought to die,

because he made himself the Son of God. 8 When Pilate therefore heard that saying, he was the more afraid; 9 And went again into the judgment hall, and saith unto Jesus, Whence art thou? But Jesus gave him no answer. 10 Then saith Pilate unto him, Speakest thou not unto me? knowest thou not that I have power to crucify thee, and have power to release thee? 11 Jesus answered, Thou couldest have no power *at all* against me, except it were given thee from above: therefore he that delivered me unto thee hath the greater sin.

What we gather from this passage is that **Pilate**, as an individual ruler within the Roman government, only had the **power...given** him **from above**, that is, from God. So it is not merely governments at large that God establishes, but in God's exercise of sovereignty, He gives or delegates authority to specific individuals, be it a Pharaoh or a governor like **Pilate**. Too many Christians imagine God's hand in action when their candidate wins, but what the Scripture testifies to is that every human government, of every nation, at every level, is ordained of God, not only as state organizations but as to each individual member. This means that the governments of North Korea and Iran are just as much ordained of God as the government of the United States, or on a more local level, the state government of Texas, and the city government of Houston where I reside. To this I hasten to add that God accomplishes his purposes for human government through the good and the bad, just as God generally accomplishes His purposes through the good and bad conduct of people. Recall how God used

Joseph's brothers' wickedness in selling Joseph into slavery to ultimately bring Joseph into power as the second-in-command in Egypt, as Joseph explained to his brothers after Jacob's death: "ye thought evil against me; *but* God meant it unto good, to bring to pass, as *it is* this day, to save much people alive." (Genesis 50:20) In fact, many of the Bible examples, like the Pharaoh of the Exodus, are bad. Consider Nebuchadnezzar, the king of the Babylonian Empire that God used to chasten Judah. God installed Nebuchadnezzar in power, referred to him as "my servant," and sovereignly protected him against his enemies:

> Jeremiah 27:6 And now have I given all these lands into the hand of Nebuchadnezzar the king of Babylon, my servant; and the beasts of the field have I given him also to serve him. 7 And all nations shall serve him, and his son, and his son's son, until the very time of his land come: and then many nations and great kings shall serve themselves of him. 8 And it shall come to pass, *that* the nation and kingdom which will not serve the same Nebuchadnezzar the king of Babylon, and that will not put their neck under the yoke of the king of Babylon, that nation will I punish, saith the LORD, with the sword, and with the famine, and with the pestilence, until I have consumed them by his hand.

So we see that God places whom He wills into power, may choose to protect their power against their enemies, and holds accountable those rulers like Pharaoh that abuse or exceed their authority. We dare not look at this through the lens of the United States only. Which governments did God ordain? The Bible tells us that God ordained every government, not just democratic republics. To put it plainly, for His purposes, God ordained monarchies, and communist and socialist governments, just as He did the government of the United States. And He will hold all of them accountable. To be sure, God is not wringing His hands in worry about who will win the next presidential election in the United States. God is sovereign and uses, in the case of presidents, our votes to fulfill His purposes, and at the end of the day the person that wins does so because God willed or permitted it. In the United States, at the time of this writing, the current presidential administration is Republican. The prior administration was Democrat. God ordained both, and specifically ordained the presidents that were elected, and both are responsible to God for how they exercise the authority delegated to them.

Getting back to Romans 13:1, Paul said **every soul must be subject unto the higher powers**. Every believer under every human government in the world, good or bad, benign or oppressive, democratic, communist or other, is obligated to obey the government where God placed them. But what if I do not approve of the government? Or I find a law it passed unreasonable? The Bible says, in effect, "so what." As a professor of mine would ask his students rhetorically, "Is God sovereign or isn't he?" When we disobey the government God ordained and delegated authority to, we disobey God, and that is sin. Not only that, when we **resist** or disobey civil government we **shall receive to** ourselves **damnation** or judgment, typically at the hand of the government we resist. That judgment may be fines, imprisonment, or even death, as Paul explained. But what if human government abuses its delegated authority? The short answer is God will deal with that also, but there are times when that abuse requires the Christian to disobey.

We find an excellent example of God dealing with those He delegated authority to in Pharaoh and Nebuchadnezzar. Of course, as recorded in the book of Exodus, God sent plagues upon Egypt, and ultimately brought Pharaoh to his knees and freed His people. Nebuchadnezzar deluded himself into believing that his kingdom was the product of his actions alone. In the book of Daniel, we read a curious episode of God schooling Nebuchadnezzar as to who brought him to power and prospered his kingdom. Daniel 4 records that Nebuchadnezzar had a dream about a tree being cut down to a stump and asking Daniel to interpret the dream, as he had done previously (see Daniel 2) with another of the king's dream. Daniel explained that God was going to bring temporal judgment on Nebuchadnezzar, and indeed, at the very moment that Nebuchadnezzar boasted, God brought him down and he spent seven years as a madman:

> Daniel 4:28 All this came upon the king Nebuchadnezzar. 29 At the end of twelve months he walked in the palace of the kingdom of Babylon. 30 The king spake, and said, Is not this great Babylon, that I have built for the house of the kingdom by the might of my power, and for the honour

> of my majesty? 31 While the word *was* in the king's mouth, there fell a voice from heaven, *saying*, O king Nebuchadnezzar, to thee it is spoken; The kingdom is departed from thee. 32 And they shall drive thee from men, and thy dwelling *shall be* with the beasts of the field: they shall make thee to eat grass as oxen, and seven times shall pass over thee, until thou know that the most High ruleth in the kingdom of men, and giveth it to whomsoever he will. 33 The same hour was the thing fulfilled upon Nebuchadnezzar: and he was driven from men, and did eat grass as oxen, and his body was wet with the dew of heaven, till his hairs were grown like eagles' *feathers*, and his nails like birds' *claws*.

Only after seven years did Nebuchadnezzar come to his senses, but during this time of insanity God protected him. When Nebuchadnezzar awoke from his madness, he recognized publicly that God can take down kings at His whim:

> Daniel 4:34 And at the end of the days I Nebuchadnezzar lifted up mine eyes unto heaven, and mine understanding returned unto me, and I blessed the most High, and I praised and honoured him that liveth for ever, whose dominion *is* an everlasting dominion, and his kingdom *is* from generation to generation: 35 And all the inhabitants of the earth *are* reputed as nothing: and he doeth according to his will

> in the army of heaven, and *among* the inhabitants of the earth: and none can stay his hand, or say unto him, What doest thou? ... 37 Now I Nebuchadnezzar praise and extol and honour the King of heaven, all whose works *are* truth, and his ways judgment: and those that walk in pride he is able to abase.

Turning again to Romans 13, Paul explained the primary purpose of human government, namely to create an environment where righteousness can flourish.

> <u>Romans 13:3</u> For rulers are not a terror to good works, but to the evil. Wilt thou then not be afraid of the power? do that which is good, and thou shalt have praise of the same: 4 For he is the minister of God to thee for good. But if thou do that which is evil, be afraid; for he beareth not the sword in vain: for he is the minister of God, a revenger to *execute* wrath upon him that doeth evil.

Paul provided a maxim, not a guaranty, that human government was **not a terror to good works**. In other words, in general, a believer who does right by God will not be punished in so doing by human government. Rather, the government is **a terror...to the evil**, meaning those who disobey civil law. For that reason, if we do not want to live in fear of the government we are under, we should **do that which is good** before men and God, for which, again as a maxim or general rule of life, we **shalt have praise of the same**. When we are living Biblically, generally the government will not be a source of fear to us, but of **praise** or commendation. In fact, human government **is the minister** or servant **of God to** us **for** our **good**. However, if we do wrong, we should be afraid because God delegated to human government the authority to punish, even to wield or **beareth...the sword**, and when government bears the sword it does so as a **minister** or servant **of** God to impose God's **wrath** (temporal judgment) **upon him that doeth evil**. Ironically, the **sword** Paul had in view, that of a Roman executioner, would be the source of his own death not too many years after he wrote these words. So pulling this together, if we obey the laws, the government will generally leave us alone. But if not, God delegated to the government the right to punish, even up to imposing the death penalty. (cf. Deuteronomy 21:18-21)

> Romans 13:5 Wherefore *ye* must needs be subject, not only for wrath, but also for conscience sake. 6 For for this cause pay ye tribute also: for they are God's ministers, attending continually upon this very thing. 7 Render therefore to all their dues: tribute to whom tribute *is due*; custom to whom custom; fear to whom fear; honour to whom honour.

As Paul continued, since God ordained human government and its right to punish, we **must needs be subject** to that government that God placed us under, both to avoid punishment or **wrath** at the hands of human government, and **for conscience sake** before God, recognizing that our obedience to government is obedience to God. On this matter of **conscience**, as believers, we should be convicted by our sin. Since God delegated authority to human governments and those governments pass laws, our disobedience to such laws is (generally) a violation of God's standards and, therefore, sin that should result in a guilty **conscience**. We are to live in obedience to the law of the land, both to avoid the civil or criminal penalty for disobedience, and to maintain a clean **conscience** before God.

And to get to the question everyone in the room has but may not ask, does this mean we must pay outrageous taxes? Yes. Paul instructed his readers to **pay ye tribute also** because **they** (government authorities, i.e., the IRS) **are God's ministers** or servants tasked with **attending continually upon this very thing**, that is, governing. Recall Jesus' words, "Render therefore unto Caesar the things which are Caesar's; and unto God the things that are God's." (Matthew 22:21) Not only that, Paul further commanded that we owe **fear to whom fear** is due and **honour to whom honour** is due. That is, the believer should **fear** government as he or she should **fear** God, and **honour** the governing authorities as he or she would **honour** God. To **honour** means to show respect.

Before turning back to 1 Peter, one more point should be made, which is that we are called to pray for those in authority. Hear Paul's words to Timothy:

> <u>1 Timothy 2:1</u> I exhort therefore, that, first of all, supplications, prayers, intercessions, *and* giving of thanks, be made for all men; 2 For kings, and *for* all that are in authority; that we may lead a quiet and peaceable life in all godliness and honesty. 3 For this *is* good and acceptable in the sight of God our Saviour.

Paul's exhortation in verse 2 is simple. We are to pray **for all men**, including **kings** and **all those that are in authority**. I am not privy to other peoples' private prayers, but I do hear many public prayers in church and other contexts. My observation is that certain people pray publicly for the president and others in government with enthusiasm when it is who they voted for. When the other guy wins, the prayers go away or are qualitatively different (deflated and rote). This is hypocrisy and it is sin. We are admonished to pray for the governing rulers—both the ones we voted for and the ones we did not vote for, the ones we like and the ones we do not like, the ones we respect and the ones we have no respect for. And in those countries where the citizens do not get to vote, or the vote is rigged, believers are still exhorted to pray for those in leadership. The command is not difficult to comprehend, and we just need to make it happen. Remember that Paul wrote these words to Timothy, as he did the words to the church in Rome that have guided this excursus, against the backdrop of an oppressive, corrupt, and frequently brutal Roman government.

## Scripture and Comments

With the foregoing excursus in mind, we turn to 1 Peter 2:13-17. Peter briefly addressed the importance of abstaining from fleshly lusts and godly conduct before others, and then focused on the issue of submission to human government. All of these issues were in the larger context of Peter's explaining the outworking of the salvation of the soul in our brief time of sojourning in this world. As Peter said, we are presently "receiving the end of [our] faith, even the salvation of [our] souls." Our faith responses to life put to our account the heavenly treasures, and in a very real sense, appropriate to us during this lifetime the inheritance to be revealed "at the appearing of Jesus Christ." (1 Peter 1:7, 9) And in the verses under immediate consideration, it is the faith responses to living among those that malign and marginalize his readers, and living under God's ordained human government, that Peter addressed.

> <u>1 Peter 2:11</u> Dearly beloved, I beseech *you* as strangers and pilgrims, abstain from fleshly lusts, which war against the soul; <u>12</u> Having your conversation honest among the Gentiles: that, whereas they speak against you as evildoers, they may by *your* good works, which they shall behold, glorify God in the day of visitation.

Peter started with a paradigm shift for his readers. As believers, we are in this world, but are not of this world or the world system. Indeed, God transferred us from the kingdom of darkness into the kingdom of His beloved son. (Colossians 1:13) We read in Philippians 3:20: "For our conversation is in heaven; from whence also we look for the Saviour, the Lord Jesus Christ." We were "called... out of darkness into his marvelous light." (1 Peter 2:9) And so it is no surprise that in this world we are mere **strangers and pilgrims**, not citizens. This world is not our permanent home. Remember the testimony of Abraham's life of faith: "By faith he sojourned in the land of promise, as *in* a strange country, dwelling in tabernacles with Isaac and Jacob, the heirs with him of the same promise: For he looked for a city which hath foundations, whose builder and maker *is* God." Abraham lived in the Promise Land in tents because he understood his real home to be in the heavenly city, the New Jerusalem. When the writer of Hebrews wrote that Abraham "sojourned," he used the verb form of the Greek word translated **strangers** here in 1 Peter 2:11. Like Abraham, we are on temporary assignment as resident aliens (**pilgrims**) and our conduct reflects on God. We are ambassadors of Jesus Christ, and should not bring him reproach.

As **strangers and pilgrims** we are not to adopt the world's agenda or thinking, for those are contrary to God. Our mandate from Jesus is to live out a Biblical agenda; we are **pilgrims** called to live out the reality of our salvation and not to let **fleshly lusts** dominate our **soul**[s]. We are to **abstain from fleshly lusts** or desires, **which** Peter warned make **war against the soul**. Here, **soul** has the same meaning as it does throughout the epistle, not speaking of our spirit but our experience of life. In 1 Peter 1:13, after introducing the concept of the salvation of the **soul**, Peter wrote: "Wherefore gird up the loins of your mind, be sober, and hope to the end for the grace that is to be brought unto you at the revelation of Jesus Christ." (1 Peter 1:13) How we think matters and right thinking is critical to this matter of the salvation of our **soul**. And in that regard, **fleshly lusts** can do us harm from the inside out. The word **lusts** is the Greek *epithumia*, which Strong's says means "a longing (especially for what is forbidden):--concupiscence, desire, lust (after)." While we should be about the business of "receiving the end of [our] faith, even the salvation of [our] souls" (1 Peter 1:9), our own **lusts** can bring ruin to our **soul**, i.e., our temporal experience of life. Indeed, when our deepest desire is not for the things of God but for the things of the world, our thought life will **war against** our **soul** and destroy our opportunity to appropriate our inheritance. Using the same term for **lust**, James explained how **lust** gives birth to sin, and that to an experience of death rather than life:

> James 1:14 But every man is tempted, when he is drawn away of his own lust, and enticed. 15 Then when lust hath conceived, it bringeth forth sin: and sin, when it is finished, bringeth forth death.

We need to understand that spiritual warfare occurs between the ears. Our thought life will direct our conduct. Yet we are in a world where people honor the "god of this world." (2 Corinthians 4:4) And how extraordinary it is in our time for a person to live above the culture. I fear it is far more common for believers to fit, and indeed to welcome, the mold of the world, which Paul warned against so strongly in Romans 12:2 saying, "be not conformed to this world." It is in our flesh to conform to the world, but by God's grace we can be different and stand out from the culture we are in. For being different and above the culture we live in, from the standpoint of Biblical thinking and living, is the essence of personal holiness that Peter urged his readers to engage. (1 Peter 1:16) And the point that Peter, James and Paul all made was that when we live according to our **fleshly lust**, that is not really living but death. In a famous verse frequently misunderstood as a justification verse, Paul wrote: "For the wages of sin is death...." (Romans 6:32) Where we direct our thought life determines whether, as believers, we experience life or death:

> Romans 8:5 For they that are after the flesh do mind the things of the flesh; but

they that are after the Spirit the things of the Spirit. 6 For to be carnally minded *is* death; but to be spiritually minded *is* life and peace.

If we cater to the flesh, our mind will center on the flesh, and if we cater to the things of God, our mind will center on the things of God. The former is an experience of death and the latter life and peace. Peter explained that in the outworking of the salvation of the **soul**, what is between our ears is critical. And if we would have our minds centered on **fleshly** or carnal **lusts**, then it will have ramifications for our **soul**, our very experience of life. Such thinking and living is characteristic of those of the world, but should not be characteristic of those who understand they are mere **strangers and pilgrims** on temporary assignment representing the King of Kings and Lord of Lords. This is similar to what Paul wrote in Romans 8. In contrast to an experience of death, right thinking will result in a life that is vindicated before those who observe us. And the key to right thinking is minding the things of the Spirit, or as Paul exhorted the Galatians, to "walk in the Spirit, that [they] shall not fulfill the lust of the flesh." (Galatians 5:16)

Peter related right thinking to right conduct. His readers should have their **conversation** or manner of living **honest among the Gentiles**. The term **honest** is the Greek *kalos*, which is typically translated as "good." The term **Gentiles** is from the Greek *ethnos* and is plural here; it can be translated races, tribes or nations depending on context. By **Gentiles**, many commentators understand Peter to have meant unbelievers or non-Christians, and for that reason the NET translation renders the language as "among the Non-christians." However, the term is almost always used in the New Testament literally of **Gentiles**, meaning non-Jews. There is no indication in the text that Peter meant non-believer. Remembering that Peter's readers lived in Jewish settlements in predominantly **Gentile** nations, it should not surprise us that Peter exhorted his Jewish readers to live right **among** their **Gentile** neighbors.

There is a potential for confusion in this passage because of the several uses of the pronoun **they**. Peter understood that his audience may experience adversity from their neighbors, but did not teach his audience to retaliate. Rather, **they** were to respond with a lifestyle that honors God, and based on what **they** (the **Gentiles**) see in the lives of these Jewish Christians, even though **they** (the **Gentles**) **speak against** the Christians **as evildoers** or wrongdoers, **they may by** the Christians' **good works, which they shall behold, glorify God in the day of visitation**. In other words, Peter said, do not retaliate against those that malign you as **evildoers** but demonstrate your godliness in how you live so that when God appears, **they** will **glorify God**.

This is reminiscent of Jesus' words in the Sermon on the Mount: "Let your light so shine before men, that they may see your good works, and glorify your Father which is in heaven." (Matthew 5:16) In fact, in that same message, Jesus taught non-retaliation. (Matthew 5:38-42) Ultimately, **in the day of visitation** when Jesus returns, the unbelieving world will give testimony to the fact that the Christians were right. Indeed, as Paul wrote to the Philippians, eventually every knee will bow. (Philippians 2:9) But it seems that some may **glorify God** because an authentic Christian who lived right (**honest**) influenced them and ultimately they were won to Christ, and this seems to be what Peter primarily had in mind. Of course, some will reject Jesus despite the evidence of radically changed lives of believers. But in the end, all will acknowledge God's glory. Our words do matter, but often it is our **honest conversation** before an unbelieving world that will make all the difference. Peter will return to this concept of influencing others by good or **honest** conduct in chapter 3 in the context a wife's conduct before her husband. And he will return to the issue of persecution from non-believers in much greater detail in chapter 4 of the epistle.

> 13 Submit yourselves to every ordinance of man for the Lord's sake: whether it be to the king, as supreme; 14 Or unto governors, as unto them that are sent by him for the punishment of evildoers, and for the praise of them that do well.

Peter next examined how **strangers and pilgrims** live in various spheres of life. Up first was the area of living under human government. Peter explained how believers should manifest their living hope not only through abstinence from lust but by submission to human government. Similar to Paul's words in Romans 13:1 that we considered in the excursus, Peter exhorted his readers to **submit...to every ordinance of man for the Lord's sake**. The word translated **submit** is the Greek *hupotassō*, which Strong's defines as "to subordinate; reflexively, to obey:--be under obedience (obedient), put under, subdue unto, (be, make) subject (to, unto), be (put) in subjection (to, under), submit self unto." Thus, to **submit** is to obey.

Peter's exhortation, then, was simply that we are to obey **every ordinance** or law **of man**, and Peter added, **for the Lord's sake**. In other words, we are to obey the laws because that pleases **the Lord**. And our obedience is appropriate both **to the king, as supreme, or unto governors**. In other words, it is the entirety of human government, at every level, that Peter had in mind when he exhorted obedience to government. The basis for that submission, just as Paul explained in Romans 13, is that human government is ordained by God. He is absolutely sovereign, and where He deems it fit to delegate authority to someone, then we are bound to obey the delegate just as we are to obey God. Thus, Peter wrote that we are to obey them **as unto them that are sent by God for the punishment of evildoers, and for the praise of them that do well**. We have in these short words God's primary purpose for human government—to create an environment where righteousness can flourish by punishing **evildoers** but approving those **that do well**. Bear in mind that Peter anticipated, as a maxim and not an absolute, that government would fulfill these basic purposes.

> 15 For so is the will of God, that with well doing ye may put to silence the ignorance of foolish men: 16 As free, and not using *your* liberty for a cloke of maliciousness, but as the servants of God. 17 Honour all *men*. Love the brotherhood. Fear God. Honour the king.

Peter explained that our submission to human government **is the will of God**. I can recall a time when I was under the impression that as believers we need to find **the will of God** for our lives, but that somehow it is hidden from us, only to be revealed in some obscure or mystical way. Looking back on much of the teaching I heard on this issue, I realize there is a great deal of confusion. For example, I once heard a missionary couple explain how they learned of their "calling" to a particular country to minister. They were driving somewhere and suddenly saw a street sign with a country name as part of the street name, and that is where they went. But the Bible does not teach us that God's **will** is hidden, or that we should determine God's **will** through street signs and the like. The Bible shows us God's **will** explicitly, and as God grows us, He will lead us by our desires, which are also confirmed later if, indeed, it was God's **will**. But before we embark on looking for street signs, we should start where God's **will** is so explicit, such as here in 1 Peter where we learn it is God's **will** to submit to human government.

Many would skip the more arduous step of diligently engaging God's Word and look for something else first, but that is not Biblical thinking. Many verses specifically state that this or that is the "will of God":

> Romans 12:2 And be not conformed to this world: but be ye transformed by the renewing of your mind, that ye may prove what *is* that good, and acceptable, and perfect, **will of God**.

> Ephesians 6:5 Servants, be obedient to them that are *your* masters according to the flesh, with fear and trembling, in singleness of your heart, as unto Christ; 6 Not with eyeservice, as menpleasers; but as the servants of Christ, doing the **will of God** from the heart;

> **1 Thessalonians 4:3** For this is the **will of God**, *even* your sanctification, that ye should abstain from fornication:
>
> **1 Thessalonians 5:18** In every thing give thanks: for this is the **will of God** in Christ Jesus concerning you.
>
> **Hebrews 10:36** For ye have need of patience, that, after ye have done the **will of God**, ye might receive the promise.

In fact, it is not only these verses that specifically use the phrase "will of God" that reveal His will for us. All of the Bible is instructive in learning God's will. As Jesus prayed his high priestly prayer in John 17, he said, "Sanctify them through thy truth: thy word is truth." It is God's will that we be set aside and changed by His word—all of it! Paul told Timothy that "[a]ll scripture *is* given by inspiration of God, and *is* profitable for doctrine, for reproof, for correction, for instruction in righteousness." (2 Timothy 3:16) So if God's **will** seems hidden, we need to get our heads in the Book where we are sure to find His **will**.

In this area of obedience to human government, Peter reinforced the point he made in verse 12, namely that others are watching. As those who claim the name of Jesus Christ, we are under the world's microscope. Our submission to God's ordained authority in human government is **well doing** before God and man and **may put to silence the ignorance of foolish men**. This, of course, is a maxim. Some people are always a critic (including believers who apparently think a constantly critical attitude is a Spirit gift), but as a general proposition, most non-believers' criticism, which God calls **ignorance of foolish men**, can be silenced. In this regard, the idea of **foolish** entails a lack of understanding. We can influence and teach by our living, walking testimony before the world. We should never underestimate the influence we can have in this way.

Remember that we are "pilgrims and strangers," essentially ambassadors on temporary assignment for Jesus in this world, but not of this world, under diplomatic immunity as regarding sin (i.e., Jesus paid it all). However, Peter warned his audience not to abuse their position. Believers are **free** from sin and death, but that freedom or **liberty** should not be used **for a cloke of maliciousness**, i.e., as a pretext for doing evil. Rather, we are **free** from sin and death to be **the servants of God**. The word **servants** is the Greek *doulos*, meaning slave. This is similar to what Paul wrote in Romans 6:18: "Being then made free from sin, ye became the servants of righteousness." We were set **free** to be slaves to God, and in this context that means especially obedience to God's delegates, that is, human government. Our freedom from sin's penalty is not a license for anarchy or civil disobedience, except in the narrow circumstance where the government prohibits doing that which God requires, or the government mandates that which God prohibits.

Bringing this all together in a memorable creedal statement about doing right before **men** and **God**, Peter exhorted his readers to **honour** or respect **all men, love the brotherhood, fear God**, and **honour the king**. We do not have to like someone to **honour** them. The term carries the idea of showing respect to someone or placing a high value upon someone. Consider Jesus' words to the hypocrites: "This people draweth nigh unto me with their mouth, and honoureth me with their lips; but their heart is far from me." (Matthew 15:8) We also are instructed to **honour** Jesus: "For the Father judgeth no man, but hath committed all judgment unto the Son: That all *men* should honour the Son, even as they honour the Father. He that honoureth not the Son honoureth not the Father which hath sent him." (John 5:22-23) And we are instructed to **honour** widows: "Honour widows that are widows indeed." (1 Timothy 5:3) In all these passages, the word carries the sense of showing due respect. And we can show respect to people that do not always deserve respect from the standpoint of how they behave or what they do. The inability to **honour** others reeks of pride.

In terms of leaders within human government, insofar as they are God's delegates, respect or **honour** is due them. This is easy to understand but hard to do when, for example, we think a leader within government has taken an action we strongly oppose, or when the leader is at odds with our political ideology, or even at odds with a Biblical worldview. Many Christians struggle with their obligation to **honour** the president, governor, senator, etc., if they did not vote for him or her. This is not about disagreeing with ideology or policy. Rather, what is occurring, especially through social media, is Christians (even pastors) posting what are at best disrespectful public statements about persons in government, and at worst, is outright slander. There seems to be a tacit assumption that the Bible does not apply to Facebook posts. But Jesus said every idle word would be judged. (Matthew 12:36) And Peter said that disrespecting those He sovereignly placed in authority within government is rebellion against His sovereignty.

We find a great example of showing **honour** based on God's delegation of authority, and not necessarily on the piety of the delegate, in the life of David. He had already been anointed by Samuel the prophet to succeed the disobedient King Saul. But so long as Saul lived, even though Saul sought to murder David, David purposed to show respect to Saul. And in 1 Samuel 24, we read an episode where David did something that embarrassed Saul, and after doing so, David acknowledged his sin:

> 1 Samuel 24:1 And it came to pass, when Saul was returned from following the Philistines, that it was told him, saying, Behold, David *is* in the wilderness of Engedi. 2 Then Saul took three thousand chosen men out of all Israel, and went to seek David and his men upon the rocks of the wild goats. 3 And he came to the sheepcotes by the way, where *was* a cave; and Saul went in to cover his feet: and David and his men remained in the sides of the cave. 4 And the men of David said unto him, Behold the day of which the LORD said unto thee, Behold, I will deliver thine enemy into thine hand, that thou mayest do to him as it shall seem good unto thee. Then David arose, and cut off the skirt of Saul's robe privily. 5 And it came to pass afterward, that David's heart smote him, because he had cut off Saul's skirt. 6 And he said unto his men, The LORD forbid that I should do this thing unto my master, the LORD'S anointed, to stretch forth mine hand against him, seeing

he *is* the anointed of the LORD. 7 So David stayed his servants with these words, and suffered them not to rise against Saul. But Saul rose up out of the cave, and went on *his* way. 8 David also arose afterward, and went out of the cave, and cried after Saul, saying, My lord the king. And when Saul looked behind him, David stooped with his face to the earth, and bowed himself.

Notice how David, after having remorse over his actions against Saul, acknowledged that Saul was his "master" and "lord" and God's "anointed" and for that reason, David had no right "to stretch forth [his] hand against him." When David saw Saul outside the cave, David "stooped with his face to the earth, and bowed himself." In the context of the time in which David lived, this was a demonstration of respect. We are called to show respect for our leaders, no matter who they are or where we live or whether we voted for them or despise their political ideology or even their character. They are God's delegates, and if they abuse God's authority He will address that in His timing. Our orders on our temporary assignment for Jesus is to **honour** those, as Jesus himself did.

We are likewise to **love the brotherhood**. This is *agape* **love**, the **love** that reflects a volitional choice to do in the best interest of others, and in this context, the **love** is directed toward our brothers and sisters in Christ. Recall that Peter had said in 1 Peter 1:22 that we should have "love one another with a pure heart fervently." This is a family obligation. We are also to **fear God**, which means that we acknowledge by our conduct God's sovereignty over our lives and our responsibilities to obey Him. And

Peter finished with the admonition that brings this short section full circle—**honour** or show due respect to **the king**. Imagine how radically different our lives would be if we could but faithfully obey 1 Peter 2:17. This appropriates the salvation of the soul looking forward to our inheritance in the world to come. In a very real way, the "now" is God's training program for the future. And how we handle the "now," especially with regard to our submission to human government, is our testimony to whether God or Satan has the right to rule.

## Closing

Organized sports seem to start at younger and younger ages. Some of my children played soccer at age 3, and I have heard of leagues starting earlier than that. Toddlers playing soccer is a wonderful blend of humor and chaos. The children primarily know two things—run at the ball and kick it. At that age, there is not teamwork, passing the ball, rules or strategies. There is running and kicking, and sometimes kicking the ball in the wrong goal.

This world is in chaos and a great many Christians do not look much different than toddlers playing soccer. They do not have a strategy to win or a focus on the right goal. They just bumble about and sometimes kick the ball in the wrong goal. An appropriate question is, "whose team are you on?" Because if you or I find ourselves kicking the ball in the wrong goal, then it looks like we are on Satan's team and not God's team. This state of confusion derives from ignorance of the Book. When Christians persist in ignorance rather than making the study of God's Word a life practice, they make messes and kick goals for the wrong team because they fall back on fleshly lusts that reflect worldly philosophies. But Peter said to set that aside, to live right before men and God, and to honor and obey human government. Playing on God's team and playing to win means setting aside old thinking and accepting a new paradigm about reality and what God expects of us. It is living a life that gives testimony to God's right of rule over His creation, including His right to rule through delegated authority to human government.

## Application Points

**MAIN PRINCIPLE:** Understanding that we are merely temporary residents in this world, we are not to buy in to the world's agendas or philosophies, but live right before men and God, and in particular, to submit to God's delegated human government except where doing so violates Scripture.

## Discussion Questions

1. What would be some indicators in your life that you see yourself as a stranger and pilgrim in this world, or that you do not?

2. Can you provide a real example from your life where you continued to exhibit good works, without retaliation, before someone who maligned you?

3. Is it acceptable (before God) for a Christian to post on social media personally disparaging statements about the president? Or governor, senator, etc.?

("disparaging" here does not mean a statement disagreeing with an ideology or policy, but is, as we say in the South, "bad mouthing")

4. Is it acceptable (before God) for a Christian to post on social media allegations about the misconduct of the president without any independent investigation of whether those allegations are true? Or governor, senator, etc.? (e.g., posting that an official takes bribes without having any evidence that the statement is true)

5. Does a Christian who lives under a Communist government have the same obligation to honor and obey that government as one who lives in the United States?

6. How does a Christian best determine the will of God?

# Chapter 6

# Transformation on the Job
## 1 Peter 2:18-25

The judge calls the witness to the stand. He has casts on both legs and one arm and is seated to testify from his wheelchair. After being placed under oath, he testifies about the accident caused to him by the defendant, how he has mounting medical bills and may never work again. Then the defense lawyer gets up to cross-examine the plaintiff and shows a series of photographs of the plaintiff, taken just days earlier, showing him walking with no casts and no wheelchair, and then a video of the plaintiff briskly walking in a parking lot. Notwithstanding the plaintiff's testimony, the jury finds he was not injured and awarded no compensation.

Christians also have two forms of public testimony. First, when we are on the witness stand under oath, we may provide testimony that God is on the throne of our lives. We affirm emphatically that God is in charge. But then on cross-examination the video of our life plays out before the jury. This is the second form of testimony, and it is the more convincing evidence. What does the movie of our life testify? Does it tell the world God is in charge? As ambassadors for Jesus, our testimony by words and conduct should affirm God's right to rule over His creation. And in certain spheres this requires us to submit to the authority of others, and even to submit in suffering.

## Outline

III. THE PLAN OF SALVATION (OF THE SOUL-LIFE) (1:13-4:19)

    a. That it would transform our character (1:13-2:10)

    b. That it would transform our conduct through submission (2:11-3:7)

        i. Our conduct in the world (2:11-17)

        ii. Our conduct on the job (2:18-25)

## Excursus on Submission

The Bible says a great deal about the issue of submission. In fact, we find in the Scriptures at least four areas in which God ordains human authority, which some call divine institutions: (1) the family; (2) human government; (3) the church; and (4) the marketplace. Our obedience to God's designated authority in these areas bears testimony to God's sovereign right to rule in the affairs of humanity. On the other hand, our refusal to submit to God's delegated authority affirms Satan's right to rule. For when we disobey God's delegate, it is rebellion to God Himself. As we proceed through the balance of 1 Peter 2 and then 1 Peter 3:1-12, we will be aided by hearing Peter's words against the backdrop of the larger canvas the Bible paints about this matter of submission.

To be sure, submission is not popular, and some would even relegate these verses to outdated cultural prejudices that the modern Christian is free to ignore. The Bible bears out, however, that submission in these areas of delegated authority is not a cultural issue, but a spiritual issue. And with that in mind, a good place to begin in understanding the larger context of submission is Ephesians 5:18 ff.

> Ephesians 5:18 And be not drunk with wine, wherein is excess; but **be filled with the Spirit**; 19 Speaking to yourselves in psalms and hymns and spiritual songs, singing and making melody in your heart to the Lord; 20 Giving thanks always for all things unto God and the Father in the name of our Lord Jesus Christ.

In this passage, we find the only place where the Bible commands us to be Spirit-filled. Using the negative illustration of how, when a person is inebriated (filled with wine), the wine influences their behavior, Paul commanded that we be **filled with the Spirit**. The word **filled** is used figuratively, as we might say that someone was **filled** with rage. It is not a literal filling, but that the rage influences or controls their actions. So it also is with **the Spirit**, that is, the notion of being **filled with the Spirit** is that we are allowing **the Spirit** to guide and influence our actions. We do well to skim through the verses that follow, for they speak in practical terms about what the Spirit-filled life looks like in various contexts, much of which comes down to obedience, submission, or putting another first: to one another (Ephesians 5:21), wives to husbands (Ephesians 5:22), husbands loving their wives (Ephesians 5:25), children obeying and honoring parents (Ephesians 6:1-2), and servants obeying masters (Ephesians 6:5). But the question must be asked, exactly how does one be Spirit-filled? Paul commanded the doing of it, explained that it has to do with the Spirit influencing and leading us, and addressed what it looks like in practical terms. But how do we get there? For that, it is helpful to turn to Colossians 3:16 ff.

> <u>Colossians 3:16</u> Let the **word of Christ dwell in you richly in all wisdom**; teaching and admonishing one another in psalms and hymns and spiritual songs, singing with grace in your hearts to the Lord. <u>17</u> And whatsoever ye do in word or deed, *do* all in the name of the Lord Jesus, giving thanks to God and the Father by him.

What becomes apparent as we read Colossians 3:16 ff. is that it parallels Ephesians 5:18 ff. (recall that generally these are parallel letters written closely together in time to two churches geographically close together). As Paul painted the picture of what a Christian life looks like when it is a Spirit-filled life and then the picture of a life wherein the word of Christ dwells richly in all wisdom, the results were the same. And the results are the same because the cause is the same. To be Spirit-filled is the flipside of letting the **word of Christ dwell in** us **richly in all wisdom**. So the Holy Spirit influences, guides and leads us by **the word of Christ**, which gives us **wisdom**. This is not merely knowing **the word**, or even memorizing it, but taking it in to the depths of our being. The **word** permeates the fabric of who we are, abides there, and dictates our thinking and thus our actions, which is why Paul added the words, **in all wisdom. Wisdom** is what you know directing what you do and how you do it. To turn this around and consider the negative, if we are ignorant of **the word**, we cannot be Spirit-filled because we lack the tools in our box for the Spirit to use to influence and direct us. Our ability to be influenced and led of the Spirit is therefore proportional to our diligently taking in the Word of God. No wonder why Paul would tell Timothy: "Study to shew thyself approved unto God, a workman that needeth not to be ashamed, rightly dividing the word of truth." (2 Timothy 2:15)

As Paul built out what a Christian life looks like under the influence of **the word** in the Colossians passage, he wrote of obedience, submission and putting others first: wives to husbands (Colossians 3:18), husbands loving wives (Colossians 3:19), children obeying parents (Colossians 3:20), and servants obeying masters (Colossians 3:22). It is especially instructive to observe what Paul wrote about servants submitting to their masters, which is what Peter took up in 1 Peter 2:18:

> Colossians 3:22 Servants, obey in all things *your* masters according to the flesh; not with eyeservice, as menpleasers; but in singleness of heart, fearing God: 23 And whatsoever ye do, do *it* heartily, as to the Lord, and not unto men; 24 Knowing that of the Lord ye shall receive the reward of the inheritance: for ye serve the Lord Christ. 25 But he that doeth wrong shall receive

for the wrong which he hath done: and there is no respect of persons.

Note how Paul connected allowing the Word of Christ to dwell within us richly to being submissive in the specific sphere of the servant / master relationship, with the result that such submission is, in fact, submission to Jesus and will appropriate our inheritance. And that is exactly what 1 Peter is all about, to wit, the appropriation of our inheritance and how the attitudes and actions that will receive the reward play out in practical terms in various spheres of daily life. Our submission to others is service to **the Lord Christ**.

While the best analog for Paul's words would be the modern employee / employer relationship, we must acknowledge Paul used the Greek term *doulos*, translated as "servant" or "bondservant" but actually meaning slave. Without chasing this rabbit too far, we do need to understand that what Paul addressed was slavery within the Roman Empire, and to be more specific, he directed his exhortation to slaves and slave-owners within the congregations at Colossae and Ephesus. There is good scholarship that as much as half of the inhabitants of Rome were slaves, and in the Empire at large, 20% to 30% of the populace were slaves. We should not import our notions of slavery from the more recent slavery in the history of the United States, but it is a worthy study to try to better understand the nature of slavery in the first century Roman Empire.

There were three main types of slaves: agricultural, household slaves, and penal slaves. Conditions were poor for agricultural and penal slaves, while those working in the homes of wealthy Romans could have considerable influence (especially as members of an honored household like Caesar's), earn money, seek to buy their own freedom or manumission (usually by the time they were in their 30's) and even own their own slaves. These slaves were often educated as their owners trained them to run various aspects of their business and household. Moreover, sometimes slaves were adopted as adults, legally becoming heirs of their owners, a legal transaction Paul referenced in his writings. In general, slaves were permitted to attend religious functions and the gladiatorial games. But at the same time, they were property and could be severely punished for running away, which in the first century had become a significant problem in the Empire. (cf. Philemon) Slaves were very expensive, and thus were a sign of personal wealth to the owner.

## Scripture and Comments

Peter did not address the issue of slaves, but the related notion of house servants. The thing about being submissive, in any sphere, is that it opens us up to being hurt. Peter was concerned both with exhorting his audience to submit in certain areas of their lives, but also that they would understand the issue of suffering. Peter would teach that to suffer in the right way for the right reasons honors God.

> 1 Peter 2:18 Servants, *be* subject to *your* masters with all fear; not only to the good and gentle, but also to the froward.

Peter used the Greek word *oiketes,* translated here as **servants**. The word means domestic help and could be a slave but would often be hired help, in other words, an employee. Thus, Peter exhorted the **servants** in the churches he writes to, and by application anyone who is an employee, to **be subject to your masters** or employers **with all fear**. The phrase **be subject** draws from the same Greek verb *hupotassō* that was used in 2:13 and translated there as "submit." The notion of being **subject to** is the same as submitting or obeying. The sense here of **fear**, given the context, is likely the notion of respect or reverence. And Peter hastened to add, this submission and respect is owed **not only to the good and gentle** employer (e.g., the ones that provide vacation times and bonuses and treat their employees with respect), but **also the froward**. The word **froward** means willfully contrary or difficult. Peter told his audience they need to obey and show reverence to their boss / employer even if he or she is a bad egg. As Jesus explained in the context of rewards in relation to our showing love for others, "For if ye love them which love you, what reward have ye? do not even the publicans the same?" (Matthew 5:46) It is, or at least should be, easy to submit to a boss or employer who treats us kindly, but it is quite a different matter to show respect for those who are difficult or even cruel. But that is exactly what Peter instructed his readers to do.

One may ask a host of "yeah but" and "what if" questions. The Bible does not teach unbridled submission to any human agent, but the exception is narrow, as we addressed previously in the context of God's ordained human government. If a boss or employer seeks to require you to do that which God prohibits, or prohibit you from doing that which God requires, then we are bound to obey God and not man. When the apostles were ordered by the Jewish leadership not to preach

Christ, Peter refused: "Then Peter and the *other* apostles answered and said, We ought to obey God rather than men." (Acts 5:29) So for example, if a boss expects the employee to steal, engage in criminal behavior, or provide sexual favors, the employee should not submit and should be looking to change jobs.

> 19 For this *is* thankworthy, if a man for conscience toward God endure grief, suffering wrongfully. 20 For what glory *is it*, if, when ye be buffeted for your faults, ye shall take it patiently? but if, when ye do well, and suffer *for it*, ye take it patiently, this *is* acceptable with God.

Peter said **this is thankworthy**, in other words, **this** finds favor with God. But what is **this**? In a word, it is **suffering**. Peter said that **if a man for conscience toward God endure grief, suffering wrongfully**, that finds favor with God. In these few words, Peter said a great deal. It is only **suffering** with the right attitude and for the right reason that **is thankworthy**.

The notion of **suffering** is from the Greek term *paschō* and means to experience pain. It is the Greek term from which we get the "paschal" lamb. The right attitude for **suffering** is **for conscience toward God**, in other words, an awareness and allegiance to obeying God, and in this context, obeying God's delegated authority. As believers, we should keep short accounts with God, confessing our sin when we are aware of it (1 John 1:9), and generally seeking to the best of our ability to obey. In this way we may maintain a "good conscience before God" (Acts 23:1), a "conscience void of offence toward God, and toward men" (Acts 24:16), and a "pure conscience" (2 Timothy 1:3).

Peter wrote of a person who for their allegiance **toward God endure[s] grief**, meaning hardship while they **suffering wrongfully**. Some Christians suffer from their employer because they are lazy (what the KJV eloquently refers to as a sluggard), abrasive or obnoxious to fellow employees, gossips (they always circle the water cooler), routinely tardy to work, steal time while on the clock, take too many sick days (usually Mondays), or flirt with other employees. It may surprise some Christians that being the jerk at work is not a Spirit gift. And if you suffer because you are a sluggard, a terrible employee, or treat other people at work poorly, that finds no favor with God. But to work diligently, dependably, and show reverence for the employer and suffer without having done anything wrong, that finds God's favor because it affirms His right to rule as He sees fit.

That is where the rub comes in—none of us want to suffer **wrongfully**. "I have rights. I'll sue. I'll take it to the highest court in the land." God says, essentially, "you can quit but while you are still in their employ you need to submit." Most of us are not good at this. But remember what Paul said when he connected being Spirit-filled to submitting. If we will not submit, we are not Spirit-filled. A critical litmus of our spiritual maturity is this issue of submission, because it reflects humility, a subject Peter took up later in his epistle.

> 21 For even hereunto were ye called: because Christ also suffered for us, leaving us an example, that ye should follow his steps:

Now Peter gets to something that, at least in our flesh, we do not want to hear. He wrote, **for even hereunto**, that is, to suffering, **were ye called**. Paul wrote in

Philippians 1:29: "For unto you it is given in the behalf of Christ, not only to believe on him, but also to suffer for his sake." As Christians, we were **called** to suffer! Let that soak in. If we were **called** to suffer then at some point in our lives, and perhaps for a protracted period of time, we will suffer. "But the television preacher said my faith assures me physical health and financial prosperity." The Apostle Peter, and indeed the witness of the entire New Testament, and most of all, the words and example of Jesus Christ, call the television preacher out as a liar. Turn off the tube and read First Peter.

Of course, this does not mean we look for suffering or cause trouble so that we will find suffering, but neither should we be surprised when suffering comes our way. While as a general principle, we will not be persecuted or ill-treated when we have done nothing wrong, even if we were perfect (we are not), conflict and suffering is inevitable because we are **called** to it. Jesus himself said, "If the world hate you, ye know that it hated me before it hated you. If ye were of the world, the world would love his own: but because ye are not of the world, but I have chosen you out of the world, therefore the world hateth you....If they have persecuted me, they will also persecute you...." (John 15:18-20) And again in Matthew 16:21: "From that time forth began Jesus to shew unto his disciples, how that he must go unto Jerusalem, and suffer many things of the elders and chief priests and scribes, and be killed, and be raised again the third day." Thus, the question is not whether we will suffer, but how we will deal with it when it comes. To be a Christian is to identify by faith with Jesus **Christ, who also suffered for us, leaving us an example** of how to suffer with the right attitude for the right reasons. Peter addressed how Jesus suffered in the verses that follow, but admonished us here to **follow his steps** in suffering correctly. Peter said, paraphrasing, "let's be like Jesus even in suffering." This assumes we know from our study of the Word something about how Jesus lived.

> 22 Who DID NO SIN, NEITHER WAS GUILE FOUND IN HIS MOUTH: 23 Who, when he was reviled, reviled not again; when he suffered, he threatened not; but committed *himself* to him that judgeth righteously:

Note first that in building out his argument about suffering correctly, Peter quoted from Isaiah 53:9. It is helpful to see this verse with a bit of the larger context of the suffering servant song of Isaiah 53 (the quoted words are bolded):

> Isaiah 53:4 Surely he hath borne our griefs, and carried our sorrows: yet we did esteem him stricken, smitten of God, and afflicted. 5 But he *was* wounded for our transgressions, *he was* bruised for our iniquities: the chastisement of our peace *was* upon him; and with his stripes we are healed.... 7 He was oppressed, and he was afflicted, yet he opened not his mouth: he is brought as a lamb to the slaughter, and as a sheep before her shearers is dumb, so he openeth not his mouth.... 9 And he made his grave with the wicked, and with the rich in his death; **because he had done no violence, neither *was any* deceit in his mouth.**

Thus, it is in the context of Jesus suffering for our sins, and not any wrongdoing of his own, that Peter reminded his readers that Jesus **did not sin, neither was guile** or deception **found in his mouth.** Jesus neither sinned by his actions or his words, yet still suffered. We must remember that Jesus did not have to suffer, and could have stopped the suffering at any time. Recall his words from Matthew 26:53 at the moment of his arrest in Gethsemane as Jesus told Peter to put away his sword: "Thinkest thou that I cannot now pray to my Father, and he shall presently give me more than twelve legions of angels?" Recall as the Roman soldiers approached, Jesus' self-identifying acclamation of "I am" (i.e., Yahweh) forced the soldiers to the ground: "As soon then as he had said unto them, I am *he*, they went backward, and fell to the ground." (John 18:6) And yet in 1 Peter 2:23, we are reminded that Jesus not only did not stop the suffering, but **when he was reviled, reviled not again.** To be **reviled** is to be maligned or vilified, in other words, to be the target of evil or insulting speech. But Jesus did not retaliate in turn. Of course, this was true throughout Jesus' earthly ministry, but especially so as he was arrested, tried, tortured and murdered.

Peter continued, explaining that **when** Jesus **suffered, he threatened not.** Remember from the prior verse that **suffered** refers to Jesus' agony and death, the worst physical suffering. Jesus could have spoke his enemies out of existence, but he did not even threaten them. We do well to reflect on what it means to follow Jesus in suffering. It is one thing to suffer when we "had it coming to us" and quite another to suffer for another. And yet it is a matter in a class of its own to suffer for no wrong without threatening, yelling, cursing, or the like.

In our flesh, we want to be vindicated. But God knows, even if no one else does, and eventually He will settle the accounts. Jesus could have stopped the pain, but instead **committed himself to him that judgeth righteously**, his heavenly Father. And that is at the heart of God's appeal to us today.

When we suffer for the right reasons and with the right attitude, it glorifies Him and affirms His right to rule in our lives even when it costs us. We have Jesus' example to follow. He suffered wrongfully but did not retaliate in words or actions, but entrusted himself to the Father. That is how we need to handle suffering. But for many professing Christians, just giving God an hour or two one day a week is asking too much. To suffer without fighting back is not an option. It is not surprising that suffering has always refined churches and strengthened them because the dead weight falls away quickly under pressure.

> 24 Who his own self bare our sins in his own body on the tree, that we, being dead to sins, should live unto righteousness: BY WHOSE STRIPES YE WERE HEALED. 25 For ye WERE AS SHEEP GOING ASTRAY; but are now returned unto the Shepherd and Bishop of your souls.

Peter again appealed to the servant song of Isaiah 53 (quoted words bolded below):

> Isaiah 53:4 Surely he **hath borne our griefs**, and carried our sorrows: yet we did esteem him stricken, smitten of God, and afflicted. 5 But he *was* wounded for our transgressions,

*he was* bruised for our iniquities: the chastisement of our peace *was* upon him; and **with his stripes we are healed.**

The Son of God **bore our sins in his own body on the tree**, meaning the cross, so **that we, being dead to sins, should live unto righteousness.** Verse 23 said Jesus **committed himself to** the Father, and that path was a path of suffering, but not without reason. Jesus suffered and died for a purpose—for us. And not merely to rescue us from sin's penalty, but from sin's power over our lives so that we **should live unto righteousness.** Peter would return to this issue and build it out in some detail in 1 Peter 4:1-7. It is helpful to note here the words of 1 Peter 4:6: "For for this cause was the gospel preached also to them that are dead, that they might be judged according to men in the flesh, but live according to God in the spirit." There, Peter explained that the "gospel [was preached] to the spiritually "dead," and by their faith they identified with Jesus, who was judged by men and murdered. But as Jesus died, then resurrected, so also those who identify with him by faith identify with his death, and his resurrection life. Jesus' death set us free from sin's penalty and dominion over us, and his resurrection empowers our life "in the spirit."

Similarly, here in 1 Peter 2:24, Peter told his audience that when Jesus suffered and died, **we** who identify by faith with Jesus also died, thus **being dead to sins** and set free to **live unto righteousness.** And in this context, Peter quoted from Isaiah 53:5, when he explained that **by** Jesus' **stripes** we **were healed.** I note here that some use these few words (not even the whole verse) as "go to" support for various teachings on physical healing, but the context of both Isaiah 53 and 1 Peter 2:24 is Jesus' death for **our sins** and not his death to heal us physically. Indeed, there is no theological reason that Jesus needed to die to provide physical healing to anyone. As sovereign creator of the universe, Jesus could heal people as he pleased. In the poetic device of Isaiah 53:5, Jesus' **stripes** refers to his death, and the healing in Isaiah 53:5 and 1 Peter 2:24 is a metaphorical healing of our sin problem. Jesus died to restore our relationship to a Holy God, and our expectation of the Christian life must include an expectation of suffering: "And if children, then heirs; heirs of God, and joint-heirs with Christ; if so be that we suffer with *him*, that we may be also glorified together." (Romans 8:17). We are qualified as heirs based on being children of God by faith, but our inheritance as heirs is tied to a life of faithful obedience that may require our willingness to endure in suffering as Jesus did, submitting to human authorities and accepting what comes from God's hand as a result of our obedience.

Finally, quoting from Isaiah 53:6, Peter recalled that his readers **were as sheep going astray** from the shepherd, but because of their faith in what Jesus did they were **now returned unto the Shepherd and Bishop of their souls**. The word **Shepherd** is the Greek *poimen* usually translated as shepherd or pastor. The word **Bishop** is the Greek *episkopos* and has the idea of being an overseer. Applying this to us, we **are now returned** to the One who provides for us (**Shepherd**) and guards and superintends (**Bishop**) our **souls**. Peter likely recalled Jesus' words: "I am the good shepherd: the good shepherd giveth his life for the sheep." (John 10:11) Again, Peter did not use soul to mean our spirit. The immediate context is that Jesus died for us and so we ought to live for God, and in so doing, God will provide for and lead our soul-lives.

## Closing

It has been observed that the Bible says more about work than worship. It is worldly thinking to see our employment merely as a means of getting a paycheck. Peter provides us a paradigm shift for how we think about work and other spheres of our lives. As Christians, we have this great living hope with a view to a salvation ready to be revealed in the last time. (1 Peter 1:3-5) Peter reminds us that this living hope has implications across the board for how we live. And in the passage covered in this lesson, Peter reminds us that we have a ministry in our place of work. We honor God by submitting to our employer, and we do so in the view of others who not only hear our testimony but see it as well. We must see our work as part of our personal ministry, and understand that our faithfulness in this sphere of our lives appropriates heavenly treasures to our account.

## Application Points

**MAIN PRINCIPLE:** Christians are to be submissive to their employers, even if this brings suffering, knowing that we are called to suffer and should follow Jesus' example in suffering for well doing with the right attitude and without retaliation.

## Discussion Questions

1. Do you have a difficult boss? How can you honor God by your attitudes, words and actions in fulfilling your employment duties under the supervision of your boss?
2. What are ways in the employer / employee context that a Christian might suffer and deserve that suffering?

3. If you are submissive to a difficult employer, how might that provide a positive testimony to your co-workers?

4. If you are kind to a difficult boss to his or her face, but bad mouth the boss privately with your co-workers, does that honor God's command to submit "with all fear"?

5. If your boss or supervisor does a wrong against you, or treats you unfairly, how might you try to resolve that conflict while still remaining submissive?

6. How does the life of Jesus provide an example of suffering in the right way for the right reasons?

# Chapter 7

# Transformation in the Home

1 Peter 3:1-7

We live in a culture where marriage is a norm, but sadly, so are failed marriages. According to a Barna Group study in 2008, 78% of adults have been married at least once, and among born again Christians, 84% get married.[1] But among adults that have been married, the Barna Group's study found that one-third were divorced at least once. That translates into one out of four American adults having experienced divorce. This reflects the average and certain groups have higher or lower percentages having experienced a divorce, with evangelicals at about 26%. Grouping evangelicals and others that consider themselves born again Christians, "their divorce figure is statistically identical to that of non-born again adults: 32% versus 33%, respectively."[2]

---

[1] The Barna Group, *New Marriage and Divorce Statistics Released*, March 31, 2008, https://www.barna.com/research/new-marriage-and-divorce-statistics-released/ (last checked 12.26.18).
[2] *Ibid.*

The trend is toward "serial" marriages where young people plan to marry but expect to be married multiple times. To these alarming statistics, I would add anecdotally that many marriages do not technically end in divorce but for all practical purposes become "marriageless marriages" leaving both partners bitter. Notwithstanding this harsh reality, most people, including some professing Christians, reject Biblical principles of marriage out of hand. It is far past time for those who identify as evangelicals to take a serious look at what God's Word says on the issue of marriage. A look at what Peter had to say in his epistle is a good start.

## Outline

III. THE PLAN OF SALVATION (OF THE SOUL-LIFE) (1:13-4:19)

    a. That it would transform our character (1:13-2:10)

    b. That it would transform our conduct through submission (2:11-3:7)

        i. Our conduct in the world (2:11-17)

        ii. Our conduct on the job (2:18-25)

        iii. Our conduct in the home (3:1-7)

## Excursus on Marriage

Before we engage what Peter said about experiencing the salvation of the soul in the context of the marriage relationship, some background concepts will be beneficial. When God created Adam and Eve, He did so with the intent that they would exercise dominion over the animals, and by extension, the planet. (Genesis 1:26-28) But God needed to educate Adam before He created Eve. God permitted Adam to begin exercising dominion by naming certain animals so that God could bring Adam to understand there was not an animal that corresponded to him.

> Genesis 2:7 And the LORD God formed man *of* the dust of the ground, and breathed into his nostrils the breath of life; and man became a living soul... 18 And the LORD God said, *It is* not good that the man should be alone; I will make him an help meet for him. 19 And out of the ground the LORD God formed every beast of the field, and every fowl of the air; and brought *them* unto Adam to see what he would call them: and whatsoever Adam called every living creature, that *was* the name thereof. 20 And Adam gave names to all cattle, and to the fowl of the air, and to every beast of the field; but for Adam there was not found an help meet for him. 21 And the LORD God caused a deep sleep to fall upon Adam, and he slept: and he took one of his ribs, and closed up the flesh instead thereof; 22 And the rib, which the LORD God had taken from man, made he a woman, and brought her unto the man. 23 And Adam said, This *is* now bone of my bones, and flesh of my flesh: she shall be called Woman, because she was taken out of Man. 24 Therefore shall a man leave his

father and his mother, and shall cleave
unto his wife: and they shall be one flesh.
25 And they were both naked, the man and
his wife, and were not ashamed.

Note that God said, "it is not good that [Adam] should be alone." But Adam needed to understand the issue from God's perspective. And so He allowed Adam to name the birds and the animals of the field. It became apparent to Adam that "there was not found an help meet for him." That is to say, Adam saw birds and animals of the field and they all come in male and female, and while they are different, they correspond. But there was no one to correspond to Adam. God taught Adam that he would need one who is different from him, yet corresponds to him. From this concept, God made Eve. Adam was made from the dirt for the dirt, meaning he had a primary design for labor. But Eve was taken from Adam for Adam, meaning she had a primary design function of being relationship oriented. Neither was superior, but neither was the same as the other. Each had strengths and weaknesses so that each would complement the other.

We further note that Adam named the woman (Genesis 2:23) as he had named the animals, and this was an exercise of God's delegated authority to him. But God's description of the relationship did not stop there as it might for the animals. God designed Adam and Eve for a unique relationship with one another. God said, "Therefore shall a man leave his father and his mother, and shall cleave unto his wife: and they shall be one flesh." (Genesis 2:24) Of course, Adam had no earthly parents, but this verse established the pattern for marriage, one of

God's divine institutions. First, the wife is to replace the husband's parents as the single most important human relationship he has. Second, the husband is to cleave to (meaning unite with) his wife and together in this union they are "one flesh." And as an aside, we should be reminded of Jesus' commentary on this passage from Genesis: "Wherefore they are no more twain, but one flesh. What therefore God hath joined together, let not man put asunder." (Matthew 19:6) And so Adam's headship within this family unit was not a license for unbridled mastery. Instead, his wife Eve was to be the most important human relationship he would ever experience, and his union with her was to be permanent. Yet some men today know by heart half of Ephesians 5:23 ("For the husband is the head of the wife...") and abuse it as a license to be a tyrant (a jerk!). The picture in Genesis 2, and in Ephesians 5, is quite different. If your wife is the most valuable relationship you have with any human being on the planet, it will show in how you think about her, speak to her, and treat her privately and publicly.

In Genesis 2, when God ordained marriage, He said, "they shall be one flesh." We know in mathematics that one plus one is two. But in marriage, God says, in effect, one plus one is one. Why? Because the two people with all their differences correspond and they commit to a union, and in this union there is a completion and wholeness that brings mutual ability and joy in their God-given roles. But, alas, sin entered the picture and everything changed. For our purposes in 1 Peter 3, we are especially concerned with what God told Eve would occur as a result of the Fall:

> Genesis 3:16 Unto the woman he said, I will greatly multiply thy sorrow and thy conception; in sorrow thou shalt bring forth children; and thy desire *shall be* to thy husband, and he shall rule over thee.

In particular, note that God told Eve her "desire shall be to thy husband, and he shall rule over thee." The first clause is not about sexual desire, but rather, that she will want to control her husband. The same language appears in Genesis 4:7, where God warned Cain that sin (by implication Satan) wanted to dominate him: "...and if thou doest not well, sin lieth at the door. And unto thee shall be his desire, and thou shalt rule over him." Yet, she will not control him, and instead, the husband will "rule over" her. This is not the headship God intended for the marriage relationship. Rather, this "rule" emphasizes domination or mastery, not care and leadership. Thus, instead of the structure God intended in a healthy marriage, our flesh nature will cater to a fight for control that all too often will result in conflicts. Accordingly, the "Christian" husband today that uses half of Ephesians 5:23 to support his abusive behavior is doing exactly what God said in Genesis 3:16 is an expression of the sin nature.

So we must ask ourselves, what is the fix for this problem? As we have already seen in the excursus in the prior chapter of this commentary, the passage about the Spirit-filling in Ephesians 5:21 ff. parallels what Paul wrote about allowing the Word of Christ to dwell in us richly in Colossians 3:16 ff. And in both cases, the result of being Spirit-filled (or allowing the Word to dwell in us richly in all wisdom) included submission in different spheres of life, including within the home or marriage:

> Ephesians 5:21 Submitting yourselves one to another in the fear of God. 22 Wives, submit yourselves unto your own husbands, as unto the Lord. 23 For the husband is the head of the wife, even as Christ is the head of the church: and he is the saviour of the body. 24 Therefore as the church is subject unto Christ, so *let* the wives *be* to their own husbands in every thing.

Paul told his audience that a Spirit-filled wife would be submissive to the leadership of her husband. As we will see, in the context of the outworking of the "salvation of the soul" that is the primary subject of First Peter, he exhorted wives to submit to their husbands. In Paul's writings and Peter's, the issue of submission is a spiritual matter to be worked out as part of the sanctification process; they are not cultural rules.

## Scripture and Comments

Just as human government and the marketplace are divine institutions that provide Christians the opportunity to submit to God by submitting to those with His delegated authority, so also the marriage context provides that opportunity. But more than that, the husband and wife have a ministry to one another as they submit to God's Word in this area. I suggested in the prior chapter that we need to accept from God's Word, and in particular from Peter's epistle, a paradigm shift in our thinking about the workplace and its relationship to the salvation of our souls. So also, we need to be challenged by God's Word with a paradigm shift in our thinking about marriage. The world is telling us to get our needs fulfilled in our marriage or divorce and move on. Such a marriage is built on selfish ambition. The Bible is telling us we have a ministry guided by honoring God's Word and ministering to the needs of our mate. Such a marriage is built on submission, and as we will see, it is not just submission of the wife.

> 1 Peter 3:1 Likewise, ye wives, *be* in subjection to your own husbands; that, if any obey not the word, they also may without the word be won by the conversation of the wives; 2 While they behold your chaste conversation *coupled* with fear.

Peter began with **likewise**, which refers back to his exhortation in chapter 2 to be submissive to human government and submissive within the employer-employee context. Peter used the term **likewise** again in 3:7 in instructing the husbands in how they treat their wives; we should keep in mind throughout Peter's instructions for marriage that the roles of husbands and wives are different but tied at the hip as each is to make the well being of the other their priority. Too often people have misunderstood the Bible's teaching about submission and marriage and distorted or caricatured the respective roles. Peter's teaching in this regard should bring clarity.

Peter wrote, **likewise** or in that same way (i.e., as in the context of human government and employers), **ye wives, be in subjection to your own husbands**. Note that her obligation is to her husband and no other men. The issue of submission is one of those concepts that we can understand better by meditating on what it is not. And so we pause here to ask what it looks like when a wife is not submissive. Or said another way, what may she do that undermines her husband's headship in the home? And while explicit control is an obvious means, there are more indirect and subtle ways a wife may respond to her husband that undermine his headship in the family or establish an environment within the home that prevents him from leading. Some of these are as follows: (1) manipulating him through her emotions (guilt trips, passive aggressive behavior, the "silent treatment," arbitrary ultimatums, turning on the tears, and being impossible to please); (2) using or withholding sex to manipulate him (cf. 1 Corinthians 7:3-5); (3) making key decisions without the husband's input; (4) using aggression to get her way; (5) micromanaging her husband's life, which may include behavior such prying questions and constant phone calls and text messages; (6) always complaining or criticizing but never encouraging or praising; (7) undermining his decisions (e.g., being the cool parent and saying yes after he said no); (8) openly engaging in flirtatious speech or behavior toward other men; (9) making comparisons of her husband to other men (e.g., his job to someone else's job, their house to someone else's much nicer house); (10) unrealistic expectations (setting a bar that he cannot possibly meet).

One may ask whether these are all things a husband might do. They are, and a husband would be wrong to do these very things. These types of behavior are by no means limited to wives and the list is not intended in that way, but I will pick on the husbands in the notes on 1 Peter 3:8. One may also have a "yeah but" objection to Peter's command of submissiveness. Such objections are usually of the "God you don't know my situation" sort. We are all (men and women) prone to lodge such objections in order to justify our disobedience to God's clear directives. But I hasten to add that there are some legitimate "yeah but" objections. As I commented regarding submission within the context of human government and the employer-employee relationship, Peter (and Paul) were not teaching a rigid submission that knows no exceptions. In particular, the husband's role as head of the home does not entitle him to make his wife do that which the Bible prohibits, or to prohibit her from doing that which the Bible commands.

But beyond this generalization, let's consider a specific example. As Christians, our counsel to people cannot just be a few simple rules at a high level with no real world wisdom where the rubber hits the road. For example, a husband may be physically abusive and present a safety threat to his wife or children. I have encountered scenarios of abuse and physical danger where theologically conservative pastors (and others) told a wife she must remain in the home with her abusive husband, fulfilling her Biblical duties toward him including being submissive, no matter what. But his beating her, or sexually abusing the children, is a violation of God's Word, a violation of man's law (remember, God ordained human government and husband and wife are both under that authority), and a wholesale abandonment of his obligations to his family. It is possible for two people to be under the same roof but one of them has, in practical terms, abandoned the marriage and all obligations to it. Nothing in the Bible requires a wife to allow physical harm to herself or the children. And rather than giving her ill-conceived advice to just stick it out, Christians ought to get involved in these situations and make sure a safe house is available and the proper authorities are involved (as the law will sometimes require). Without speaking to the issue of divorce, there is unquestionably a time to get out of the house for physical safety.

To consider another example, imagine a man who is a human tick. He is drunk more often than he is sober. His life has become the proverbial ship in the bottle, but it is a bottle of booze. He rarely or never works, provides little or no contribution to the marriage, and he will never leave his wife so long as she will wait on him hand and foot and perhaps even provide for him financially, just like a tick will not leave the dog while there is still more blood. The wife's duty of submission to his headship surely does not include enabling a deadbeat husband's alcoholism. And again, without getting to the issue of divorce, the wife in this scenario should refuse to be the enabler of the husband's alcoholism. Enabling that lifestyle is not love and God's Word is clear about the issue of drunkenness. God's delegated authority to her husband does not entitle him to demand submission in a way that violates God's Word.

We can easily imagine other scenarios, perhaps situations we have encountered or experienced. I have seen, within local churches, husbands consumed by pornography, husbands who routinely hire prostitutes, husbands abusing the wife and children, and other sordid and outrageous behavior involving men who polish themselves up on Sunday morning before engaging in this conduct on Sunday afternoon. And often he is able to gain support from other church members despite his conduct. All of this is to say that while we must acknowledge the straightforward directive of Scripture on this issue of submission, we must not view this as a rigid absolute. There are times when being submissive is the wrong thing to do because submitting to the husband's sinful demands violates Scripture, or violates the law, or may put someone in danger. Just as with human government, when a husband would require a wife to do that which God prohibits or would prevent her from doing that which God requires, she can and should do what is right before God first, and this may require her to defy the husband.

With all this said, I turn back to what Peter wrote and it is clear. He wrote, **ye wives, be in subjection to your own husbands**. As previously noted, to submit is to obey, and to obey is to submit. And right at that point, the world and many Christians object: "This is just old-fashioned. This is something for a culture of the past but not today." But nothing about the text tied what Peter stated to a cultural accommodation. The background, as already shown, was directly from the opening chapters of Genesis, which Peter's Jewish Christian audience would have understood. In any event, it is interesting that in a culture today in which so many marriages fail, and in which people struggle generally with maintaining healthy relationships, that what the Bible teaches about marriage comes under such tremendous attack. Many Christians fare no better than non-believers in this area. They move from one failed relationship to another, taking the same deficient skill set to each new relationship expecting a different outcome. Decisions are made on the basis of hormones and selfish ambition and not Biblical principles. And when a relationship fails, putting this in the language of the South, the Christian fishes the same pond again, convincing themselves they will catch a trout in a pond full of catfish.

Against our nation's dismal track record in this regard, the Biblical blueprint for family and marriage issues deserves a fresh look. The Bible says a great deal that is counter-cultural. For a Christian to decide to engage God's Word and be a Biblical Christian is to put most everything he or she does in life at odds with the world's wisdom. And this is all the more true with issues involving the home, marriage, and parenting.

Having stated the basic principle of submission, Peter anticipated a particular problem, which frankly is extremely common today, namely where the wife desires to grow in the Word and live to glorify God, but her husband does not. There is no reason to assume Peter has in mind a non-believing husband since the book is directed throughout to believers. Peter directed his attention to addressing the best means for a wife in this scenario to positively impact her wayward husband, noting **that, if any** husband **obey not the word** of God, **they also may without the word be won by the conversation** or conduct **of the wives**. Simply stated, Peter explained that it will be the wife's conduct and not her words, that will impact her husband. Peter no doubt had in mind not just talking, but nagging, i.e., setting him straight, because that is the flesh nature that bends toward dominating the husband. Peter said that nagging will not work, and if the wife truly wants to influence her husband, she will do it by her lifestyle, which her husband will observe, that is, **while** he **behold[s] your chaste conversation coupled with fear**. I can assure you that in much of the Christian marriage counseling today, this is not what people are being told. Today, Peter would rarely have anyone return for a second session. People want to be vindicated, and being submissive does not do that.

This pictures a wife whose **chaste** or pure behavior is **coupled with** a respectful attitude toward her husband. Their home is a classroom on godliness, yet **without a word**. Obviously, Peter did not have silence in mind, but what he warned against was lecturing, manipulating, nagging or threatening. The husband in this situation will observe a godly woman who is not selfish, lives under the influence of the Holy Spirit (recalled the material on being Spirit-filled), is not domineering but instead submits to his headship in the home, and who wants to build a God-centered family. This would be easy to do if he were a model husband (if that species exists). Yet Jesus taught in the Sermon on the Mount that godliness is not just loving those who are easy to love but those who are not:

> Matthew 5:44 But I say unto you, Love your enemies, bless them that curse you, do good to them that hate you, and pray for them which despitefully use you, and persecute you; 45 That ye may be the children of your Father which is in heaven: for he maketh his sun to rise on the evil and on the good, and sendeth rain on the just and on the unjust. 46 For if ye love them which love you, what reward have ye? do not even the publicans the same?

In short, Peter taught that a wife's best strategy for influencing her wayward or spiritually immature husband is by her godly example. She cannot nag him into godliness, but her influence by godly living is a powerful thing.

> 3 Whose adorning let it not be that outward *adorning* of plaiting the hair, and of wearing of gold, or of putting on of apparel; 4 But *let it be* the hidden man of the heart, in that which is not corruptible, *even the ornament* of a meek and quiet spirit, which is in the sight of God of great price.

The godly wife who will positively influence her husband must be beautiful! But what is real beauty? Peter explained that her **adorning** should **not be that outward adorning of plaiting the hair, and of wearing of gold, or of putting on of apparel**. The word **adorning** is the Greek *kosmos* that is often translated "world." (See John 3:16, "For God so loved the world [*kosmos*]...") The first definition provided for this term in BDAG is "that which serves to beautify through decoration, adornment, adorning." And so we understand that Peter directly addressed beauty and what is beautiful to God, and indeed, what should be beautiful to godly men. In short, that which is on the outside does not determine beauty from God's perspective. In view of this, it is hardly surprising that the world is obsessed with outward beauty. Peter said real beauty is not about **plaiting** or elaborate braiding of **the hair**, nor the **wearing of gold** jewelry, **or of putting on of apparel** or fine clothes. These things our outward and say nothing about a woman's character.

Before moving to verse 4, two critical comments are in order. First, there are those that teach from 1 Peter 3:3 that women are prohibited from wearing make-up and jewelry or doing their hair. But if Peter's point was to prohibit fixing their hair and wearing jewelry, then he also prohibited **putting on of apparel**. Obviously, God did not prohibit women from wearing clothing. The point Peter made was simply that women may put a great deal of their attention to these outwards things when it is the inward that matters most and it is the inward character that is true and lasting beauty. But there is nothing wrong with a woman doing her hair and dressing well, and in fact, in the Song of Solomon, Shulamit was complimented for her beauty including her clothing and jewelry that she wore to please her beloved. (Song 1:10-11) Second, if God says (and He does) that true beauty is within, then men who are considering marriage need to think about whether they are making a glandular decision or a godly decision in who they ask to marry them.

Thus, God said through Peter that the wife who will influence her husband to godliness has class, and while there is nothing wrong with physical beauty (after all, God is the source of that), having class is more than what a woman looks like on the outside. The woman that wins the beauty contest God judges has beauty in **the hidden** or inner **man of the heart, in that which is not corruptible**. Remember that as human beings we are material (our physical body) and immaterial. The **heart** refers to that aspect of our immaterial person from which our character and personality derive. The physical body may have beauty but time will rob that away, yet **the heart…is not corruptible**. So this beauty within the inner person does not fade with time. And more than anything, inner beauty looks like **a meek and quiet** or peaceable **spirit**. The word **meek** is humble, self-unassuming, and gentle, the opposite of which is selfish ambition. A wife with selfish ambition will dominate her husband to fit her agenda, and certainly will use her words and perhaps forms of manipulation rather than her godly conduct to influence him. A **quiet**

**spirit** refers to a peaceable character. Peter wrote that **a meek and quiet spirit...is in the sight of God of great price**, in other words, this type of beauty is valuable to God. Recall the wisdom of Proverbs 31:10: "Who can find a virtuous woman? for her price is far above rubies." But I would note here that this is a godly quality for all people, and in fact, most of 1 Peter 5 was devoted to the issue of humility or meekness. There is never spiritual maturity without humility.

> 5 For after this manner in the old time the holy women also, who trusted in God, adorned themselves, being in subjection unto their own husbands: 6 Even as Sara obeyed Abraham, calling him lord: whose daughters ye are, as long as ye do well, and are not afraid with any amazement.

Peter observed that **after this manner in the old time**, meaning that consistent with what he wrote about true beauty there were women in the Old Testament who exemplified this type of character. There were **holy women...who trusted in God, adorned themselves** with inward beauty, especially in the area of submission **unto their own husbands**. As a specific example familiar to Peter's Jewish readers, Abraham's wife **Sara obeyed** or submitted to him, **calling him lord**. This does not mean a wife today needs to call her husband **lord**, but in the time and place where **Sara** and **Abraham** lived, this term connoted her recognition of his headship over the family. It is interesting that the Bible specifically noted Sara's (or Sarai's) physical beauty. (Genesis 12:11) But what Peter drew his readers' attention to was her inner beauty, best exemplified in her submission to **Abraham** by which she honored his position, and in so doing, honored God.

The women in Peter's audience, and women today, should follow Sara's example of submission and in so doing are her **daughters, as long as** they **do well**, that is, do what is right by God, **and are not afraid with any amazement** or alarm. The latter phrase simply means that they should do so without being intimidated. It is never easy to submit because in whatever context we do so, we make ourselves vulnerable to the one we submit to. It may seem safer to maintain a wall, but in the marriage context especially, a wall will not do. God's best for us requires us to risk being hurt, and if suffering comes, then to follow Christ's example and respond appropriately.

> 7 Likewise, ye husbands, dwell with *them* according to knowledge, giving honour unto the wife, as unto the weaker vessel, and as being heirs together of the grace of life; that your prayers be not hindered.

Now to pick on the husbands! The **likewise** parallels 3:1, and refers back to Peter's exhortation in chapter 2 to be submissive to human government and submissive within the employer-employee context and his exhortation in 3:1-6 regarding the wife's submission in the home. Having just addressed wives, Peter turned his attention to husbands, and while he did not command submission, what he commanded was intended to parallel the submission already addressed. That parallel is critical to balancing and not distorting what the Bible says about submission in a marriage context.

Peter wrote, **likewise** or in the same way, **ye husbands, dwell with** your wives **according to knowledge** or understanding. The world seeks to eradicate the differences between men and women under the guise of equality, arguing that any differences are the result of environmental conditioning, but the Bible affirms there are differences. As we saw from the early chapters of Genesis, these differences are not merely physical, but are part of God's design intent. The point is not that one gender is superior or more valuable than the other, but merely that the two are different by design. And so in the immediate context of Peter's admonition to **husbands** and how they interact with their wives, Peter said to every husband, in effect, "you need to understand your wife." Peter did not say, "you need to understand women," but that "you need to understand your wife specifically." There is no marriage class that will give you all of the information you need. You are going to have to observe and listen (for a long time) and take notes (in your head).

Peter then added, **giving honour unto the wife, as unto the weaker vessel**. Just as there are differences between men and women, so there are between vessels. The maker of the vessels designs and makes different vessels for different purposes. The reference to the **wife** as, metaphorically, **the weaker vessel**, is not speaking of physical weakness or character weakness, but as a **vessel** different from men. A **weaker vessel** in the first century was one made for a special purpose, it typically had more value, and would receive special care, much in the way as a family today might keep the "fine china" in a special place and reserved for special meals. Thus, Peter's point to each husband was that he should understand how his wife is wired, her unique strengths and weaknesses, and her needs. This last part is critical—figure out her most important needs. To **dwell** or live with her with **knowledge** is to understand her talents and encourage her, and understand her needs and meet them as best you are able.

In the book *His Needs, Her Needs*, by Willard Harley, Jr., the author used the example of a "love bank" in explaining this matter of meeting needs. Simply put, when a husband meets a wife's needs, or the wife meets the husband's needs, it is like making a deposit in their spouse's love bank. The balance grows. But when needs are not met, debits are made. And when needs are not met for a prolonged period, the marriage may begin to run on credit, a very dangerous situation. Using the language of this helpful illustration to paraphrase Peter's words, Peter said that **husbands** need to be making deposits, not just withdrawals, and you cannot do that effectively if you are not deliberate about knowing her needs and doing what you can to meet them. It is beyond the scope here to pursue this issue of meeting needs much further, but it is obvious that men and women may have some common needs, but that does not mean they would prioritize them the same. Husbands and wives tend to assume their needs are the same and are prioritized in the same way. They are not. When needs are never met, the love boat runs aground, and often stays aground a while before both spouses realize it. This is important stuff for every married couple, and it is a lot easier if you marry your best friend and keep it that way. But if our sole agenda is meeting our own needs, the other partner's love bank will be overdrawn, and no healthy marriage can exist for long on credit. An experienced counselor / teacher I had always said that people divorce for the same reason they marry. It took some years for that to soak in, but it is a dependable maxim. People marry expecting certain needs to be met, and tend to divorce when those needs are not met.

As noted in the earlier notes on Genesis, the husband's relationship with the wife is to be the most important relationship he has with any human being, and this is born out in Peter's exhortation that he **dwell with** her **according to knowledge**, as well as the exhortation that he give **honour** or respect to his **wife**. The husband that knows half of Ephesians 5:23 and fancies himself a king in his castle and the other members of the household his servants violates Peter's directive and is living a sinful lifestyle. Wives are due such **honour...as being heirs together** or joint-heirs **of the grace of life**. The salvation Peter elaborated on throughout the epistle so far—the salvation of the soul—is enjoyed by all Christians equally, men and women. And all Christians have an important place in the world to come and all are qualified to inherit as joint-heirs.

Accordingly, the wives are special to God and as such ought to be special to their husbands. If a husband does not treat his wife as he should (as 1 Peter 3:7 requires), his **prayers** will be **hindered** or blocked. There will be temporal negative consequences for his behavior. As a husband treats his wife poorly and prays for his personal blessing, God's answer will be a resounding NO every time. Men who feel that their needs in a marriage are not met would do well to meditate on what their wives' five most important needs are and how well they are meeting those needs. Then, if you are a risk taker, ask your wife what her five most important needs are and whether you are meeting them. That's what leadership in the home looks like. Start with the person in the mirror before trying to do corrective surgery on the other person.

As we try to put this all together, it becomes apparent that a lot of misunderstanding about the issue of submission within a marriage is rooted in failing to see how the teachings to the **husbands** and wives correspond. While the **husbands** are not commanded to submit, they are commanded to make their relationships with their wives the single most important relationship they have, and to work toward understanding their wives' needs and meeting them. She comes first. And while that is not the same as submission, neither is it all that different. She is commanded to submit to his leadership, and he is commanded to make her wellbeing the top priority of his life in terms of human relationships, and that glorifies God.

Backing out from the immediate context of 1 Peter 3:1-7, and remembering the "salvation of the soul" umbrella under which Peter wrote, a healthy marriage operating in accordance with God's design parameters is one where both husband and wife are laying up treasure in heaven by honoring God's sovereign rule within their marriage. This relationship models Christ's love for the church (Ephesians 5) and teaches their children how to form and maintain healthy relationships. A strong Christian marriage is a tremendous testimony to the world that God's wisdom in the area of the home is right. And this type of marriage provides the best opportunity to develop the most deep and intimate relationship we can have with another human being. Husband and wife become, as Professor Harry Leafe would tell his students, the dynamic duo in life and ministry.

## Closing

In ancient Greek mythology, the story is told of Pygmalion, a sculptor who gave up on human women, but fell in love with a woman he sculpted out of ivory. But of course, the statue was lifeless. At a festival for Aphrodite, Pygmalion made offerings at the altar and wished for a bride that would be the living image of his statue. When he returned home, Aphrodite had granted his wish in that when he kissed the statue, it came to life and he married his perfect woman. A great many people marry their perfect Prince Charming or Princess Lots of Hair on the basis of primarily glandular motivations, only to learn later that not all that glitters is gold. The frog is just a frog. When that happens, they wish to sculpt from a real and flawed human being the perfect mate. But we cannot change other people, nor require them to be someone else so that we may be happy. Peter presented a wholly different framework for marriage, which is not based on finding our perfect soul-mate or changing other people, but ministering to our spouse as we function in our God given roles. In this way, and by the grace of God, two imperfect people can sculpt a beautiful marriage that enjoys a deepening level of intimacy and love, and that honors God by their example before a broken world.

## Application Points

- **MAIN PRINCIPLE:** Christian wives are to submit to the headship of their husbands in the home, and if the husband is spiritually immature or off track, the wife should seek to influence him by her godly conduct and example.

- **SECOND MAIN PRINCIPLE:** Christian husbands are to diligently study their wives' needs and seek to meet those needs, and always privately and publicly show their wives honor and respect.

- Genuine female beauty begins with a character of humility and gentleness, which beauty God highly values.

## Discussion Questions

1. Does the Bible prohibit a woman from fixing her hair and wearing jewelry and nice clothes? If not, is there a way for a lady to do so that is God-honoring? (the intent here is to explore not only what is worn but for whom and for what purpose)

2. What are specific examples for how a wife may undermine her husband's headship in the home?

3. Does a wife being submissive to her husband mean she is weak? (explain)

4. Review Proverbs 31:10-31 and list the qualities of the virtuous wife from God's perspective and explain how that picture of a godly wife fits (or does not fit) with Peter's picture of a godly wife in 1 Peter 3:1-6.

5. What does a meek and quiet spirit (1 Peter 3:4) look like in real life? It helps to consider some examples of what it does not look like.

6. How should a husband go about learning his wife's most important needs?

# Chapter 8

# Courageous Suffering
1 Peter 3:8-22

In a speech Winston Churchill gave to the House of Commons on June 4, 1940 after the successful evacuation of over 338,000 Allied troops to England, he stated: "We shall go on to the end, we shall fight in France, we shall fight on the seas and oceans, we shall fight with growing confidence and growing strength in the air... we shall fight on the beaches, we shall fight on the landing grounds, we shall fight in the fields and in the streets, we shall fight in the hills...." But if you did not have the larger context of his speech, and only caught these words, you might conclude this was commentary on a family vacation. And if you have been through a church split, you might see Churchill's words as commentary on what you witnessed among good Christian brothers and sisters engaged in civil war. Everyone thinks they are right, and being right justifies hateful words, secret meetings, anonymous letters to the pastor, and a host of other absurd behaviors. It should not surprise us that Peter, in addressing various spheres of practical living, in the context of receiving the salvation of our souls, would address how we treat our fellow brothers and sisters in Christ. We are born again, and one of the implications of that is that we have family obligations. And we also have obligations to represent Jesus well before those outside the family.

## Outline

III. THE PLAN OF SALVATION (OF THE SOUL-LIFE) (1:13-4:19)

    a. That it would transform our character (1:13-2:10)

    b. That it would transform our conduct through submission (2:11-3:7)

    c. That it would transform our conduct through suffering (3:8-4:19)

        i. Suffering without fear (3:8-22)

            1. With the right attitude (3:8-15a)

            2. With a good testimony to non-believers (3:15b-17)

            3. With a commitment to God (3:18-22)

## Scripture and Comments

The Bible addresses different aspects of our salvation, and broadly speaking, addresses deliverance from the penalty of sin, the power (influence) of sin, and the presence of sin. The focus of First Peter is our deliverance from the power of sin over our lives, and more specifically he was focused on the deliverance of our soul-life from the power of sin. This entails how we meet the challenges and trials of life by faith, and how our faith responses (or proof of faith or proven character) to life are both an experience of deliverance from the power of sin and a credit of heavenly treasure to our account. To this point, Peter specifically addressed the salvation of our souls in the sphere of our interaction with and attitude toward human government, in the sphere of the marketplace, and in particular in our interaction with and attitude toward our employers, and in the sphere of the home with our interaction with and attitudes toward our spouses. It is apparent that Peter envisions our living hope as a motivation to a whole new paradigm for living, and this paradigm naturally applies in the sphere of our brothers and sisters in Christ. This most likely presumes a local church setting and a church family that Peter's readers interact with regularly.

> 1 Peter 3:8 Finally, *be ye* all of one mind, having compassion one of another, love as brethren, *be* pitiful, *be* courteous:

Peter wrote **finally** to mark the culmination of his treatment of the spheres of personal interactions that are part of the shared experience of his readers. What Peter saved for last is interactions within a local church context, which is implicit in his charge to **be ye all of one mind**. This is similar to Paul's exhortation to the Philippians: "If *there be* therefore any consolation in Christ, if any comfort of love, if any fellowship of the Spirit, if any bowels and mercies, Fulfil ye my joy, that ye be likeminded, having the same love, *being* of one accord, of one mind." (Philippians 2:1-2) Paul used the words "likeminded...one accord...one mind." Neither Peter nor

Paul meant that we are to be the same. Oneness is not "sameness." But this idea of **one mind** means that we are in harmony about our primary purpose. We should have the same high-level goals and objectives for our lives as God's children and for the local church we belong to. In the immediate context, the behavior patterns Peter described in 3:8-11 are the types of basics we should all be of **one mind** about. But beyond that, there seems to be little doubt such would include glorifying God, and the best means of that is carrying out the Great Commission.

One may ask whether we ought to be of **one mind** on doctrine. The difficulty is that as we study, we will form views on issues about which the Bible says a great deal and things about which the Bible does not say a great deal (or says nothing expressly). And over time our views may change. And within a local church, there will be members with various levels of knowledge of the Word. For this reason, it seems unlikely Peter could have envisioned broad agreement on all matters of doctrine. But some have mistakenly concluded from our inability to agree on everything that doctrine is unimportant or too divisive to have an important role in the life of a local church. However, the Bible plainly teaches that doctrine is critical and we are to study and teach doctrine. (Romans 6:17, 16:17; 2 Timothy 4:2; Titus 1:9, 2:1; Hebrews 6:1-2) Paul told Timothy that "scripture...is profitable for doctrine." (2 Timothy 3:16) And he even warned against immaturity characterized by being "carried about with every wind of doctrine." (Ephesians 4:14) Paul told Timothy he should be "nourished up in the words of faith and of good doctrine." (1 Timothy 4:6) But regarding those that would minimize doctrine, Paul's words cut to the chase: "For the time will come when they will not endure sound doctrine; but after their own lusts shall they heap to themselves teachers, having itching ears." (2 Timothy 4:3) So unquestionably the proclamation of doctrine should be one of the central purposes of a local church, and as Christians we ought to engage doctrine. But regarding the issue of being of **one mind** about doctrine, it seems that we ought to be likeminded on the fundamentals of the faith such as the inerrancy of the Bible and the content of the gospel message.

Unfortunately, Christians are frequently unable to agree on what is fundamental and what is secondary. What is apparent is that we are not going to have all Christians everywhere in agreement, and it is unlikely that is what Peter had in mind. Peter was writing to churches, and his exhortation should be understood as being of **one mind** within each respective local church. We should plant ourselves in a local church where we have **one mind** on the fundamentals with that assembly, especially on the core Biblical objectives for believers and the local church. In this context, the following statement from Bishop Burnet in the preface to the book *The Life of God in the Soul of Man* is apropos:

> There is scarce a more unaccountable thing to be imagined, than to see a company of men professing a religion, one great and main precept whereof is mutual love, forbearance, gentleness of spirit, and compassion to all sorts of persons, and agreeing in all the essential parts of its doctrine, and differing only in some less material and more disputable things, yet maintaining those differences with zeal so disproportional to the value of them, and

prosecuting all that disagree from them with all possible violence; or if they want means to use outward force, with all bitterness of spirit. They must needs astonish every impartial beholder, and raise great prejudices against such persons' religion, as made up of contradictions; professing love, but breaking out in all the acts of hatred.

So we may conclude on this matter of doctrine that if every hill is a hill to die on, then you have a serious pride problem.

Peter continued, adding that we ought to have **compassion one of another**. The word **compassion** includes notions of empathy so that we may empathize with the trials others are going through. Such an exhortation assumes a level of personal involvement with **one another**, and again suggests a local church setting is in view. We need to walk alongside folks and help carry their hurts. Peter also said to **love as brethren**, emphasizing the family concept within a local church. Notably, **love** is an adjective, not a verb, so the sense is to be **brethren** characterized by **love**. We are also to be **pitiful**, meaning full of pity. This is not a negative thing, but has the idea of being heartbroken for other people who are suffering. The opposite would be coldness, an attitude James rebuked in James 2:15-16: "If a brother or sister be naked, and destitute of daily food, And one of you say unto them, Depart in peace, be *ye* warmed and filled; notwithstanding ye give them not those things which are needful to the body; what *doth it* profit?" We need to be willing to pray with others, help carry their hurts, and shed tears with them. Shame on us if we are hard-hearted to the trials our brothers and sisters have been called upon to endure.

Finally, Peter instructed his readers to **be courteous**. The idea of courtesy here is to yield to others. The Greek word means humble. Peter thus exhorted his readers to be self-unassuming, humble, or meek. Peter no doubt recalled Jesus' words: "Blessed are the meek: for they shall inherit the earth." (Matthew 5:5) The opposite would be selfish ambition, but a humble person need not be self-promoting. For those who serve God faithfully with excellence and the right heart attitude to bring glory to Him, God takes care of the promoting where it is necessary, as we can observe from the lives of Joseph, Nehemiah and Daniel. This issue of being humble is probably the single greatest challenge we all face in striving to become more Christ-like. When the Hollywood "stars" make movies, often they fight over who will get top billing, whose name comes first in the credits, or whose name is written in the larger letters on the movie poster. When someone in a local church (including the pastor) always needs top billing, there is a serious problem. Humble people are ok with someone else getting top billing, and they do not fall to pieces when they do not get their way.

While this is not the place for a full discourse on the issue of being humble or meek, I would note that this should not be confused with the notion of being weak. In our country, we vote on people who look "presidential" and who are alpha types. When they debate, we want our gladiator to verbally beat down the other. Yet in Scripture, one of the greatest leaders that ever lived was

Moses, and God said of him: "Now the man Moses was very meek, above all the men which were upon the face of the earth." (Numbers 12:3) And if we may turn a page and look at 1 Peter 5:6: "Humble yourselves therefore under the mighty hand of God, that he may exalt you in due time." Civil wars in churches happen when people lack humility and the willingness to resolve conflicts Biblically.

> 9 Not rendering evil for evil, or railing for railing: but contrariwise blessing; knowing that ye are thereunto called, that ye should inherit a blessing.

Having stated several affirmative or positive directives, Peter moved to the negatives. That he even felt it necessary to write these things means that people in churches who call themselves Christ-followers do these terrible things to one another. Thus, he wrote, do not return **evil for evil, or railing for railing**. The term **railing** means reviling or insulting. Recall that Jesus said in the Sermon on the Mount: "But I say unto you, That ye resist not evil: but whosoever shall smite thee on thy right cheek, turn to him the other also." (Matthew 5:39) And again, Jesus said, "...bless them that curse you, do good to them that hate you, and pray for them that despitefully use you, and persecute you." (Matthew 5:44) In other words, Jesus said, "don't retaliate, don't get the last word, don't get them back, but love." All of that sinful behavior derives from pride (not being humble). **But contrariwise**, in other words, in contrast to **rendering evil** and **railing** on one another, be a **blessing**. We are called to be a **blessing** to those around us—**knowing that ye are thereunto called**. So what does being a **blessing** look like?

It is the opposite of the negatives Peter referenced. Instead of **rendering evil** we render good to others. Instead of **railing** we speak words of edification, encouragement, kindness, life and love.

Note the words Peter added to his exhortation to be a **blessing**. He said, **that ye should inherit a blessing**. Simply stated, we must be a **blessing** to other people in order to **inherit a blessing** from God. We cannot be a jerk and expect God's **blessing**. Note that the idea of **inherit** suggests receiving the **blessing** in the future, in connection with Jesus' return that is so frequently alluded to in First Peter. Note again Peter's words from 1 Peter 5:6, that God "may exalt you in due time." Peter does not guarantee an immediate return **blessing**, but that one will be inherited. Much of the Christian life is about laboring now and receiving the promises and rewards later. This is our living hope.

> **10** For HE THAT WILL LOVE LIFE, AND SEE GOOD DAYS, LET HIM REFRAIN HIS TONGUE FROM EVIL, AND HIS LIPS THAT THEY SPEAK NO GUILE: **11** LET HIM ESCHEW EVIL, AND DO GOOD; LET HIM SEEK PEACE, AND ENSUE IT. **12** FOR THE EYES OF THE LORD *ARE* OVER THE RIGHTEOUS, AND HIS EARS *ARE OPEN* UNTO THEIR PRAYERS: BUT THE FACE OF THE LORD *IS* AGAINST THEM THAT DO EVIL.

Here, Peter quoted from Psalm 34:12-16, providing three keys to obtaining a blessing. One may interpose: "But I thought God pours out blessings on us no matter what?" To which I would respond, "Lots of things that preach well ain't so." The person that **will love life, and see good days**, in other words the person that wants to continue enjoying God's blessings, must **refrain his tongue from**

**evil, and his lips that they speak no guile** or deceit. So principle one is that we have to watch our mouth! James addressed the issue of our speech in each of the five chapter of his epistle. Here are some helpful verses from James on speech:

> James 1:25 But whoso looketh into the perfect law of liberty, and continueth *therein*, he being not a forgetful hearer, but a doer of the work, this man shall be blessed in his deed. 26 If any man among you seem to be religious, and bridleth not his tongue, but deceiveth his own heart, this man's religion *is* vain.
>
> James 3:5 Even so the tongue is a little member, and boasteth great things. Behold, how great a matter a little fire kindleth!

James said it is doing God's Word (obedience) that leads to blessing, to which he added that if you cannot control your words, your religion is useless. Indeed, the person that lacks self-control over his speech is deceived about his spiritual maturity. Our speech (this includes what we say on social media) is a litmus for the level of our maturity, and our inability to control our words shows we lack maturity. This issue is critically important, James would add, because our words can cause great injury. They are like a small spark that can take down a hundred acres of land. And the thing about words is that once they are out there, you can never un-ring the bell, just as you cannot take back the words after the hundred acres are scorched black. Our words can build people up and tear them apart. We especially cause harm when we speak lies, so Peter stated that our speech should contain **no guile**. This is more than just a prohibition of lies, but of taking part in any deception. Sometimes we try to walk a line by leaving out details that render our words misleading. We need to be people of integrity and that should be a guiding principle for our speech.

So to experience the blessing of God we need to (1) control our **tongue** (speech), (2) **eschew** or turn away from **evil, and do good** and (3) **seek peace, and ensue it**. It is not enough to just refrain from **evil**, but Peter said, turn away from it and instead **do good**. Do what is right. He further said to be a peacemaker. This is like what James wrote about a Christian who lives by God's wisdom: "And the fruit of righteousness is sown in peace of them that make peace." (James 3:18) And Jesus said: "Blessed *are* the peacemakers: for they shall be called the children of God." (Matthew 5:9) Godly people by their words and actions sow peace and the harvest from that planting is righteousness in themselves and others. Those who do these three things, Peter wrote, are blessed. In fact, **the eyes of the Lord are over the righteous**, meaning God gives divine favor to **the righteous**. Moreover, God's **ears are open unto their prayers**. The term **ears** is an anthropomorphism to explain God in human terms. The point is that God favorably hears the **prayers** of those that do these three things, those that are **righteous**, which implies He does not grant the prayers of Christians who behave wickedly toward other Christians. This should sound a sobering alarm for all of us. There are a host of consequences for our sin, and one is that God may not grant our prayers.

Moreover, **the face of the Lord is against them that do evil**. This describes discipline on God's children who choose not to live like God's children should. To those that would teach that God blesses believers who just have enough faith, Peter's words are a siren call to awaken from the heretical stupor. How we live matters, now and when the Lord returns. When Christians reject God's Word as their standard for living, He is **against them**. Yet too many believers are under the impression that they may pick and choose the parts of the Bible they would live by. The Bible says a great deal, for example, about sexuality, but I think it no exaggeration that in our culture most believers refuse to follow the Bible's guidance on these issues. "I will do it my way....God please bless my relationship with [him or her]. Amen." This a la carte approach to the Bible is unacceptable and God is not going to bless our rebelliousness. The key to blessing in each area of our lives is obedience to God in our words and actions.

> 13 And who *is* he that will harm you, if ye be followers of that which is good?

Not only will our obedience to God lead to His blessing us, but as a general maxim, it will meet with approval among people. But that is not always true; sometimes we can do good and still suffer, which is an issue Peter previously visited in his epistle. Suffering can arise from several sources, including other believers, human government, or even those close to us. Peter asked rhetorically, **who is he that will harm you, if ye be followers of that which is good?** In other words, Peter argued that as a general principle or maxim, people do not **harm you** for doing **good**. Those who are obedient to

God's Word, who "eschew evil, and do good" (1 Peter 3:11), will usually not suffer **harm** from others. But this is not a guarantee, because as Peter already addressed in chapter 2, Christians can suffer (e.g., 1 Peter 2:12, 2:20) even when they have done nothing wrong.

Much in the same way, Paul taught, as a maxim that is not true 100% of the time, that Christians will not suffer oppression from human government if they do "good": "For rulers are not a terror to good works, but to the evil. Wilt thou then not be afraid of the power? do that which is good, and thou shalt have praise of the same: For he is the minister of God to thee for good. But if thou do that which is evil, be afraid; for he beareth not the sword in vain: for he is the minister of God, a revenger to *execute* wrath upon him that doeth evil." (Romans 13:3-4) And as we will see in the next verse, Peter provided instruction for those times when, despite doing right, suffering still comes. But that Peter would address doing good in connection with the blessing of God, and in the next breath, doing good and still suffering as the hands of men, necessarily means that God's blessing on our lives does not mean we will not suffer. Recall, Peter already said Christians are called to suffer. (1 Peter 2:21) Many believers assume God's blessing always takes the form of something material or at least something that is pleasant and enjoyable. What if God's blessing may be to permit a trial that grows you to a greater level of maturity? We need to refrain from putting a worldly spin on what is meant by the blessing of God.

> <u>14</u> But and if ye suffer for righteousness' sake, happy *are ye*: and BE NOT AFRAID OF THEIR TERROR, NEITHER BE TROUBLED;

Acknowledging the reality that believers may suffer despite doing nothing wrong, Peter explained that **if ye suffer for righteousness' sake, happy are ye**. The **if** is a Greek first class condition, meaning that Peter assumed the reality of his statement. There will be a time when we suffer having done nothing wrong, and indeed, for **righteousness' sake**, that is, we will suffer for doing what is right before God. And for those times, we must understand that Peter considered such suffering a blessing from God. This is foreign to our thinking. When we pray for God's blessing, we usually have something like a good job or good health in mind, not suffering for doing good. Yet Peter said it was a blessing, and when he revisited the issue of suffering in chapter 4, he said it is a cause to "rejoice," connecting the rejoicing now to the rejoicing at the return of Christ. (1 Peter 4:13) Peter likewise, in the prologue, connected suffering in trials to our inheritance when Jesus returns. (1 Peter 1:6-7) The notion of a blessing is an internal sense based on confident assurance, and in this context our confidence is in the imminent return of our Lord and Savior who will reward the saints and settle accounts. Does God bless believers materially? James wrote in James 1:17: "Every good gift and every perfect gift is from above, and cometh down from the Father of lights, with whom is no variableness, neither shadow of turning." But we need to understand that the primary blessing Peter had in mind was in connection with our living hope, spiritual growth, and the salvation ready to be revealed to us in the last time.

Peter then quoted from Isaiah 8:12, exhorting his readers to **be not afraid of their terror, neither be troubled** or disturbed. Notably, Isaiah said in 8:13 to let God be "your fear, and let him be your dread." The point of Peter's quoting Isaiah 8:12 was to encourage his readers not to **be...afraid** of the things non-believers fear, i.e., **their terror**, which usually is about what other people can do or say against them. In other words (my paraphrase), "do not let what strikes fear in the heart of the unsaved have the same result in your hearts." The non-believers fear men, but as Isaiah 8:13 said, we are to fear God instead. In the midst of the suffering, Peter essentially said, "understand your blessing and lean in to God and not fear of men."

> **15** But sanctify the Lord God in your hearts: and *be* ready always to *give* an answer to every man that asketh you a reason of the hope that is in you with meekness and fear:

In contrast to being afraid of men, we are to **sanctify** or set apart **the Lord** Jesus as **God in** our **hearts**. This is the antidote to fear of what other people can say or do against us. We have to remember who is in charge. Regardless of our circumstances, Jesus is **Lord** and **God**. He is number one and everyone else is not. But it is one thing to say this as our profession and quite another to own it in our **hearts**. The word **hearts** refers to the immaterial aspect of our person that is the seat of our feelings and thought life. How we think always establishes who we are. As Solomon said, "For as he thinketh in his heart, so is he...." (Proverbs 23:7) Jesus is to be the centerpiece of our worldview and the primary focus of our loyalty. With that mindset, others have no weapon to cause us to fear, no attack that may steal away who we are and what we have in Christ.

But shame on us if these are just words. Shame on us if we say Jesus is at the center of our **hearts** but our words and actions show Jesus is only in the picture when we find it convenient. It is possible for us to express that we want Jesus on the throne of our lives but at most we let him get one cheek on the chair because we will not budge. The person who sets apart Jesus as **God in** their **hearts** will be radically different in the words they choose, the company they choose, the priority they place on material things, their devotion to Jesus' church, their time management, and their choices. A great many believers today talk the talk but they go to church when nothing else interferes. All it takes is a little league game and then Jesus is not first. Or a really great weather day for some bass fishing and then Jesus is not first. The apostle Paul's words ought to convict us: "Be not deceived; God is not mocked: for whatsoever a man soweth, that shall he also reap." (Galatians 6:7) And it bears saying that what Peter is talking about is not for Moses and Paul, but us; it is intended to be the norm for Christian living, not the exception. The bar for genuine devotion to Jesus Christ is indeed a high one. "But Jesus, I will follow you when there is ...[no soccer game, nothing that keeps me out too late Saturday before, a different guy preaching, no rain...]" Peter had in mind throughout this epistle that every one of us will one day account to Jesus for how we invested our lives, whether we invested our moments with a view to the deliverance of our lives at the bema or for our own personal agendas. Peter would say to us today, "don't squander your soul-life for a [ball game, fill in other excuses here]." Make Jesus number one. Period.

The thing about making Jesus central in our **hearts** is that, by the by, others will notice, and in fact, our right living may bring us into conflict with others. And because of this, they may ask why we are the way we are. Peter said of this issue, when they ask, **be ready always to give an answer to every man that asketh a reason of the hope that is in you with meekness and fear.** The expression **be ready always** means to prepare ourselves and remain prepared; we are to maintain a state of readiness, and that cannot be done apart from diligent study of the Word of God.

The word **answer** is the Greek *apologia* from which we get the English term "apologetics" but it generally means an answer or a defense. We popularly use the word apologetics to refer to defending the faith. But often we think of apologetics only in terms of speaking to skeptics about issues like Darwinism or the resurrection. But the context here focuses on, in the midst of suffering, answering for or providing **a reason** for **the hope that is in** us. The **hope that it in us** refers to our steadfast confidence in Jesus Christ and his word, especially about this matter of the salvation of the soul (recall, this is the content of the living hope of 1 Peter 1:3). This **hope**, as Peter previously explained in the context of human government, employers, marriage, and even suffering, should be transformative. After all, we will only receive such questions because we have followed Peter's instruction in 3:15 to **sanctify** Jesus as **God in** our **hearts** or thinking. Why have we done that? Why have we anchored who we are on Jesus? But the questions people ask can vary widely. While we cannot have an answer to every possible question, we ought to know enough about the Bible to speak of the effects of sin, our need for a savior, life beyond the grave, and how to become a child of God, just for starters.

As one of my professors frequently said to his students (my paraphrase), what a sad state of affairs if after many years of professing Christ all that we know of him could be put in a tea cup and there would barely be enough to rattle it around and make a little noise. Referring someone to your pastor for an answer is not being prepared. God expects us to be people of the Book and not people that did everything else available to entertain ourselves but never made knowing the Book a priority. It is only by diligently studying the Bible that can we work out our salvation with fear and trembling. (Philippians 2:12) The writer of Hebrews made a similar statement to what Peter said here:

> Hebrews 5:10 Called of God an high priest after the order of Melchisedec. 11 Of whom we have many things to say, and hard to be uttered, seeing ye are dull of hearing. 12 For when for the time ye ought to be teachers, ye have need that one teach you again which *be* the first principles of the oracles of God; and are become such as have need of milk, and not of strong meat.

The writer of Hebrews wrote to Jewish believers who were under persecution from non-believing Jews, and in the face of that persecution had backslidden. The KJV translates the Greek perfect as a present when it says, "seeing ye are dull of hearing," but the sense is that they had previously fallen from a state of being able to hear to being dull of hearing and presently remained so. The concept of hearing, in this context, is the ability to comprehend the deeper things of God like the doctrine of the priesthood of Melchisedec. Yet the writer said their reversion to immaturity occurred at a point in time when they "ought to be teachers" such that they now "need that one teach...again which be the first principles of the oracles of God." Peter told his audience they should be prepared **always** to **give an answer**, meaning a Biblical defense for their **hope**. The writer of Hebrews told his readers each should be capable of teaching the Word of God. He did not mean in a public sense necessarily, but in a one-on-one conversation they ought to be able to explain truth from the Word of God to others. Unquestionably, the Bible writers expected first century Christians to learn the Word of God well enough they could teach it to others. If someone asks us questions like what happens to us when we die, what about the promise of Jesus' return, why do bad things happen to good people, etc., we ought to be ready and willing to **give an answer**.

How easy it is to fake it though. We can attend church, dress in our Sunday best, carry a Bible, and sing the great hymns of the faith (e.g., "I surrender all..."), but what happens when we are called upon to **give an answer**? It is not the pastor's job, it is mine and yours according to Peter. And he added, how we **give an answer** matters. There is a segment of Christians that look for opportunities to **given an answer** on their pet doctrines. They like to debate and show how smart they are. They can dot the I's and cross the T's with proof texts and confidence but they have no prosperous ministry because pride does not win people. Peter said we are to **answer...with meekness and fear**. The word **meekness** means humility and includes the notion of gentleness. In this context, **fear** is respect. If you have a rotten attitude or a prideful attitude, no one will listen because they cannot get beyond your personality. Even to those that disagree with us, and even if their approach is testy, our directive is to be gentle and respectful. It must be understood that in these situations a central part of giving an **answer** is being willing to listen, not interrupting and speaking over others, not debating, and generally to meet people where they are. We do not know how God might use our encounter with this person to change their heart, but we can rest assured that we will strike out if our **answer** is about showing how smart we are, or proving ourselves right, or being the better debater, and not about teaching God's Word in love with clarity.

Listen to Paul's admonition to Timothy in the context of this very issue when dealing with fellow believers who have caught hold of bad doctrine:

> 2 Timothy 2:24 And the servant of the Lord must not strive; but be gentle unto all *men*, apt to teach, patient, 25 In meekness instructing those that oppose themselves; if God peradventure will give them repentance to the acknowledging of the truth; 26 And *that* they may recover themselves out of the snare of the devil, who are taken captive by him at his will.

Paul plainly said, "the servant of the Lord must not strive," that is, engage in heated disputes. Instead, he or she must be gentle to everyone, willing to teach (not beat down), patient, and meek or humble. And it is worth noting that good teachers always (1) have something from God's Word to say, (2) care about their audience, and (3) are humble. Flee the rest of them.

> 16 Having a good conscience; that, whereas they speak evil of you, as of evildoers, they

may be ashamed that falsely accuse your
good conversation in Christ.

In the process of providing an answer with meekness and fear, we need to keep **a good conscience**. The **conscience** refers to our moral **conscience** before God. Sin soils a **good conscience**, and so having a **good conscience** is a matter of obedience to the Word and dealing with sin as it occurs in our lives (1 John 1:9). We are to keep short accounts with God. When we do this, even though **they speak evil of** us, slandering us **as... evildoers, they may be ashamed that falsely accuse** our **good conversation** or conduct **in Christ**. It is critical in this verse that Peter assumes a **good conscience** and that the accusations are lodged at our **good conversation** and, therefore, are misplaced accusations. In that event, we have nothing to be **ashamed** of, but the slanderers do, and it is likely Peter had in mind their being **ashamed** when they face judgment by Jesus Christ for their works, including their slander.

> <u>17</u> For *it is* better, if the will of God be so,
> that ye suffer for well doing, than for evil
> doing.

Peter concluded that **it is better, if the will of God be so, that ye suffer for well doing, than for evil doing**. Peter previously pointed out that it is a good to suffer for the right reason and with the right attitude: "For this *is* thankworthy, if a man for conscience toward God endure grief, suffering wrongfully. For what glory *is it*, if, when ye be buffeted for your faults, ye shall take it patiently? but if, when ye do well, and suffer *for it*, ye take it patiently, this *is* acceptable with God." (1 Peter 2:19-20) And that is his point here. But Peter added another nuance to this issue of suffering. He stated in 3:14 that it is a blessing to "suffer for righteousness' sake." And here Peter added the notion that it may be **the will of God** concerning our suffering. God permits suffering to come into our lives for His purposes, but His purposes may be that we face the consequences of poor choices or sinful conduct, what Peter referred to as **evil doing**. But God also permits suffering to come our way as a result of **well doing**, and that is **better** than suffering **for evil doing**. The reason it is **better** is that we glorify God when we suffer for **well doing** (1 Peter 2:12, 4:16) and in the midst of our suffering we can experience the blessing of God (1 Peter 3:14) and grow by facing the challenge on the basis of the Word of God (1 Peter 2:2).

> 18 For Christ also hath once suffered for sins, the just for the unjust, that he might bring us to God, being put to death in the flesh, but quickened by the Spirit:

Peter earlier stated, "Christ also suffered for us, leaving us an example, that ye should follow his steps." (1 Peter 2:21) Peter pointed out that Jesus was reviled, but neither reviled back nor threatened, "but committed himself to him that judgeth righteously." (1 Peter 2:23) And Jesus did not suffer for his sins, but "his own self bare our sins in his own body on the tree, that we, being dead to sins, should live unto righteousness...." (1 Peter 2:24) Jesus exemplified how to suffer for the right reasons and without retaliation. The world condemned him, but God used his sufferings for our benefit and ultimately exalted Jesus. Here, Peter built on Jesus' suffering, adding that Jesus **Christ also hath once suffered for sins, the just for** the unjust... being put to death in the flesh, but quickened by the Spirit. The term **once** is the Greek *hapax*, and the point here is that Jesus' death was a one-time event and no second or third death was necessary. The writer of Hebrews said it this way: "By the which will we are sanctified through the offering of the body of Jesus Christ **once** for all." (Hebrews 10:10)

Jesus is **the just** who died **for the unjust**, meaning here the innocent one who died for the guilty. And he did this to **bring us to God**. In the Old Testament, the sacrifices did not remove sin and so they had to be repeated: "And every priest standeth daily ministering and offering oftentimes the same sacrifices, which can never take away sins." (Hebrews 10:11) The payment for sin must involve death but also have sufficient value in accordance with the sin that was committed. Only the blood of the Son of God had sufficient value to address humanity's sin problem. Again, the writer of Hebrews explained: "For by one offering he hath perfected for ever them that are sanctified...And their sins and iniquities will I remember no more. Now where remission of these is, there is no more offering for sin." (Hebrews 10:14, 17-18) We could never pay the price Jesus paid, but we can identify with his sacrifice by faith. And we do this knowing that Jesus did not stay dead, but was **quickened** or made alive (i.e., resurrected **by the** Holy **Spirit**). Jesus' resurrection shows the Father's acceptance of and satisfaction in the offering. We do well to recall John the Baptizer's words upon seeing Jesus and realizing he is the Christ: "Behold the Lamb of God, which taketh away the sin of the world." (John 1:29) In taking away the sin, Jesus brought **us to God** who identify with him by faith.

> 19 By which also he went and preached unto the spirits in prison; 20 Which sometime were disobedient, when once the longsuffering of God waited in the days of Noah, while the ark was a preparing, wherein few, that is, eight souls were saved by water. 21 The like figure whereunto *even* baptism doth also now save us (not the putting away of the filth of the flesh, but the answer of a good conscience toward God,) by the resurrection of Jesus Christ:

These verses are probably the most debated verses in First Peter. The key to interpreting them, as with all the Bible, is context. Peter began with **by which also**. The use of **which** refers back to an antecedent, and shows Peter was building on the implications of Jesus' suffering and being resurrected by the Spirit. The antecedent of **which** is the Holy Spirit, and so Peter stated that **by** the Holy Spirit **he went and preached unto the spirits in prison**. The interpretational difficulties drove Martin Luther to write in his commentary on the text, "A wonderful text is this, and a more obscure passage perhaps than any other in the New Testament, so that I do not know for a certainty just what Peter means."[1] Because the passage is so debated, there is some value in surveying the more common interpretations and providing some critique of each position. Like Luther, I will refrain from any dogmatism as to the proper interpretation of this

---

[1] Martin Luther, *Commentary on Peter & Jude* (Grand Rapids: Kregel, 1990), 166.

challenging passage, but I intend to argue that the better view is that Christ **preached** by the Holy Spirit through **Noah** in the days preceding the Flood, and it is those people that rejected the message that were in Peter's day spirits in prison, under judgment for their rejection of the word of God.

In his commentary on First Peter, Wayne Grudem summarizes the five most popular views of the text:

> *View 1:* When Noah was building the ark, Christ 'in spirit' was in Noah preaching repentance and righteousness through him to *unbelievers who were on the earth then* but are now 'spirits in prison' (people in hell).
>
> *View 2:* After Christ died, he went and preached to *people in hell*, offering them a second chance of salvation.
>
> *View 3:* After Christ died, he went and preached to *people in hell*, proclaiming to them that he had triumphed over them and their condemnation was final.
>
> *View 4:* After Christ died, he proclaimed release to *people who had repented just before they died in the flood*, and led them out of their imprisonment (in Purgatory) into heaven.
>
> *View 5:* After Christ died (or: after he rose but before he ascended unto heaven), he travelled to hell and proclaimed triumph

over the *fallen angels* who had sinned by marrying human women before the flood.²

In addition, Thomas Schreiner offers and advocates a sixth view that is a variation on Wayne Grudem's View 5:

> ...the majority view among scholars today is that the text describes Christ's proclamation of victory and judgment over the evil angels. These evil angels, according to Gen. 6:1-4, had sexual relations with women and were imprisoned because of their sin. The point of the passage, then, is not that Christ descended into hell but, as in 3:22, his victory over evil angelic powers.³

I advocate View 1, but will first address reasons to reject Views 2 through 6. As we have already seen, Peter's epistle has a central theme of the proper Christian response to suffering in the larger context of our living hope with a view to the salvation of our souls. And Peter began verse 18 with these words: "For Christ also hath once suffered for sins...." The critical interpretive grid to be applied to this difficult passage is the context and flow of Peter's argument that suffering may come our way even when we do what is right before God, the sort of living that receives the salvation of our souls. Any proposed solution must not only make sense syntactically, but must further and bolster Peter's argument that it is better to suffer for righteous living

---

[2] Wayne A. Grudem, *Tyndale New Testament Commentaries: 1 Peter* (Downers Grove: Intervarsity Press 2009), 212-13.

[3] Thomas R. Schreiner, *The New American Commentary: 1, 2 Peter, Jude* (Nashville: Broadman & Holman Publishers 2003), 185.

and have the favor of God now and in the world to come than to live unrighteously and face the judgment of God. Moreover, the solution must make sense of Peter's connecting the death and resurrection of Christ with "spirits" (whoever that was) that were disobedient in the days of Noah. And finally, the solution must be something Peter's audience could have grasped without a seminary education. With this in mind, I will turn to Wayne Grudem's View 2.

The View 2, again, is as follows: "After Christ died, he went and preached to *people in hell*, offering them a second chance of salvation." Thomas Schreiner rightly criticizes this view as not fitting the context:

> The view that Christ offered salvation to those who died in the flood suffers from some of the same weaknesses as the first [view]. Such a view also reads the term "spirits" to refer to human beings, but we have seen that this is unlikely. If Christ descended into hell before his resurrection, the word "went" seems superfluous when used of Christ's "spirit." If the journey below is placed after the resurrection, at least Christ has a body with which to make the trip. This interpretation has another fatal problem. It makes no sense contextually for Peter to be teaching that the wicked have a second chance in a letter in which he exhorted the righteous to persevere and to endure suffering. Indeed, we have seen in many places throughout the commentary that eternal life is

> conditioned upon such perseverance. All motivation to endure would vanish if Peter now offered a second opportunity for death. The benefit of braving suffering is difficult to grasp if another opportunity to respond will be offered at death.[4]

While I disagree that, in the epistle, Peter conditioned eternal life on perseverance—rather, the salvation of one's soul-life is in view—but Schreiner is fundamentally correct that the motivation for enduring in suffering righteously is diminished or devalued, or in any case not bolstered, by the argument that the evildoers get a second chance. It must also be noted that the text does not say that Jesus **preached** the gospel, and indeed, Peter did not explicitly state the content of the preaching. But as J. Ramsey Michaels points out in his commentary on First Peter, the Greek term translated "preached" is used only here in First Peter, and where Peter spoke of preaching the gospel he used a different word (1 Peter 1:12, 25; 4:6).[5] Those who advocate this view usually teach that everyone gets a second chance at salvation, but that neither fits the flow of Peter's argument here nor finds any support elsewhere in the Bible.

The fourth view is thematically similar to the second, and shares some of the same failings: "After Christ died, he proclaimed release to *people who had repented just before they died in the flood,* and led them out of their imprisonment (in Purgatory) into heaven." This view is purely speculative in that there is no indication in the

---

[4] Thomas R. Schreiner, 187–88.
[5] J. Ramsey Michaels, *Word Biblical Commentary: 1 Peter* (Nashville: Thomas Nelson 1988), 209.

text of any repentance. Rather, the text only describes these **spirits** as having been disobedient, and nothing in the Flood account in Genesis suggests that anyone repented and yet died in the Flood. The great mark of repentance would surely have been to have heeded Noah's preaching and entered the ark. Moreover, this view assumes a notion of Purgatory that finds no support in the Scripture and runs contrary to the notion that, on the cross, Jesus paid it all. Jesus could not very well have exclaimed, as we find recorded in John's Gospel, "It is finished," if in fact, it was not finished and something remained to be done to deal with sin.

The third view is more appealing than those already considered: "After Christ died, he went and preached to *people in hell*, proclaiming to them that he had triumphed over them and their condemnation was final." This view at least fits the flow of Peter's argument insofar as it builds on the contrast of the spiritual blessings to the righteous versus judgment or condemnation for the unsaved. The difficulty with this view is that it does not adequately relate to what Peter follows with in verse 20: **Which sometime were disobedient, when once the longsuffering of God waited in the days of Noah, while the ark was a preparing, wherein few, that is, eight souls were saved by water.** As J. Vernon McGee explains in arguing his view, the term **when** is critical here:

> This has been a most misunderstood passage of Scripture. The key word to this entire passage is in verse 20; it is the little word *when*—
>
> When did Christ preach to the spirits in prison? "When once the longsuffering of

God waited in the days of Noah." In Christ's day, the spirits of those men to whom Noah had preached were in prison, for they had rejected the message of Noah. They had gone into *sheol.* They were waiting for judgment; they were lost. But Christ did not go down and preach to them after He died on the cross. He preached through Noah "when once the longsuffering of God waited in the days of Noah." For 120 years Noah had preached the Word of God. He saved his family but no one else. It was the Spirit of Christ who spoke through Noah in Noah's day. In Christ's day, those who rejected Noah's message were in prison. The thought is that Christ's death meant nothing to them just as it means nothing to a great many people today who, as a result, will also come into judgment.[6]

Putting aside for the moment whether McGee's interpretation is the right one, he is correct that any proffered interpretation must make good sense of the phrase, **when once the longsuffering of God waited in the days of Noah**. As it is presently stated, View 3 is unsatisfactory.

The fifth and sixth views are substantially similar and may be treated together. View 5 states: "After Christ died (or: after he rose but before he ascended unto heaven), he

---

[6] J. Vernon McGee, *Thru The Bible: 1 Corinthians Through Revelation* (Nashville: Thomas Nelson Publishers 1983), 701-2.

travelled to hell and proclaimed triumph over the *fallen angels* who had sinned by marrying human women before the flood." View 6 affirms the message and the audience, but locates the place of the preaching as somewhere related to Jesus' ascent, but not hell. Unlike the third view, these views give more credence to the phrase, "when once the longsuffering of God waited in days of Noah," but rather than placing the preaching in the days of Noah (as I will advocate below), it only connects the audience (fallen angels) with the days of Noah. Those advocating this view rely primarily on two arguments: (1) the use of the term "spirits" is rarely used of people as opposed to angels and (2) Peter places the preaching within the context of Jesus' death, resurrection and ascension, giving no indication that the preaching occurred in Noah's day. Supporting the latter point, they would point out that if Jesus merely preached through Noah, then Peter would not have used the term "went." But as N.M. Williams explained, that Jesus "went" need not necessarily imply a physical journey:

> Great weight has been attached to this word in support of the view that Christ *went in person* to the prison of the lost. But the word does not necessarily imply personal locomotion. See Gen. 11:5-7, and especially Eph. 2:17. Such language would have been entirely admissible (for it would have been in harmony with the genius of the Greek tongue), had Peter desired to say that Christ brought himself into connection with the persons in question,

either by his Spirit, or by means of some pious inhabitant of the earth.[7]

Moreover, the term **spirits** can be used of people (see Hebrews 12:23) and so the context should drive our interpretation rather than any artificial assumptions. The thrust of Peter's argument was the contrast between Christians suffering for righteousness sake and evildoers, with warnings that there will be consequences for evildoers. It seems far more likely, then, that the term **spirits** refers to the **spirits** of human evildoers, not angels. Advocates of the fifth and sixth views are quick to point out and relate the reference to **spirits** in verse 19 to **angels** in verse 22, but the reference in verse 22 to **angels** cuts against their position. If Peter had in mind the fallen angels of Genesis 6 and wanted to make the connection to the **angels** in verse 22, then it seems more likely that he would have used **angel** or **spirits** both times. Indeed, Peter referred to these angels explicitly in his second epistle, calling them the "angels that sinned." (2 Peter 2:4) Moreover, we find no indication in Genesis 6 or elsewhere in the Bible that the fallen angels of Genesis 6 persecuted the faithful for living righteously. We know from the Flood account and here in 1 Peter 3 that only eight lives were saved from the Flood. Had these fallen angels persecuted those eight for their righteous living, it would seem to be a glaring omission from the Flood narrative.

Measuring these proposals against the context and flow and Peter's argument and against the backdrop in Genesis, the fifth and sixth views, while plausible, do not

---

[7] H. H. Harvey et al., An American Commentary On The New Testament Volume VI (Valley Forge: The Judson Press 1890), Ch. 3, 51.

provide the most satisfactory solution. This leaves View 1 for consideration: "When Noah was building the ark, Christ 'in spirit' was in Noah preaching repentance and righteousness through him to *unbelievers who were on the earth then* but are now 'spirits in prison' (people in hell)." Verse 19 begins with **by which also.** As Grudem explains, this refers back to the Spirit in verse 18:

> *In which* refers back to 'in the spirit' in verse 18. It means 'in which realm, namely, the spiritual realm.' It does not necessarily mean 'in the resurrection body' (which Peter could easily have said, had he wanted to), but rather 'in the realm of the Spirit's activity' (the realm in which Christ was raised from the dead, v. 18).[8]

As we press forward, that the actions of Christ occur in the spirit is critical, and it is the primary point of attack for those that reject this view. As J. Vernon McGee points out, the **when** is critical. As with McGee, commentator N.M. Williams also advocates that the preaching in view occurred at the time of the disobedience, not later at the time of the resurrection:

> The preaching occurred at the time of the disobedience, not thousands of years afterward. That it occurred long after the disobedient were swept away has been taught by the majority of expositors, including some recent distinguished interpreters of Germany. The common view is held in most remarkable disregard

---
[8] Wayne A. Grudem, 164-65.

> of the construction of the Greek ... The spirits who were in prison when Peter was writing those words were persons who lived their earthly life in the days of Noah.[9]

Advocates of views 5 and 6 insist that the **when** refers back to when the **spirits** were disobedient but not when the preaching occurred. The problem with this view is that it does not provide the best fit for the situation of Peter's audience. Peter implored his readers to live righteously even if it entails underserved suffering brought about by other people, to wit, to rejoice despite their trials (1:6-7), to gird up the loins of their minds as obedient children (1:13-14), be holy in all of their conduct knowing everyone's works will be judged by God (1:15-17), set aside sin in favor of the "sincere milk of the word" that endures forever (1:25-2:2), offer spiritual sacrifices to God (2:5), abstain from fleshly lusts (2:11), to have a good reputation among Gentiles (2:12), and to submit and suffer for doing good (2:20-25). Peter's readers must have felt overwhelmed by their circumstances, and he recalled for them another group of believers who faced a like situation, namely Noah and his family.

Of Noah, the "preacher of righteousness" (2 Peter 2:5), we read in Hebrews 11:7: "By faith Noah, being warned of God of things not seen as yet, moved with fear, prepared an ark to the saving of his house; by the which he condemned the world, and became heir of the righteousness which is by faith." From the description in Genesis 6, Noah lived in a morally decayed world in rebellion to God, and it must have been a tremendous trial as he and his family lived in that time by faith in

---

[9] H. H. Harvey et al., 51-52.

God's Word. But in the end, they were blessed and the evildoers faced the judgment of God. Likewise, in Peter's time, his readers would face undeserved suffering for living out the Word of God, but they ultimately would have deliverance and blessings in Jesus Christ. They were hearing the Word of Jesus Christ in their day through Peter and others just like those in Noah's day heard it through Noah. This finds support especially in 1 Peter 1 where Peter explained that it was the "spirit of Christ" that preached the word of God through the Old Testament prophets.

> <u>1 Peter 1:10</u> Of which salvation the prophets have enquired and searched diligently, who prophesied of the grace *that should come* unto you: <u>11</u> Searching what, or what manner of time **the Spirit of Christ which was in them** did signify, when it testified beforehand the sufferings of Christ, and the glory that should follow.

The prophets wrote with the understanding that the Spirit of Christ superintended their writing. Those persons Jesus preached to through Noah that rejected his message are now suffering as spirits in prison, awaiting their future judgment. (Revelation 20:11-15) Likewise, in Peter's day, the believers who were suffering for their faith would find future blessings, but the evildoers would face a certain judgment. The same Spirit who preached to people in both eras raised Christ and, thereby, proclaimed victory over all those opposed to him, and by implication, a future salvation for those like Peter's audience who presently suffer as a result of identifying with the Christ.

Thomas Schreiner dismisses the view that Christ spoke through Noah, pointing out the primary objection typically raised against the view, namely that the term **went** does not make sense if Christ only spoke through Noah rather than journeying somewhere:

> First, the idea that Christ spoke by means of the Spirit through Noah suffers from a number of problems. First, it does not explain adequately the participle (*poreutheis*) translated "went" in v. 18 and "has gone" in v. 22. In v. 22 it is clear that it refers to Jesus' ascension to God's right hand, showing that it is a post-resurrection event. The word "went" seems out of place and strange for those who defend the Augustinian view, for Christ does not really go anywhere if he preaches "through" Noah. There are instances in the New Testament where the word "went" (*poreuomai*) refers to the ascension of Christ (Acts 1:10-11; John 14:2, 3, 28; 16:7, 28), while it nowhere refers to his descent into the underworld. We also noticed in v. 18 a clear reference to the resurrection of Christ. The "going" in v. 19, therefore, also most naturally refers to what is true of Christ's resurrection body. It is obviously the case that Christ did not need his resurrection body to preach through Noah by means of the Spirit. Indeed, the reference to Christ's going in v. 19 demonstrates the implausibility of the first view since it is only through the Holy Spirit. This piece of

evidence alone shows the first view is implausible.[10]

But as pointed out before, **went** (*poreutheis*) need not indicate physical locomotion. Peter himself used the term figuratively in 1 Peter 4:3 (*walked* in lasciviousness, lusts,...), 2 Peter 2:10 (*walk* after the flesh), 2 Peter 3:3 (*walking* after their own lusts), and the term was used also by Jude in Jude 11 (*gone* in the way of Cain), Jude 16 (*walking* after their own lusts), and Jude 18 (*walk* after their own ungodly lusts). In this sense, the term does not carry the sense of a journey at all, but stresses the characteristic of the person by describing the sphere of their activities. In 1 Peter 3:19, the point is not that Jesus journeyed anywhere, but that in the realm of the Spirit or by the Spirit he **preached**.

The passage under consideration presents substantial challenges, but as with any passage, context is key. Peter's epistle focused on the issue of Christians' undeserved suffering. Such suffering is to be met with righteousness, knowing that there will be future blessings as the soul-life is delivered into eternity (1 Peter 1) and there will be judgment for the evildoers. Of the six views considered, the only view that both fits within Peter's argument and makes sense of the language is the view that Jesus **preached** through Noah the Word of God and those that rejected it are now **spirits in prison**. Likewise, in Peter's day, Christ **preached** the Word of God through Peter and others. As in the days of Noah, Peter's audience could expect that living by the word would entail suffering, but the end of it would be blessings, whereas those rejecting the word would in the end face judgment at the hand of God.

---

[10] Thomas R. Schreiner, 186.

Peter next showed a typology concerning **the ark** that was a **baptism** that saved **eight souls...by water**. Peter explained, **the like figure**, a reference to **the ark**, is a type for the **baptism** that **doth also now save us**. While it is not uncommon to hear it expressed that **baptism** means to submerse in water, the word has a broader meaning of placing one thing inside another, and like many words, it can be used figuratively. In the context of water, it does mean to sink or submerse within the water. As always, context is critical. Here, Peter hastens to add concerning this **baptism** that it is **not the putting away of the filth of the flesh**, in other words, it is not water **baptism**. Instead, Peter explained, this **baptism** that **now saves** or delivers **us** is **the answer of a good conscience toward God**. As we have noted before, the word **saves** generally means to deliver or rescue and context determines from what one is delivered or rescued from, and to what. Also, the word **answer** is not the Greek *apologia* that was translated "answer" in 3:15 and had the idea of a defense, but instead is the Greek *eperotema* that has the sense of a commitment or pledge. The **baptism** in view is a pledge **of a good conscience toward God**. Peter used the same term when he referenced a "conscience toward God" in 1 Peter 2:19 and "having a good conscience" in 1 Peter 3:16. Recall that a **good conscience** is the result of obedience to God's Word and addressing sin (1 John 1:9) by confession and repentance when it arises. Thus, the **baptism** here is a commitment of faithful obedience. This helps us to understand that the **now saves you** does not refer to justification (deliverance from sin's penalty) but the deliverance of our soul-life that is the central theme of the epistle that Peter first referenced his prologue and built upon throughout his epistle. Noah's **answer of a**

**good conscience toward God** led him to build the ark that saved his and his family's lives. Our **answer of a good conscience toward God** likewise saves our soul-lives.

This makes good sense. We know from other passages that salvation in the sense of justification or deliverance from sin's penalty is not grounded in a commitment to obedience, but a trusting in Jesus and him alone for the forgiveness of sins based on his finished work at Calvary. But Peter assumed throughout his epistle that his readers were believers, and his focus was on the "what next?" and, in particular, on the notion of living in such a way that we exchange our lives for the inheritance reserved in heaven for us. (1 Peter 1:4) Indeed, Peter said in the prologue that we were born again "unto a lively [or living] hope by the resurrection of Jesus Christ form the dead, to an inheritance incorruptible...." (1 Peter 1:3-4) And so also here, Peter saw the physical deliverance or saving of the lives of Noah and his family—who were believers before they entered the ark—as prefiguring a deliverance for believers' soul-lives today. This deliverance is empowered **by the resurrection of Jesus Christ** (just as in 1 Peter 1:3) and is realized on the basis of a commitment to obedience to God. As we handle life on the basis of God's Word, our lives are being delivered from sin's power and we are appropriating our share in the inheritance reserved in heaven for us. Peter would similarly explain in 1 Peter 4:6 that the gospel was preached to the spiritual dead so that they might "live according to God in the spirit." It is this resurrection-enabled living according to God in the spirit that delivers our lives and appropriates our inheritance.

**22** Who is gone into heaven, and is on the right hand of God; angels and authorities and powers being made subject unto him.

Building on the concept of Jesus' resurrection, Peter added that Jesus has **gone into heaven, and is on the right hand of God.** The New Testament elsewhere confirms the reality of Jesus' exalted position at **the right hand of God.** (Romans 8:34; Ephesians 1:20; Colossians 3:1; Hebrews 1:13, 8:1, 10:12, 12:2) Interestingly, the writer to the Hebrews explained that "when [Jesus] had by himself purged our sins, [he] sat down on the right hand of the Majesty on high; Being made so much better than the angels, as he hath by inheritance obtained a more excellent name than they." (Hebrews 1:3-4) And in fact, as Son, Jesus was appointed "heir of all things." (Hebrews 1:2) Paul referenced Jesus' position at the "right hand in the heavenly places, far above all principality, and power, and might, and dominion, and every name that is named, not only in this world, but also in that which is to come." There, as here, Jesus' resurrection was followed by his exaltation and receipt of an inheritance and authority. Peter wrote, **angels and authorities and powers being made subject unto him.** In the "world to come" (Hebrews 2:5) or "that which is to come" (Ephesians 1:21), Jesus will exercise that authority over his inheritance, but it is his now. The inheritance we have to look forward to is a share in Jesus' inheritance. (Romans 8:17; Colossians 3:24) Following Jesus' example, we also may suffer now, but in due time God will exalt us as we receive our portion of the inheritance. As Peter later stated: "Humble yourselves therefore under the mighty hand of God, that he may exalt you in due time." (1 Peter 5:6)

## Closing

As Peter already touched upon in his epistle, and would revisit in the next chapter, suffering is a part of the Christian experience. And in particular, suffering for the name of Jesus Christ should not come as a surprise to us. But with all that said, there should be some safe havens where persecution and suffering are not the norm. One such place should be the marriage relationship. This is not to say that a marriage should be free from conflict, but it should be a safe place where each partner can be open and vulnerable rather than hiding behind a wall. If the marriage is not a safe place, then it will not be all that God wants for us. Another safe place ought to be the local church. Safe does not mean that publicly flaunted sin will be condoned. But the local church should be a place where there is Christian tolerance (see 1 Peter 4:8) and acceptance and where people are not judged on the basis of externalities that say nothing about a person's standing before God or their spiritual walk. We should expect to see people of different backgrounds, colors, and preferences, some with office jobs and others that work outside, some that love to hunt and fish and others that do not, some that love sports and others that could care less, some with ink and some without, some with blue or green hair and some with natural hair colors, some wearing cowboy boots and a hat and other dressed differently, some blended families, some interracial marriages, some adopted children, and some people with physical handicaps. And among all of these, with all their differences, there should be unity of purpose and love because they are all family in Jesus Christ, and all of them should experience a safe place within their local church community.

## Application Points

- **MAIN PRINCIPLE:** Christians should be a blessing to others within the local church, setting apart Jesus as the centerpiece of their thought-life that motivates their words and actions, and if they suffer for doing right, they should be prepared to provide a Biblical response to questions from non-believers about their faith.

- The Christian's pledge of a good conscience before God will save his or her soul-life, just as Noah's pledge of obedience to God's Word in building the ark saved his and his family's physical lives.

## Discussion Questions

1. What are some practical ways you can be a blessing to someone at your church that you have seen but have not yet met?

2. What kinds of persecution against Christians are happening in the United States at this time?

3. How do we "sanctify the Lord God in [our] hearts?" And if we do that, how should that affect the things we think about, what we read, the music we listen to, the entertainment we take in, the people we hang around with, how we prioritize our time and family commitments, and other areas of our lives?

4. What are you personally doing to be prepared to give an answer to the person that asks you for a reason for your hope? (1 Peter 3:15)

5. Will there be consequences to you if you choose to do little or nothing to be prepared to give an answer to the person that asks you for a reason for your hope?

# Chapter 9

# Out with the Old, in with the New
1 Peter 4:1-11

There were seven mandatory Biblical feasts for national Israel in the Old Testament. Probably the most well known among Christians is the Passover, but there was a seven-day feast immediately following the Passover called the Feast of Unleavened Bread. (Exodus 12:15-20; Leviticus 23:6-8, 14-15; Numbers 28:17-25; Deuteronomy 16:3-4, 8, 16) During the seven days, there was to be no leaven in the home, or indeed, within the borders of the country, and the people only ate unleavened bread. Part of the ritual for each family was a thorough cleaning of their home to ensure that every bit of leaven was removed. Of course, Jesus' death on a Roman cross fulfilled the Passover for the whole world. (John 1:29; 1 Corinthians 5:7) As the famous hymn goes, "Jesus paid it all, All to Him I owe; Sin had left a crimson stain, He washed it white as snow." But what about the day after Passover? Is it back to the old ways?

The week-long Feast of Unleavened Bread, in removing the leaven from the homes, represented a complete cleansing away of sin. The sin was not swept under the rug, nor was a little of it permitted to remain in the closets. It all had to go! And the New Testament teaches that we should keep this Feast. Hear Paul's words: "Purge out therefore the old leaven, that ye may be a new lump, as ye are unleavened. For even Christ our passover is sacrificed for us: Therefore let us keep the feast, not with old leaven, neither with the leaven of malice and wickedness; but with the unleavened *bread* of sincerity and truth." (1 Corinthians 5:7-8) Paul identified Christians as "unleavened" because "Christ our Passover is sacrificed for us." He paid it all, but what now? We need to be unleavened in our experience. Paul said, "purge out therefore the old leaven," that leaven that represents who we were and not who we are now. Out with the old! Now every day going forward we should "keep the feast" only eating unleavened bread. We should not eat "the old leaven" of who we were in the past nor "the leaven of malice and wickedness," but should eat only "the unleavened bread of sincerity and truth." What a beautiful picture of Christians abandoning their former lifestyle and embracing holiness, a whole new way of living made possible by our Passover.

## Outline

III. THE PLAN OF SALVATION (OF THE SOUL-LIFE) (1:13-4:19)

    a. That it would transform our character (1:13-2:10)

    b. That it would transform our conduct through submission (2:11-3:7)

c. That it would transform our conduct through suffering (3:8-4:19)

   i. Suffering without fear (3:8-22)

   ii. Finished with the former lifestyle (4:1-6)

   iii. Loving and ministering to the brethren (4:7-11)

## Scripture and Comments

Peter labored to explain to his readers the "what next" regarding their being born again as God's children. Peter moved from justification to the outworking of our salvation in our lives on a day-by-day basis. Peter referred to this as the salvation or deliverance of our soul-lives. We are delivering our soul-lives into eternity as we live in faithful obedience to God's Word, exchanging our moments in this mortal life for our inheritance in Christ. With each moment we decide to live for ourselves and according to the philosophies of the world and lusts of our flesh (what Paul called wood, hay and stray) or for Christ according to God's Word (what Paul called gold, silver and precious stones). But even if we do right by God, Peter warned that we should expect suffering to come our way. In the material that follows, we will see that Peter begins to make more explicit what was always in the background, namely the return of Christ and the judgment. Peter expected his readers to live in light of the future. We are on temporary assignment, the fuse it lit, and the clock is counting down.

> 1 Peter 4:1 Forasmuch then as Christ hath suffered for us in the flesh, arm yourselves likewise with the same mind: for he that hath suffered in the flesh hath ceased from sin;

This is a "therefore" verse where Peter drew a conclusion from the materials stretching back at least to 1 Peter 3:13. There, Peter explained that Godly living may bring suffering, but that if we suffer for righteousness sake then we are blessed (3:14). Peter further explained that we must set aside Jesus as Lord in our hearts (3:15), making the person and works of Jesus the centerpiece of our thinking. And more than that, we must be prepared to provide a verbal defense for what we believe (3:15). Indeed, Jesus was the supreme example of suffering, and we have by faith identified with Jesus Christ.

With all of this in mind, Peter began the "therefore" to build the implications of the preceding material. Thus, he concluded, **forasmuch then as Christ hath suffered for us in the flesh**. We must pause here and recognize that while Jesus suffered in various ways throughout his life, Peter wrote here specifically of the Savior's death on a Roman cross. Jesus **Christ** died **for us in the flesh**. Jesus fully appreciated the ramifications of what he did **for us in the flesh** and Peter exhorted his audience (and us by application) to **arm yourselves likewise with the same mind**. We need to take up the same resolve or mindset, that is, we need to comprehend the implications **for us** of his death **in the flesh** as a substitute for our own death. From God's perspective, our identification by faith with the One who died **in the flesh** accomplishes our death **in the flesh** and on that basis, we have **ceased from sin**. We are set free! But it is not enough to be free; we must understand and **arm** our minds with this truth.

Paul addressed this very issue in Romans 6, where Paul explained the implications of being dead to sin and alive to God.

> Romans 6:4 Therefore we are buried with him by baptism into death: that like as Christ was raised up from the dead by the glory of the Father, even so we also should walk in newness of life....7 For he that is dead is freed from sin. 8 Now if we be dead with Christ, we believe that we shall also live with him: 9 Knowing that Christ being raised from the dead dieth no more; death hath no more dominion over him. 10 For in that he died, he died unto sin once: but in that he liveth, he liveth unto God. 11 Likewise reckon ye also yourselves to be dead indeed unto sin, but alive unto God through Jesus Christ our Lord. 12 Let not sin therefore reign in your mortal body, that ye should obey it in the lusts thereof.

Note how Paul taught that our identification with the Savior is an identification with his death and his resurrection life. And just as Peter taught in 1 Peter 4:1, Paul explained that "he that is dead" (i.e., identified by faith with Jesus' death) "is freed from sin." And the implication is that this freedom is liberty to live in "newness of life." Paul continued about this newness of life:

> Romans 6:20 For when ye were the servants of sin, ye were free from righteousness. 21 What fruit had ye then in those things whereof ye are now ashamed? for the end of those things *is* death. 22 But now being made free from sin, and become servants to God, ye have your fruit unto holiness,

> and the end everlasting life. 23 For the wages of sin *is* death; but the gift of God *is* eternal life through Jesus Christ our Lord.

Paul said that before we were believers ("when ye were the servants of sin") we "were free from righteousness." But the things we did as non-believers only brought about the experience of "death." As believers, that has all changed because we are "being made free from sin" moment-by-moment as we experience our freedom in real time. Our freedom is not a license to sin but instead a transfer of our allegiance to God as we are now "servants of God" with the intent that the fruit of our lives be characterized by "holiness." In so doing, rather than experiencing "death" we will experience "everlasting life." Understand, the issue here is not a believer's destiny, but their experience moment by moment in their earthly sojourn. Will it be death or life? Paul warned believers, in a verse commonly plucked from its context and set out on the "Romans Road," that believers are free but how they use their freedom will affect their experience of what they have in Jesus Christ. If a believer continues in sin, he or she will experience "death." But what is available is "the gift of God is eternal life through Jesus Christ our Lord."

Imagine if a slave were set free but one or two or three years later he still remained at the salt mines where he toiled for years in bondage. Imagine a prisoner finishing his sentence and when he exits the prison he just hangs around by the gates day after day. Or imagine a person was kidnapped, their hands bound behind their back and their mouth gagged. Hours after being rescued by law enforcement and unbound, that person still keeps his hands behind his back and will not speak. All of these are absurd, and so also it is absurd to be set free by the Son from sin and death so that we can experience life, and yet choosing to continue in sin and have as our Christian experience what Paul called death. We have a dual capacity as believers. We can make decisions conforming to God's Word and in the next moment act "like the devil." We are experiencing life then choose death.

> 2 That he no longer should live the rest of *his* time in the flesh to the lusts of men, but to the will of God.

Peter said that the result of this freedom from sin should be that the believer **no longer should live the rest of his time in the flesh to the lusts of men**. To do that would be to experience death (using Paul's word), which is not experiencing freedom. It is being set free but choosing to stay in the cage like a fool. And note that Peter did not call out specific external sins here, but instead referred to **the lusts of men**. It is the fleshly desires in our mind that are a great danger to us. We will choose in each moment to live by God's Word or fall back on worldly philosophies and our own internal **lusts**. According to James, it is our own **lusts** that draw us to sin, and then to an experience of death:

> James 1:14 But every man is tempted, when he is drawn away of his own lust, and enticed. 15 Then when lust hath conceived, it bringeth forth sin: and sin, when it is finished, bringeth forth death.

Rather than give in to **lusts**, Peter exhorted his readers to **live the rest of** their **time in the flesh...to the will of God**. This mirrors what Paul said in Romans 6—free from sin to be a slave to righteousness. The practical outworking of our reckoning ourselves free from sin (1 Peter 4:1) is that we are free to spend our remaining time about the business of doing **the will of God**. In that way, we are stewards of our time, cognizant that we have one candle to burn and life is serious business. As Paul wrote in Ephesians 5:16: "Redeeming the time, because the days are evil." And similarly in Colossians 4:5: "Walk in wisdom toward them that are without, redeeming the time." We must resolve each day to make this day count for the Lord.

> 3 For the time past of *our* life may suffice us to have wrought the will of the Gentiles, when we walked in lasciviousness, lusts, excess of wine, revellings, banquetings, and abominable idolatries:

Peter continued, saying in essence that at whatever age a person becomes a believer, they already had enough time living like the devil. Thus, **for the time past of our life**, that is, while we were non-believers, **may suffice us to have wrought the will of the Gentiles, when we walked in lasciviousness, lusts, excess of wine, revellings, banquetings, and abominable idolatries**. Peter's readers lived in the diaspora among pagan Gentile cultures and, like in the book of Judges, took on the lifestyle and idolatry of their Gentile neighbors. They previously **walked** or lived **in lasciviousness** and other sins. The word **lascivious** refers to debauchery or completely unrestrained behavior. The word **lusts**, as we have already seen, refers to evil or wicked desires. The phrase **excess of wine** means drunkenness. The word **revellings** means orgies. The word **banquetings** means drinking parties.

And the phrase **abominable idolatries** captures the idea of unbridled idolatry, the sin that plagued the Jewish people during so much of the Old Testament period. Whatever amount of time they had as non-believers to engage in this behavior was more than enough of sin. But when a Christian changes and no longer does those things he or she once did, not everyone will be happy about it, to which Peter turned next.

> 4 Wherein they think it strange that ye run not with *them* to the same excess of riot, speaking evil of *you*: 5 Who shall give account to him that is ready to judge the quick and the dead. 6 For for this cause was the gospel preached also to them that are dead, that they might be judged according to men in the flesh, but live according to God in the spirit.

Certainly, God's appeal to us as His children is that we walk with Jesus. Our lives as believers ought to be quite different than before our relationship with the Savior. And not just in external matters like going to church. We ought to think differently, prioritize our time differently, have different goals and aspirations, treat our relationships differently, and generally have a different life focus. But as we engage in all of this, people close to us will take notice. And in fact, the more fleshly we were in our lifestyle before knowing Christ, the more profound the change may appear. The old crowd we hung out with and perhaps even family members may not be happy at all with our decision. Indeed, **they think it strange** or they are astonished or surprised **that we run not with them to the same excess of riot**. In other words, they fail to comprehend why we will not engage in the behavior we used to do with them, and as a result, they get angry and speak **evil** of us. I have on several occasions heard the testimony of someone within a "religious" family who came to Christ only to have their family say, "you are dead to us." In one instance, the family considered it a moral obligation to murder a young man that converted to Christianity.

Those that **speak evil** of believers because of their changed lifestyle **shall give** an **account to** Jesus who **is ready to judge the quick** or living **and the dead**. (see also Matthew 12:36) Note that there is a wordplay here with **dead** in verses 5 and 6. In verse 5, the word **dead** is physical death. There will be a future time when Jesus will **judge** everyone, whether they are physically alive at the time or already **dead**. But in verse 6, Peter used the term **dead** in a spiritual sense when he wrote that **for this cause was the gospel preached also to them that are dead, that they might be judged according to men in the flesh, but live according to** the will of **God in the spirit**. In other words, the believer who is maligned by the old crowd or family should not be surprised, and indeed should understand that this proves the purpose of **the gospel** has been fulfilled in their lives. Namely, **the gospel** was **preached** to the spiritually **dead** (Peter's readers and by application us) to the end **that they might** identify by faith with Jesus who was **judged according to men in the flesh** and crucified so that we could be made alive with Jesus and thus **live according to** the will of **God in the spirit**. Those who are alive in the flesh (verse 5) are condemned, but those who are dead in the flesh (verse 6) are made alive **in the spirit**. That the old crowd speaks **evil of** a believer for refraining from their old lifestyle is confirmation of the power of the **gospel** to change lives, that it has specifically made them **live according to God in the spirit**.

> 7 But the end of all things is at hand: be ye therefore sober, and watch unto prayer.

Peter referenced the coming judgment in verse 5, and here explicitly called his audience's attention to the reality that **the end of all things is at hand** or near. We do well to keep in mind, especially if Peter wrote his epistle relatively early (A.D. 40's) that God would still reveal a great deal more about things future than what Peter may have known at the time. If Peter wrote his epistle early, then Paul's writings on the rapture (or gathering up) and John's writing of the Revelation were not completed yet. But Peter knew what Jesus revealed during his earthly ministry, and Jesus taught that believers should be ready for his return as it may be at any time:

> Matthew 24:42 Watch therefore: for ye know not what hour your Lord doth come... 44 Therefore be ye also ready: for in such an hour as ye think not the Son of man cometh.

Peter expected Jesus' return imminently and that has consequences for everyone. How we live matters and the day of reckoning may be right around the corner. But the skeptics were already saying in the first century, and doubly so now, that Jesus is not returning:

> 2 Peter 3:9 The Lord is not slack concerning his promise, as some men count slackness; but is longsuffering to us-ward, not willing

> that any should perish, but that all should come to repentance. 10 But the day of the Lord will come as a thief in the night; in the which the heavens shall pass away with a great noise, and the elements shall melt with fervent heat, the earth also and the works that are therein shall be burned up. 11 *Seeing* then *that* all these things shall be dissolved, what manner *of persons* ought ye to be in *all* holy conversation and godliness, 12 Looking for and hasting unto the coming of the day of God, wherein the heavens being on fire shall be dissolved, and the elements shall melt with fervent heat?

Peter addressed the skeptics in his second epistle, reminding them and us that the entire world was previously judged (by the Flood), and the coming "day of the Lord" will just as surely occur. Any delay in the coming judgment is a result of God's longsuffering for the lost, not His being dilatory and not because there is no coming judgment. From God's perspective, **the end...is at hand**. As a believer, that should be our perspective. In particular, we should **therefore** be **sober, and watch unto prayer**. To be **sober** (Gr. *sophreneo*) is to be alert and ready, of sound mind or in the right mind. Notice how this important term is used in the following verses:

> Luke 8:35 Then they went out to see what was done; and came to Jesus, and found the man, out of whom the devils were departed, sitting at the feet of Jesus, clothed, and **in his right mind**: and they were afraid.

> Romans 12:3 For I say, through the grace given unto me, to every man that is among you, not to think *of himself* more highly than he ought to think; but **to think soberly**, according as God hath dealt to every man the measure of faith.

In the verse from Luke, a man freed of a demon, and who was previously roaming the tombs as a madman, was said to be "in his right mind." And in Romans 12, Paul exhorted his audience not to think too highly of themselves, but in contrast, "to think soberly," clearly indicating sound judgment about themselves. And our **sober** or right thinking should be coupled with **prayer** that reflects our readiness (**watch**) for the Lord's return. Unfortunately, I think the reality is we may go extended periods of time without bringing to mind the Lord's return may be tomorrow. This is one of those areas where the theology of our profession does not match the theology of our experience. So instead of being ready and of a right mind, we get distracted and lethargic concerning the ramifications of the Lord's return. When that happens, we live like practical skeptics.

> 8 And above all things have fervent charity among yourselves: FOR CHARITY SHALL COVER THE MULTITUDE OF SINS.

Having exhorted his audience to live according to the will of God and be alert and of sound mind concerning the end, Peter reminded his readers that **above all things**, as of a first priority, **have fervent charity** or love **among yourselves**. This is essentially what Peter said in 1:22: "Seeing ye have purified your souls in obeying the truth through the Spirit unto unfeigned love of the brethren, *see that ye* love one another with a pure heart fervently."

As Christians, and especially in the context of a local church, we are to live to God, and that especially should be apparent in our relationships with our brothers and sisters in Christ. But someone may know a Christian they do not particularly like. Peter reminds us, quoting from Proverbs 10:12, that love **shall cover the multitude of sins**. This has nothing to do with atoning for sins, but with Christian tolerance. Our ability to love others has nothing to do with them and everything to do with our relationship with Jesus. That is why Jesus could teach that we should love our enemies: "But I say unto you, Love your enemies, bless them that curse you, do good to them that hate you, and pray for them which despitefully use you, and persecute you." (Matthew 5:44) And if we are to love our enemies, then this love is not about them but our allegiance to Jesus and his command. This should be all the more so when it comes it comes to fellow Christians, who should never be our enemies. Our Christ-like love should be strong enough to overlook some flaws (or perceived weirdness), and our humility (if we have it) should recognize we sometimes (or often) need some tolerance from others about our own flaws (or eccentricities). So if we are to love others, we can overlook some faults. Not everything has to be brought up.

According to an old Hebrew story, the patriarch Abraham was sitting outside his tent one evening when he saw an old man, weary from age and his long journey, coming toward him. So Abraham rushed out to greet him and then invited him in for some rest and hospitality. Abraham washed the old man's feet and fed him. But as the old man ate, he neither prayed nor blessed the food. Abraham asked, "don't you worship God?" But the old man said, "no, I worship fire only and reverence no other god." Angry at what he heard, Abraham threw the man out into the night air and he departed. Then God asked Abraham where the stranger went and Abraham explained the he sent him away because he did not worship God. God replied, "I have suffered him these eighty years although he dishonors me. Could you not endure him one night?" The word "tolerance" gets a bad rap in our culture because of its misuse, but Christian tolerance is Biblical, right here in First Peter!

> 9 Use hospitality one to another without grudging.

Building on this matter of Christian charity or love, Peter instructed that we should provide **hospitality one to another without grudging**. In the first century, **hospitality** often took the form of providing food and lodging to travelers. It is one thing to be hospitable and quite another to do it without complaining. We can say "your welcome" while we are thinking "you don't deserve this" or "you inconvenienced me." And our attitude matters to God. Some of us will be hospitable if it makes us look good, but not when it is difficult or comes at a real cost or inconvenience to us.

I have found, to my great surprise (yes, this is sarcasm), that my children despise raking up the pine needles that accumulate from the dozen or so large pine trees in our front yard. I have considered buying shirts for each of them that read, "I love yard work." They could wear the team shirts while doing the yard work. But of course, whatever our shirt says, God knows our hearts. If we are doing for the local church or providing for someone but doing so grudgingly, it does not count in terms of laying up treasure in heaven.

10 As every man hath received the gift, *even so* minister the same one to another, as good stewards of the manifold grace of God.

Staying with the general context of our relationship to our fellow Christians in a local church setting, Peter next addressed stewardship. Peter said, **as every man** (Christian) **hath received the gift, even so minister the same** gift **one to another**. The **gift** in view is what is usually referred to as spiritual gifts. Unquestionably, in the early church, the Holy Spirit gifted believers. It is usually assumed that this gifting occurred at the moment a person trusted Christ, although no verse says that. In any event, Paul explained that there are numerous gifts that come from the "same Spirit":

> 1 Corinthians 12:4 Now there are diversities of gifts, but the same Spirit. 5 And there are differences of administrations, but the same Lord. 6 And there are diversities of operations, but it is the same God which worketh all in all. 7 But the manifestation of the Spirit is given to every man to profit withal. 8 For to one is given by the Spirit the word of wisdom; to another the word of knowledge by the same Spirit; 9 To another faith by the same Spirit; to another the gifts of healing by the same Spirit; 10 To another the working of miracles; to another prophecy; to another discerning of spirits; to another *divers* kinds of tongues; to another the interpretation of tongues: 11 But all these worketh that one and the selfsame Spirit, dividing to every man severally as he will.

Paul also referenced spiritual gifts in Romans 12:6-8. There is an in-house debate among Christians as to whether the Spirit continues to gift all believers today. Some say there are no longer spiritual gifts, while others say the so-called "sign gifts" like prophecy are no longer operative but other "non-sign" gifts like wisdom are, and still others say all the gifts are operative today. In some churches, people take a spiritual gift assessment (test) to help them determine what their gift is. I note that no verse tells us to discover what our gift is; the Biblical authors assume that is apparent. Also, no passage delineates sign gifts from non-sign gifts. Nor do any verses suggest honing or developing such gifts. It is incredulous to think God's gift would be half a gift that needs years of work, but that teaching is out there (but not Scriptural). It seems preferable that these gifts were from God and were immediately usable and obvious to those that had them, just as with the Old Testament parallel when the Spirit enabled people with the skills to build the Tabernacle and its contents:

> Exodus 31:1 And the LORD spake unto Moses, saying, 2 See, I have called by name Bezaleel the son of Uri, the son of Hur, of the tribe of Judah: 3 And I have filled him with the spirit of God, in wisdom, and in understanding, and in knowledge, and in all manner of workmanship, 4 To devise cunning works, to work in gold, and in silver, and in brass, 5 And in cutting of stones, to set *them*, and in carving of timber, to work in all manner of workmanship. 6 And I, behold, I have given with him Aholiab, the son of

> Ahisamach, of the tribe of Dan: and in the hearts of all that are wise hearted I have put wisdom, that they may make all that I have commanded thee; 7 The tabernacle of the congregation, and the ark of the testimony, and the mercy seat that *is* thereupon, and all the furniture of the tabernacle, 8 And the table and his furniture, and the pure candlestick with all his furniture, and the altar of incense, 9 And the altar of burnt offering with all his furniture, and the laver and his foot, 10 And the cloths of service, and the holy garments for Aaron the priest, and the garments of his sons, to minister in the priest's office, 11 And the anointing oil, and sweet incense for the holy *place*: according to all that I have commanded thee shall they do.

When there was a need for artisans who could build the contents of the Tabernacle, the Spirit gave certain people immediately usable skills they did not previously have. In my view, this matter of spiritual gifts is the same in the New Testament, that is, in the early church and in the absence of a completed New Testament cannon, there was a need for teachers and others to have a specific skillset for immediate use. Such gifts were prevalent primarily in the first generation of Christians and waned quickly as the New Testament was written. It is curious that, if such gifts continued, we do not find considerably more references to them. The most developed teaching is in 1 Corinthians, which is among Paul's earliest writings, likely written around AD 50. His prison epistles that come much later do not mention gifts, and neither do other later epistles like 1 and 2 John. But regardless of how you come down on this issue, which Peter does not answer in the passage at hand, it is apparent that everyone has different strengths and weaknesses. We call those strengths "talents" and recognize that people are born with natural abilities that can be further developed. And such talents are not limited to things like public teaching. Talents usable within the local church certainly include teaching, but also such things as cooking, singing, photography, various artistic abilities, rocking babies to sleep in the nursery, and many other things. What are you good at? Use that in the local church to serve others.

Accordingly, whether we apply 1 Peter 4:10 to spiritual gifts, or see its primary application today to God-given talents, the application is the same. Every believer has some abilities they are good at, and Peter taught that we should use those abilities to **minister** or serve **one another**. Peter assumed no Christian is an island, but is instead engaged in a local church where they are around **one another** so that they can love, be hospitable and serve **one another**. This is required of all believers **as good stewards of the manifold grace of God**, that is, the varied (that's what **manifold** means) gifts, talents, and abilities we have from God. If you are not in a local church, or in a local church but do not serve, shame on you. Peter says here in 1 Peter 4:10, get with God's program. He gifted you so you can serve. No excuses. Just do it. Remember that we are strangers and pilgrims on temporary assignment (1 Peter 2:11) for Jesus, and during this short time we have a mission that is centered around our participation in Jesus' building of the church.

> 11 If any man speak, *let him speak* as the oracles of God; if any man minister, *let him do it* as of the ability which God giveth: that God in all things may be glorified through Jesus Christ, to whom be praise and dominion for ever and ever. Amen.

In verse 11, Peter brought the "therefore" (or "forasmuch") that started in 4:1 to a conclusion. First, Peter addressed the issue of speech. **If any man speak, let him speak as the oracles of God**. Our speech ought to reflect God. We all do well at that on Sunday mornings, but do we have a "God talk" that we keep in our pockets only to take it out on Sundays, or is our speech consistent? Peter did not limit his directive to Sunday chatter.

The fact is that, as believers, the way we talk to other people ought to be different, and people who listen to us for very long ought to hear something of God in our talk. That means that what we say ought to be true and ought to edify the hearer. It is not that we just quote Scripture, or only discuss theology. But if we have made Jesus the centerpiece of our thinking (see 1 Peter 3:15), our speech will reflect that reality even when we are not directly addressing Scripture. This rules out lies, gossip, slander, insults, most sarcasm, evil or vulgar speech and jokes, and a whole lot more. This also rules out all of our conversations being about politics, sports and the weather. Our speech ought to be encouraging, honest, instructive and edifying. This is similar to Paul's admonition in Ephesians 4:29: "Let no corrupt communication proceed out of your mouth, but that which is good to the use of edifying, that it may minister grace unto the hearers."

Likewise, when we **minister** or serve others, we ought to do so **as of the ability** or talent **which God giveth**. We cannot do this in our own strength. To use the abilities God gave us to bless others glorifies God, and so Peter added, **that God in all things may be glorified through Jesus Christ, to whom be praise and dominion for ever and ever.** Our service honors God, and it is **through Jesus Christ** because, recalling 4:6, the gospel was preached to us that we might "live according to God in the spirit." Jesus' sacrifice made it all possible, freed us from sin to serve righteousness, and for that reason Jesus deserves our **praise** and he received from the Father **dominion for ever and ever.** The writer of Hebrews wrote of Jesus: "God...hath in these last days spoken unto us by his Son, whom he hath appointed heir of all things...." (Hebrews 1:1-2) And as Peter emphasized in 4:5 and 4:7, Jesus return approaches; in the meantime we should live in anticipation of Jesus' return. Are you ready?

## Closing

Peter closed the unit of thought contained in 1 Peter 4:1-11 with an exhortation to serve to the glory of God. But some would rather be served than serve. It is fascinating that as Jesus was preparing to go to the cross in a matter of days, his disciples were quibbling about who would have a higher position of authority in the Kingdom.

Just before the triumphal entry, the mother of James and John, the sons of Zebedee, made a request of Jesus that her sons "may sit, the one on the right hand, and the other on the left, in thy kingdom." (Matthew 20:20-21) But when the other apostles heard about this, "they were moved with indignation against the two brethren." (Matthew 20:24) With this in the background, Jesus shared the last supper with his apostles, and then arose "from supper, and laid aside his garments; and took a towel, and girded himself...and began to wash the disciples' feet...." (John 13:4-5) Peter initially refused because he found it unbecoming for Jesus to wash his feet. (John 13:6) Then we read Jesus teach them the lesson he had for them about service:

> John 13:12 So after he had washed their feet, and had taken his garments, and was set down again, he said unto them, Know ye what I have done to you? 13 Ye call me Master and Lord: and ye say well; for *so* I am. 14 If I then, *your* Lord and Master, have washed your feet; ye also ought to wash one another's feet. 15 For I have given you an example, that ye should do as I have done to you. 16 Verily, verily, I say unto you, The servant is not greater than his lord; neither he that is sent greater than he that sent him. 17 If ye know these things, happy are ye if ye do them.

In the first century Jewish culture, washing another's feet was the menial task of a slave or lowly servant, but the Lord willingly took that role. It was not only service, but the type of service that gets neither notice nor applause.

Some would serve in church in a position of notoriety or in the public eye, but changing diapers in the nursery or doing the lawn work or cleaning the building between Sundays will never happen. They would never have knelt down with Jesus and washed feet alongside him. But as one of my professors, Dr. Bill Boyd, taught us about this passage, we need to join membership in the Order of the Towel, just like Jesus. He even distributed small and simple key chains made from strips of a towel to us. He reminded us that when we do not feel like our service is becoming of who we are, or when we do not feel we are being adequately appreciated and noticed, to reach in our pockets and feel the small piece of a towel and be reminded anew that we are called to be members of the Order of the Towel, kneeling beside Jesus in washing others' feet.

## Application Points

- **MAIN PRINCIPLE:** Christians are freed from the lusts of the flesh to live out the will of God in the Spirit in anticipation of the Lord's return, but the old crowd and even family may not approve of the new lifestyle and this could become a source of conflict and suffering.

- During Christians' temporary sojourning, they are to love others and minister to them with the gifts God gave them.

## Discussion Questions

1. What are the implications of identifying by faith with Christ's death on the cross?

2. Why might the old crowd or your family not approve of you living in a way that honors God but is not the same as you formerly lived? If that happens, how should you respond to them?

3. Who will give account to Jesus for their conduct? (1 Peter 4:5)

4. What is authentic hospitality and what does not count as such?

5. What are your gifts and how are you presently using those gifts in your local church?

6. In practical terms, what should people be hearing from you if you are speaking "as the oracles of God"?

# Chapter 10

# Suffering and the Judgment
## 1 Peter 4:12-19

Jesus said: "For the Son of man shall come in the glory of his Father with his angels; and then he shall reward every man according to his works." (Matthew 16:27) There is an end of the tunnel, a final accounting when our experience of life (our soul-life) will come into judgment, and that should affect how we engage God's Word and live today. But how will we face the decisions and challenges God has for us tomorrow when God turns the page? We have an opportunity every day to take the Word of God and work the problems of life.

I have taught mathematics for over 20 years at the college level. There are a great many things I do not understand, but I know something about math students. Usually the question I get in a frantic email (or nowadays, in a text) is something like this: "Hey Professor. I am completely lost in chapter 2 and I am behind on the homework and don't know what to do." My standing response: "Have you read chapter 2 in the textbook before trying to work the problems?" And if there were a way to text crickets chirping, that would often be the text I would get back. In studying mathematics, you have to read the textbook, get your hands around the formulas, then work problems by applying what you read and especially those formulas to the problems. It would be foolhardy to believe that, without any effort to understand the formulas or the process (like factoring polynomials), one could just go directly to the homework problems and be able to solve them. But that is what Christians do when they face what God has for them without spending time in the Word of God. What then happens is that they fall back on worldly wisdom—they wing it. And winging it does not work well for math or Biblical living.

In the next unit of thought in Peter's epistle, he built on the issue of suffering and trials, especially suffering for the name of Christ. If we are going to face trials, and the Bible and our experience confirm that will be the case, we need to face it on the basis of God's instruction and wisdom. As we do so, we lay up treasure in heaven by the product of our life well lived. Much of that instruction and wisdom is right here in 1 Peter 4.

### Outline

III. THE PLAN OF SALVATION (OF THE SOUL-LIFE) (1:13-4:19)

    a. That it would transform our character (1:13-2:10)

    b. That it would transform our conduct through submission (2:11-3:7)

c. That it would transform our conduct through suffering (3:8-4:19)

   i. Suffering without fear (3:8-22)

   ii. Finished with the former lifestyle (4:1-6)

   iii. Loving and ministering to the brethren (4:7-11)

   iv. Suffering for being a Christian (4:12-19)

      1. With rejoicing (4:12-14)

      2. In view of the coming judgment (4:15-19)

## Scripture and Comments

Recall that Peter already stressed in the first half of chapter 4 the return of Christ and the judgment to follow. Peter wrote in 4:5: "Who shall give account to him that is ready to judge the quick and the dead." And again in 4:7: "But the end of all things is at hand: be ye therefore sober, and watch unto prayer." In a manner of speaking, Peter held before his audience the reality that there is a coming time of accounting. That judgment makes how we live now a matter that is serious to God and ought to be serious to us. What we do with the time allotted us has consequences. But it also puts our suffering into perspective. The concept of Christian suffering is not a new topic at this point, for Peter referenced the issue already in 1:6-7, 2:19-23, 3:14-18, and 4:4. Indeed, Peter must have anticipated the issue of suffering to be real and relevant for his audience. Yet for Christians in the United States, suffering for Christ may seem foreign to us or at least uncommon. But we do not know what tomorrow may bring. Peter would tell us to expect a "fiery trial" and deal with it appropriately in light of the coming judgment already emphasized in chapter 4. Our lives now should be dramatically affected by our conviction that God will in His timing judge everyone's works.

> 1 Peter 4:12 Beloved, think it not strange concerning the fiery trial which is to try you, as though some strange thing happened unto you:

In one verse, Peter categorically rejected the all too common American brand of Christianity that promises a smooth ride to every faithful believer. Contrary to such nonsense, Peter addressed his audience as **beloved**, revealing his pastor's heart for those he wrote to, and the reason he had to tell them the truth. They should not **think it...strange concerning the fiery trial which is to try** or test them. While there are various kinds of trials, it will become apparent that the context here is persecution. And Peter put the issue of suffering out there and said do not be astonished or surprised when the **fiery trial** happens. Peter did not tell them to seek the trial or pray for the trial to come, but he reminded them candidly that such trials are to be expected in the life of a child of God. Professor Harry Leafe always told his students that it is like God is turning the pages of a book, and we don't know what is on the next page for our lives. Some pages are going to bring pop quizzes, and others will bring major exams. And then he would ask: "How are you going to handle it?" And that is the question—will we handle the pop quizzes and major exams on the basis of the Word of God or on the basis of worldly thinking?

Rather than keeping us from trials, God permits **the fiery trial** for a purpose, and that purpose is that it **try** us. The word **try** is the Greek *peirasmos* and Strong's defines it as "a putting to proof...." The primary definition in BDAG is "an attempt to learn the nature or character of something, *test, trial*."[1] And **the fiery trial** that causes suffering can come in all shapes and sizes. (see James 1:2) It may be a personal attack in the workplace in how people talk to you or about you, or trouble in the home with your spouse or children, or it could be an illness. But whatever it will be, Peter said (my paraphrase), "do not be surprised because this is normal Christian living." These things happen to non-believers also, but when God permits them to come our way, He tests or tries our faith. I do not mean by this that we are being tested as to whether we are Christians. Rather, as the illustration above about pop quizzes and major exams suggests, the issue being tested is how will we handle life. That is not so hard in the absence of suffering, but when suffering comes, will we apply God's Word and deal with the issues Biblically, or will we abandon that and fall back on worldly wisdom? The former proves our faith and appropriates our inheritance, but the latter leads to more trouble.

> 13 But rejoice, inasmuch as ye are partakers of Christ's sufferings; that, when his glory shall be revealed, ye may be glad also with exceeding joy.

In contrast (the word **but** makes the contrast explicit here) to being astonished by the trial when it comes our way, Peter said **rejoice**. The word **rejoice** translates the Greek verb *chairō* that essentially means to be cheerful.

---

[1] William Arndt et al., *A Greek-English Lexicon of the New Testament and Other Early Christian Literature* (Chicago: University of Chicago Press, 2000), 793.

And in the very same context, James wrote to his readers that they should "count it all joy when" they face trials. (James 1:2) But why rejoice? Why be cheerful? The answer is that God permits the trials for a purpose, and if we understand that purpose and our role in the training program of God then we can rejoice in what God is doing and will do. Thus, Peter explained that **inasmuch** or to the degree that we **are partakers of Christ's sufferings** during this lifetime, **that, when** Jesus' **glory shall be revealed,** we **may be glad also with exceeding joy**. The word **revealed** is the Greek *apokalupsis* and has the idea of something being disclosed, made manifest, or unveiled. And here it is Jesus being **revealed**, a reference to his return in **glory**. Peter twice made reference to this before, which is important in seeing how all of the first four chapters cohesively form a unit:

> 1 Peter 1:7 That the trial of your faith, being much more precious than of gold that perisheth, though it be tried with fire, might be found unto praise and honour and glory **at the appearing of Jesus Christ**:

> 1 Peter 1:13 Wherefore gird up the loins of your mind, be sober, and hope to the end for the grace that is to be brought unto you **at the revelation of Jesus Christ**;

Notice how in the prologue of the epistle (1:7) Peter connected the testing of our faith to the return of Jesus. And then Peter exhorted his readers to be prepared and focused on when the Lord returns (1:13). Indeed, Peter made multiple references to the return of Christ and the coming judgment, even earlier in this chapter. (1 Peter 4:5-7) Putting all of this together, Peter said **rejoice** now so that you can rejoice (**may be glad also with exceeding joy**) when Jesus returns. To **rejoice** now is to suffer with understanding, with the right attitude, and for the right reasons, sharing in or being **partakers of Christ's sufferings**. For such suffering, we will be rewarded at his return as our life (soul) is exchanged for our inheritance. In this way, we **rejoice** now so that we will rejoice later at the bema. In this context, Paul reflected on the fact that our suffering in this present time cannot be compared to the glory to come when Jesus returns and we lay hold of our inheritance:

> <u>Romans 8:17</u> And if children, then heirs; heirs of God, and joint-heirs with Christ; if so be that we suffer with *him*, that we may be also glorified together. <u>18</u> For I reckon that the sufferings of this present time *are* not worthy *to be compared* with the glory which shall be revealed in us.

Having told his readers that partaking in **Christ's sufferings** is a cause for rejoicing, Peter went a step further and explained that this suffering is a blessing.

> <u>14</u> If ye be reproached for the name of Christ, happy *are ye*; for the spirit of glory and of God resteth upon you: on their part he is evil spoken of, but on your part he is glorified.

Although Peter previously mentioned suffering at the hands of others (1 Peter 3:16), what is new here is that Peter explicitly addressed persecution **for the name of Christ**. To be **reproached** is to be reviled, vilified, defamed, taunted or insulted. All of these reflect verbal assaults. Having already indicated that suffering can be a basis for rejoicing, Peter added that if you are **reproached for the name of Christ, happy** or blessed **are ye**. The term **happy** is the Greek term *markarios* that is almost always translated "blessed," as we see, for example, in the Beatitudes. (Matthew 5:3-11). As throughout Peter's teaching on suffering, it is suffering in the right way for the right reasons that is a blessing. And the right reason is **the name of** Jesus **Christ**. By **name**, Peter did not speak of the word **Christ**. Remember that **Christ** is the Greek term for the Hebrew *Messiah*. In this context, the **name** speaks of reputation or fame based on the person and their accomplishments. Put simply, Peter spoke of the blessing of being **reproached** for one's testimony or witness of Jesus. It is evident in Scripture that persecution for providing a testimony of Jesus will get worse and worse. (See Revelation 6:9-11 and 20:4) Peter learned verse 14 directly from Jesus in the famed Sermon on the Mount, where Jesus (like Peter here) directly linked being reproached to blessing and rewards:

> Matthew 5:11 Blessed are ye, when *men* shall revile you, and persecute *you*, and shall say all manner of evil against you falsely, for my sake. 12 Rejoice, and be exceeding glad: for great *is* your reward in heaven: for so persecuted they the prophets which were before you.

In the Sermon, Jesus taught his disciples that they are "blessed" to suffer "for [his] sake" when they are reviled (same term translated **reproached** in 1 Peter 4;14). Such blessing / suffering was reason to "rejoice, and be exceeding glad" because of their "great...reward in heaven." Not only may we rejoice because of the reward in heaven, but Peter added, we are **blessed** because the **spirit...of God resteth upon** us. Recall that in Isaiah 11:2, the prophet wrote of Jesus that "the spirit of the LORD shall rest upon him." If we suffer after the example of Christ, we are blessed and the Holy **Spirit** remains upon us. This suggests enablement from God through his **Spirit** to endure.

Peter continued, explaining in reference to those that revile us, **on their** or the revilers' **part** Jesus **is evil spoken of**. It is not merely that they revile us, but they revile the Jesus of whom we testify by our words and our lives. And yet, **on** our **part** Jesus **is glorified** by our steadfast testimony in the face of the persecution. While Christians ought not to be looking for a fight, there is a time to be courageous. There is a time to stand. Recall Mordecai's words to Esther, "and who knoweth whether thou art come to the kingdom for such a time as this?" (Esther 4:14) The Bible is full of history about people who took a stand in the face of opposition. Think of the courage of Puah and Shiphrah who disobeyed Pharaoh's orders to kill the male Hebrew babies:

> Exodus 1:15 And the king of Egypt spake to the Hebrew midwives, of which the name of the one *was* Shiphrah, and the name of the other Puah: 16 And he said, When ye do the office of a midwife to the Hebrew women, and see *them* upon the stools; if it *be* a son, then ye shall kill him: but if it *be* a daughter, then she shall live. 17 But the midwives feared God, and did not as the king of Egypt commanded them, but saved the men children alive.

When Nehemiah set out to fulfill the will of God for his life by seeing to the restoration of the wall of Jerusalem, he was opposed by Sanballat the Horonite. (Nehemiah 2:10) We read in Nehemiah 4 how this wicked man mocked (reproached) Nehemiah, the very issue Peter had in mind. True to form, Nehemiah prayed then returned to his work on the wall.

> Nehemiah 4:1 But it came to pass, that when Sanballat heard that we builded the wall, he was wroth, and took great indignation, and mocked the Jews. 2 And he spake before his brethren and the army of Samaria, and said, What do these feeble Jews? will they fortify themselves? will they sacrifice? will they make an end in a day? will they revive the stones out of the heaps of the rubbish which are burned? 3 Now Tobiah the Ammonite *was* by him, and he said, Even that which they build, if a fox go up, he shall even break down their stone wall. 4 Hear, O our God; for we are despised: and turn their reproach upon their own head, and give them for a prey in the land of captivity: 5 And cover not their iniquity, and let not their sin be blotted out from before thee: for they have provoked *thee* to anger before the builders. 6 So built we the wall; and all the wall was joined together unto the half thereof: for the people had a mind to work....

We find yet another powerful example in the book of Daniel. Daniel decoded the king's dream in Daniel 2, explaining that the golden head of the statue was Nebuchadnezzar's kingdom but the silver chest and other portions represented successive kingdoms. Nebuchadnezzar did not like the message and hoped his dynasty would never end, so in chapter 3 he built a statute like the one from the dream, but all of gold, which in his mind represented the perpetuity of his dynasty over Babylon. Then he went a step further and decreed that those who would not bow to the statue would be executed. Predictably, Daniel's three friends would not bow. They stood even when it might cost their lives.

> <u>Daniel 3:13</u> Then Nebuchadnezzar in *his* rage and fury commanded to bring Shadrach, Meshach, and Abednego. Then they brought these men before the king. <u>14</u> Nebuchadnezzar spake and said unto them, *Is it* true, O Shadrach, Meshach, and Abednego, do not ye serve my gods, nor worship the golden image which I have set up? <u>15</u> Now if ye be ready that at what time ye hear the sound of the cornet, flute, harp, sackbut, psaltery, and dulcimer, and all kinds of musick, ye fall down and worship the image which I have made; *well*: but if ye worship not, ye shall be cast the same hour into the midst of a burning fiery furnace; and who *is* that God that shall deliver you out of my hands? <u>16</u> Shadrach, Meshach, and Abednego, answered and said to the king, O Nebuchadnezzar, we *are* not careful to answer thee in this matter. <u>17</u> If it be *so*, our God whom we

> serve is able to deliver us from the burning fiery furnace, and he will deliver *us* out of thine hand, O king. 18 But if not, be it known unto thee, O king, that we will not serve thy gods, nor worship the golden image which thou hast set up.

Daniel's friends did not know if they would be delivered, but were not afraid to answer the king and told him that whether or not God delivered them, they would not bow to his idol. What tremendous courage, and yet even under these circumstances they did not revile the king. They were courageous and ready to suffer with the right attitude. But there is always the danger that in our Christian walk we might suffer for wrongdoing and deceive ourselves into believing it was for our faith.

But an important question is who was doing the persecuting of Peter's readers? There is no indication in the text of formal (Roman or governmental) persecution. Since the persecution is for being a Christian, I would argue that the persecution Peter anticipated was the same he personally experienced in Jerusalem, from non-believing Jewish people, as recorded in the early chapters of the book of Acts. We see substantial evidence of this type of persecution in the New Testament prior to the Roman persecution that began with Nero.

The first century recipients of Hebrews faced persecution from non-believing Jews, which was pressing them to abandon their participation in local churches and return to Judaism. (see Hebrews 10:26-36, 12:3-4, 13:10-14) In his letter to the Thessalonians, Paul referenced his readers' persecution from other Greeks being like the persecution of the churches in Judea from other Jews. (1 Thessalonians 2:14) Indeed, even during Jesus' earthly ministry, the Jewish leadership in Jerusalem determined that those who would affirm Jesus as the Christ would be excommunicated from the synagogue, which meant exclusion from the Jewish community and had far-reaching ramifications. In John 9, Jesus healed a blind man who was blind from birth, which the Pharisees taught that only Messiah could do. So when it happened, they had to move quickly to disprove what Jesus had done, and thus they interrogated the healed man, and then his parents, who affirmed their son was born blind and could now see but would not affirm that Jesus healed their son. John added this commentary: "These *words* spake his parents, because they feared the Jews: for the Jews had agreed already, that if any man did confess that he was Christ, he should be put out of the synagogue." (John 9:22) This Jewish effort to marginalize or punish Jews who affirmed Christ began during Jesus' earthly ministry and continued during the early ministries of the apostles (e.g., Acts 5:17-42, 8:1-3), much at the hands of Saul (later Paul) before his conversion. It should come as no surprise that believing Jews of the diaspora would eventually share a similar experience of persecution.

> 15 But let none of you suffer as a murderer, or *as* a thief, or *as* an evildoer, or as a busybody in other men's matters.

Peter next presented the negative side of suffering, that is, suffering for the wrong reasons. That Peter would even have felt it necessary to say these words reminds us there is no conduct a Christian cannot do. It is not uncommon for a Christian to comment that another person cannot possibly be a Christian because they have (at least allegedly) engaged in some sinful conduct. Yet Peter warned Christians not to **suffer as a murderer, or as a thief, or as an evildoer** or criminal, **or as a busybody in other men's matters**. No doubt it was not Peter's point to be exhaustive, but to remind his audience that suffering comes for different reasons, and while it is a blessing to suffer for the right reasons, there is no blessing for suffering as a result of sin. This does not honor God.

> <u>16</u> Yet if *any man suffer* as a Christian, let him not be ashamed; but let him glorify God on this behalf.

But in contrast to suffering as a sinner, **if any man suffer as a Christian**, then he or she should **not be ashamed**. The notion of suffering **as a Christian** complements the notion from verse 14 of being "reproached for the name of Christ." The term **Christian** (Gr. *Christianos*) is only employed in two other places in the New Testament, both in the Acts. First, we learn in Acts that "the disciples were called Christians first in Antioch." (Acts 11:26) Then later in Luke's history, as Paul preached to Agrippa, he responded to Paul's preaching, "Almost thou persuadest me to be a Christian." (Acts 26:28) The latter affirms that early in church history Christ followers were called Christians. To be identified with this group at the time Peter wrote was to put oneself at risk, but that identification was nothing to **be ashamed** of. Paul would write to the Romans that he was "not ashamed of the gospel of Christ." (Romans 1:16) It is equally so that we should not be **ashamed** of being identified with Jesus Christ by the label **Christian** even if the persecutors use the term as a word of derision.

At different times and in different places, this label has caused people to be subject to ridicule and persecution, but such was sharing in the sufferings of Christ, which glorifies God (4:14). It is noteworthy that today a common label is evangelical, which means different things to different people. Whatever you may think of that label, the one we should embrace without hesitation is **Christian**, but not merely by profession. That profession is important, but it is only has value to the extent the label fits our walk in life. If we are like the Christ, then the label is rightfully ours.

So Peter wrote (much like Paul in Romans 1:16) that there is no shame in being a **Christian**. We should take a stand for all that being a **Christian** rightfully represents. The idea here of being **ashamed** suggests allowing other persons' responses to our well doing to push us back or intimidate us. Peter said, "don't do that." Instead, **glorify God on this behalf**, that is, in bearing this label. In other words, make the label authentic by doing with our lives what honors God.

> 17 For the time *is come* that judgment must begin at the house of God: and if *it* first *begin* at us, what shall the end *be* of them that obey not the gospel of God? 18 And IF THE RIGHTEOUS SCARCELY BE SAVED, WHERE SHALL THE UNGODLY AND THE SINNER APPEAR?

Here, Peter again reminded his readers (as in 4:5, 7, 13) of the nearing judgment when every person will account for their works. Yet, unfortunately, this verse supplies one of those "half verses" that has been subjected to exegetical abuse. In one way or another, many have taken the first half of the verse to speak of retributive judgment on "the church" or a church. But nothing in the four chapters up to this point suggested a context of God's retributive judgment on Peter's readers, nor is the notion of punishment inherent in the term **judgment**. The notion of making a **judgment** has to do with reaching a determination based on the evidence or information available. And when we find the term **judgment** in the Bible, we must look at the context to determine the nature of the **judgment** and not merely assume God is dishing out punishment. Indeed, as we have previously considered, there is a future **judgment** for every Christian (2 Corinthians 5:10), but not with a view to their eternal destiny. The eschatological **judgment** of a believer always has to do with inheritance and rewards. (Matthew 16:27; 1 Corinthians 3:11-15) And the trials that cause suffering that Peter addressed over and again in this epistle are not with a view to punishment, but training and rewards. (Hebrews 12:11)

Peter's point here was that if God judges His own people first (at the bema), what will become of His enemies when He judges their works (not at the bema). This is a common style of Rabbinic argument called a *qal vachomer* argument. The argument is from lesser to greater, and here, from the lesser judgment on God's people to the greater judgment on God's enemies. Peter even quoted Proverbs 11:31 from the Septuagint (LXX). In the KJV, that verse reads: "Behold, the righteous shall be recompensed in the earth: much more the wicked and the sinner." This mirrors the *qal vachomer* argument of the prior verse. Peter wrote that **the righteous**, meaning God's people, are **scarcely...saved** or **saved** with difficulty. In order for us as Christians to experience being delivered from sin's power in our day-to-day lives and ultimately enjoy the salvation of our soul-life at the bema for our inheritance, the Son of God had to die. (1 Peter 4:5-6) But what of those who reject the Son. It is with that in mind that Peter wrote, **where shall the ungodly and the sinner appear**? In other words, what shall become of the non-believers? This, of course, is a rhetorical question. If God's people are barely delivered through the Son, those that reject the Son will not be delivered at all.

> 19 Wherefore let them that suffer according to the will of God commit the keeping of their souls *to him* in well doing, as unto a faithful Creator.

The first four chapters of 1 Peter form the main body of the epistle, with chapter 5 providing related closing remarks, like a postscript. Thus, the **wherefore** at the head of 1 Peter 4:19 not only concludes the immediate unit of thought regarding suffering that began at 1 Peter 4:12, but also generally the preceding material. Peter wrote, **wherefore let them that suffer according to the will of God**. Pausing there, we must ask who these people are. And no doubt in this context they are not those that suffered for being a murderer, thief or some sort of criminal. (1 Peter 4:15) Instead, they are those that are "partakers of Christ's sufferings" (1 Peter 4:13), "reproached for the name of Christ" (1 Peter 4:14), and who suffered "as a Christian" (1 Peter 4:16). These all suffered in the line of duty, as it were, for living **according to the will of God**.

Peter's instruction to those courageous Christians was to **commit the keeping of their souls**, that is, their lives or soul-lives, **to** God **in well doing**. In the suffering, Peter wrote, trust your soul-life to God and continue **in well doing** even in the face of persecution. Do not stop what you are doing, but endure and press forward in good works even if it cost you, just like the Old Testament examples of Puah, Shiprah, Nehemiah, and Daniel's three friends Shadrach, Meshach and Abed-Nego. Rely on God's faithfulness to deliver your soul-life! Peter does not here promise physical protection, for the very context assumes the suffering will be experienced. But Peter pressed them to endure with the understanding that their lives are being entrusted to God's keeping for deliverance at the bema where their **well doing** will be richly rewarded.

## Closing

One cannot help but notice that in all Peter had to say about suffering, he never instructed his readers to pray for the suffering to go away. I am not suggesting such a prayer would be inappropriate, but rather, questioning whether our prayer during trials ought to better mirror the reality that Peter taught about suffering. Peter said suffering for Christ is a blessing from God and a reason for rejoicing because of what God is doing in and through us during the trial. King David was beset with trials at different periods in his life and we can learn a great deal from his prayer life. No doubt, he prayed for deliverance, but he prayed for more. In Psalm 61, David cried out in great emotion: "Hear my cry, O God; attend unto my prayer. From the end of the earth will I cry unto thee, when my heart is overwhelmed: lead me to the rock that is higher than I." (Psalm 61:1-2) David prayed for God's leading "to the rock that is higher than I." This was not a prayer for a way out, but for direction to a closer relationship with and increased reliance on God. David saw God as high and exalted over the affairs of mankind, and the place of safety from his enemies was the place closer to God. And so David prayed during his trial to be closer to God, "to the rock higher than I." We have to face the reality that our circumstances may not go away any time soon, but we can live above our circumstances. When our heart is overwhelmed, as David's heart was, it is refocusing on God's promises and provision that takes us to a rock higher than ourselves, higher than our troubles, a place of refuge within the trial.

## Application Points

**MAIN PRINCIPLE:** Christians should face trials, especially suffering for Christ, with rejoicing at what God is doing in and through their lives, looking forward to the return of Christ when his glory is revealed and they share in his inheritance.

## Discussion Questions

1. On what Biblical basis can any Christian teach that those who have "faith" will be financially and physically blessed when Peter taught that Christians should expect to suffer, and that such suffering is the blessing?

2. Thinking back on a trial you faced, how could you rejoice during the trial? After the trial?

3. Why do you think Peter nowhere taught his readers to pray that the suffering would end?

4. In light of Peter's teaching on suffering, what do you think we should pray for when we are in the trial? (see James 1:5 for one idea)

5. In light of Peter's teaching on suffering, how should we pray for other believers when they face trials?

6. How can a person be a Christian and also be a murder or thief? (1 Peter 4:15)

# Chapter 11

# The Enemies of Salvation
1 Peter 5:1-14

In the prologue, Peter introduced the great living hope that everyone who has been born again enjoys. (1 Peter 1:3) His entire epistle centered on the living hope and its implications for our lives. The content of this living hope is the "salvation ready to be revealed in the last time." (1 Peter 1:5) That salvation is not justification, but instead refers to the deliverance of our soul-lives—the temporal experience of our mortal lives—into eternity in the form of our "inheritance incorruptible, and undefiled, and that fadeth not away, reserved in heaven" for us. (1 Peter 1:4) We presently appropriate the outcome of our faith, even the salvation of our souls, as we meet the challenges and decisions of life with faith responses on the basis of the Word of God, and in that way exchange each moment for our share in the inheritance to be revealed when the Lord returns. In this way, how we live now will have continuing significance and value in the world to come. But there are enemies that war against our living by the Book so that we may exchange our soul-lives for our inheritance. The specific enemies Peter addressed were pride, anxiety, and the devil.

## Outline

IV. ENEMIES OF OUR SALVATION (5:1-11)

   a. Lead with humility (5:1-4)

   b. Clothe yourself with humility (5:5-7)

   c. Resist your adversary the devil (5:8-9)

   d. God will bind the wounds of suffering (5:10-11)

V. POST-SCRIPT (5:12-14)

   a. Stand in God's grace (5:12)

   b. Written from Babylon (5:13)

   c. Love and peace (5:14)

## Scripture and Comments

Peter spent four chapters building the theology of our living hope in the salvation of our souls, and how we should live well, and even suffer well, in light of that hope. In this closing chapter, Peter began by addressing an exhortation to elders, and it will become clear that the bottom line of his exhortation was the need for humility. This is not surprising since Peter said so much about submission in various contexts, and submission demands humility.

> <u>1 Peter 5:1</u> The elders which are among you I exhort, who am also an elder, and a witness

of the sufferings of Christ, and also a partaker of the glory that shall be revealed: **2** Feed the flock of God which is among you, taking the oversight *thereof,* not by constraint, but willingly; not for filthy lucre, but of a ready mind.

Peter exhorted **the elders which are among you**, and even though Peter never used the word "church" in his epistle, this exhortation seems to confirm that Peter anticipated his epistle being delivered to local churches. Peter identified himself as **also an elder, and a witness of the sufferings of Christ, and also a partaker of the glory that shall be revealed**. By these words, Peter confirms his being an **elder** like those he was specifically addressing at this point in his epistle, and he no doubt pointed this out to say that he understands the burden and responsibility of that role in a local church. Peter further identified himself as an eyewitness of Jesus' sufferings and **a partaker of the glory that shall be revealed**, meaning that he anticipates a share in the inheritance to be revealed in the last time. (1 Peter 1:5; see also Matthew 19:28) The word **elder** is the Greek *presbuteros* and refers to an office within the local church, and while it is beyond the scope of these notes to build out this concept in detail, it will be helpful to draw some observations from the immediate text and some other New Testament references.

Peter exhorted the **elders** to **feed the flock of God which is among you, taking the oversight thereof**. The verb **feed** is the Greek *poimanō* and means to tend as a shepherd or pastor; it is the verb form of the noun *poimen* which is a shepherd or pastor. Thus **feed** is like "pastoring" and in this context means to instruct the congregation in the Word of God. The phrase **taking the oversight** translates the Greek verb *episkopeō* and means to oversee or manage (the noun form of this word is sometimes translated "bishop"). So what Peter was saying is that the function of the **elder** is both pastoring or shepherding as well as overseeing or managing, within the local church. In Acts 20, Paul called the elders from Ephesus to him in Miletus and referred to them as "overseers" and exhorted them to "feed the church of God." (Acts 20:28) So both Peter and Paul used the term **elders** for the office within the local church with responsibility for pastoring and overseeing.

Peter exhorted **the elders** to carry out their roles **not by constraint, but willingly**. In other words, they should not have an attitude that they are being compelled to do the tasks inherent in their roles as **elders**, but should serve the Lord in this way **willingly**. I have heard testimonies from pastors about their calling where they explained they never wanted to do it but basically God cornered them and thrust the role upon them. Probably they should resign. Peter said to only do the role **willingly**, which is an entirely different mindset than those in the office that insist they never wanted the office. Indeed, Paul wrote: "This is a true saying, If a man desire the office of a bishop, he desireth a good work." (1 Timothy 3:1) Paul anticipated an elder desiring the post. In any event, Peter continued, explaining that **elders** should do their service **not for filthy lucre, but of a ready mind** or eagerness to serve.

Most **elders** today do not make nearly enough money for anyone to accuse them of being in it for the money, although that accusation will still get made by some people under the impression the preacher works 3 hours per week and ought to be paid just for those 3 hours. If anything, those in ministry are usually not paid enough. Many churches demand high levels of formal and expensive seminary education—there is no Biblical basis for that being a qualification for being an elder—but do not want to compensate the position commensurate with experience and education. That said, there are also some people unquestionably in it for the money, who prey upon the flock. Many of them appear on television and run their "ministry" like a 24/7 fundraiser promising blessings and payer cloths to those that give. One of the underlying problems is that in many circles there is little or no regard for what the Bible actually says about ecclesiology (study of the church), and for that reason, the role of the elder or pastor is often distorted, the roles of deacons (who in the Bible have zero authority over the local church) are distorted, and issues of abuse are more prevalent. Where we have guidance, as we do here in 1 Peter 5, we need to follow God's blueprint for church matters.

At this point, we do well to note that Peter's theme is not so much church administration but with what spirit or attitude do the **elders** function in their roles. And it will become apparent in 1 Peter 5:5 that it is a spirit of humility that Peter was most concerned with because **elders** with humility will do what they do **willingly** and **not for filthy lucre, but of a ready mind**. We tend to hear teaching that love is the most important quality for a Christian to have. I will not debate that point, but would say that what gets left out too often is that humility is probably the most significant quality of spiritual maturity. Jesus himself said: "Blessed *are* **the meek**: for they shall inherit the earth." (Matthew 5:5) And of himself said: "Take my yoke upon you, and learn of me; for **I am meek and lowly in hear**t: and ye shall find rest unto your souls." (Matthew 11:29) And at the triumphal entry, we read: "Tell ye the daughter of Sion, Behold, thy King cometh unto thee, **meek**, and sitting upon an ass, and a colt the foal of an ass." (Matthew 21:5) In each of these verses, the term "meek" is the Greek *praus* and has the ideas of humble, gentle, meek, and self-unassuming. For some reason, we may think of "meek" as weakness, a person that lets others run over them, but according to God, humility is not weakness at all, but a needful quality in a leader. We read in Numbers 12:3 that Moses was the most meek man on the planet: "(Now the man Moses *was* very meek, above all the men which *were* upon the face of the earth.)" In the Septuagint, the word *praus* is used to translate this verse.

Humility emphasizes an attitude of the heart that motivated Jesus, and so should motivate us. Yet I would suggest that humility is among the rarest of jewels even among Christians. Paul admonished his disciple Timothy to "follow after righteousness, godliness, faith love, patience, meekness." (1 Timothy 6:11) He similarly instructed his disciple Titus to show "all meekness unto all men." (Titus 3:2) The opposite of this attitude is selfish ambition—the very thing that motivates some "pastors" to do what they do for **filthy lucre**. The Pharisees exemplified this, as Matthew 23:1-12 demonstrates:

> Matthew 23:1 Then spake Jesus to the multitude, and to his disciples, 2 Saying, The scribes and the Pharisees sit in Moses' seat: 3 All therefore whatsoever they bid

> you observe, *that* observe and do; but do not ye after their works: for they say, and do not. 4 For they bind heavy burdens and grievous to be borne, and lay *them* on men's shoulders; but they *themselves* will not move them with one of their fingers. 5 But all their works they do for to be seen of men: they make broad their phylacteries, and enlarge the borders of their garments, 6 And love the uppermost rooms at feasts, and the chief seats in the synagogues, 7 And greetings in the markets, and to be called of men, Rabbi, Rabbi. 8 But be not ye called Rabbi: for one is your Master, *even* Christ; and all ye are brethren. 9 And call no *man* your father upon the earth: for one is your Father, which is in heaven. 10 Neither be ye called masters: for one is your Master, *even* Christ. 11 But he that is greatest among you shall be your servant. 12 And whosoever shall exalt himself shall be abased; and he that shall humble himself shall be exalted.

Jesus taught to do as the Pharisees said but not to follow their example because they act out of selfish ambition. Their actions betray their heart attitudes, and in particular, that they think they are better than everyone else (Matthew 23:4), they do what they do to be noticed (23:5), and to gain accolades and places of honor (23:6-7). They crave titles like "Rabbi" so that they may be promoted higher than another. But critically for understanding First Peter, Jesus concluded his criticism of the Pharisees with this principle: "And whosoever shall exalt himself shall be abased; and he that shall humble himself shall be exalted." (Matthew 23:12) The Greek word *tapeinoō* is the verb that captures idea of the outworking of humility (see Strong's 5012), and it is the word that Peter would use when he explicitly introduced the concept in 1 Peter 5:5.

> 3 Neither as being lords over *God's* heritage, but being ensamples to the flock. 4 And when the chief Shepherd shall appear, ye shall receive a crown of glory that fadeth not away.

Peter continued his exhortation to the elders, that in addition to fulfilling their roles willingly, they should do so **neither as being lords over God's heritage**. In other words, they should not "lord" their authority over others. If you have to demand submission, that is not humility. Unquestionably, the Bible teaches that elders have authority in the local church and her members should submit to that authority, but it is a rookie mistake to believe church members will do what the elder / pastor wants simply because of his title. It has been well said, "If you want to know if you are leading, looking behind you to see if others are following." Leadership in this context is leading sheep (pastoring), not driving cattle. And so Peter wrote, lead by **being ensamples** or models **to the flock**. Lead by example! This type of leadership, in contrast to lording authority over others (to get your way), reflects an attitude of humility with compassion toward the needs of the flock. Remember, Moses was one of the greatest leaders ever; he gave his life to serving others and was humble.

The elders should carry out their service knowing that **when the chief Shepherd shall appear**, they **will receive a crown of glory that fadeth not away**. The word **crown** is the Greek term *stephanos*, which refers to the prize in the games or a symbol of honor, and was essentially a wreath. This is not a diadem, indicating authority. Early in this epistle Peter introduced the issue of our inheritance, and here he made a specific application to the service of the elders in the local church. Their faithful service with the right attitude of humility will result in their receiving a reward (portion of their inheritance presently reserved in heaven) when **the chief Shepherd** Jesus returns.

## Excursus On Engaging the Word With Humility

It is worth briefly contemplating at this point the importance of engaging God's Word with an attitude of humility, and only placing ourselves under teachers and **elders** who do the same in their approach to the Word and how they interact with the flock they are charged with feeding the Word to. So what does humility have to do with engaging the Word of God? Simply put, according to the Bible, proud people are fools, and fools are not teachable.

Paul warned the Romans, "Be not wise in your own conceits." (Romans 12:16) The Proverbs warn, "Seest thou a man wise in his own conceit? There is more hope of a fool than of him." (Proverbs 26:12) In other words, the prideful are worse off than fools. Pride works in pernicious ways in relation to learning the Word of God. Proud people already know and so cannot learn. Paul warned that "knowledge puffeth up" and the proud believe they already have the knowledge they need. (1 Corinthians 8:1) Yet God's Word says that if someone "seemeth to be wise in the world, let him become a fool, that he may be wise." (1 Corinthians 3:18) The Bible learning process requires that we jettison the world's wisdom that we all have as we come into a right relationship with God, then replace such "wisdom" with God's wisdom. But this means admitting there are areas where our thinking is deficient and our conduct is wrong, and it takes humility to do that. It takes humility to be like the Ethiopian, who when asked if he understood what he was reading from Isaiah, said, "How can I, except some man should guide me?" (Acts 8:30)

The Bible says, "Give instruction to a wise man, and he will be yet wiser: teach a just man, and he will increase in learning." (Proverbs 9:9) Wise people are teachable and fools are not. As Christians, no matter how much Bible we may think we know and no matter how much time we have put into diligent study, we must remain humble in order to remain teachable. Some Christians seem to know something of the Bible but they stopped learning long ago and are unaware of it. May that not be us! We must always remain learners, looking to God by His Holy Spirit not only to teach us more, but to correct us in areas where our thinking is not in line with His thinking. We must expect God to use not only those we think are the greatest Bible teachers ever but those we mistakenly assume have nothing to teach us, and indeed, sometimes even our enemies to teach us (there is often a bit of truth in their harsh criticism). Learning should lead to change; to learn we must be willing to let go of bad thinking even where we may have invested time and energy into that bad thinking or passed along our bad thinking to others. We have to be humble or we are done growing.

In addition to learning the Word of God with humility, we must be careful in how we interact with others about the Word, and especially when we take on the role of a teacher. A critical part of the learning process is placing ourselves under good teachers of the Word of God, especially in a local church context. But what constitutes a good teacher of the Bible? Being well-spoken, well-dressed, and confident *do not make* a good teacher, although those are obviously not bad qualities. Good teachers (1) have something to say from the Bible (knowledge), (2) a desire to communicate the Word for the edification of those under their ministry, and (3) are grounded in humility. If there is no humility there, there will be pride. No one is 100% immune from pride, but the Bible teacher that exhibits pride in his words and actions and is oblivious to his pride or embraces his pride is dangerous. This pride may manifest in several ways (I use "he" below for convenience but these comments are not limited to male teachers):

- He is critical of virtually every Bible teacher (especially well known teachers) but usually has one or two in whom he places nearly unbridled confidence.
- He holds beliefs on Bible issues that require nearly every Christian throughout church history to be wrong so that he can be correct.
- He not only has an answer for everything, but will vigorously defend it—there is never room for disagreement.
- He will espouse that there are doctrines about which reasonable people can differ because of limited revelation in the Bible, but in practice he is an island to all but those that agree with him on virtually everything.

- His teaching is monopolized with addressing others' wrong teaching.

- When he is challenged on his view of a Bible passage or verse, he will "move the goal post" by retreating to other Bible verses rather than defending the particular passage at issue or admitting that there may be room for disagreement.

- On social media, he is a "keyboard warrior" who readily spews out unkind words everyone would be embarrassed about if he spoke them from the pulpit or front of the Sunday School room.

- He readily labels a broad range of people or groups as "heretics" or the like.

- He prefers to think those that disagree with him are not saved or are not "real Christians."

- He loves debating.

- He cannot receive criticism.

It is imperative to your Bible learning process that you place yourself under a good pastor and good teachers—those that have something to say, care about your spiritual growth, and are humble. If they are not humble, no matter how articulate they are, run!

## Scripture and Comments

> 1 Peter 5:5 Likewise, ye younger, submit yourselves unto the elder. Yea, all *of you* be subject one to another, and be clothed with humility: for GOD RESISTETH THE PROUD, AND GIVETH GRACE TO THE HUMBLE.

Peter next addressed the church members, but in so doing he made explicit that the issue of **humility** is what he had foremost in mind in the preceding verses addressed to the elders. Peter wrote **likewise, ye younger, submit yourselves unto the elder**. Possibly Peter used **elder** in a non-technical sense, in other words, that the **younger** people in the church should be submissive to the older people in the church in the sense of showing respect. But given the immediate context from the prior four verses and Peter's prior usage of **submit** to mean obey, Peter likely instructed the other churches members, viewed as **younger** in the faith, to **submit** to the church **elders**. Such submission is an expression of the outworking of an attitude of humility. The **likewise** is reminiscent of Peter's prior directives beginning in 1 Peter 2 that his readers submit to God's ordained human government (2:13), that employees submit to employers (2:18), that wives submit to their husbands (3:1), and that the husbands "likewise" dwell with their wives with understanding and give them honor (3:7). But in the more immediate context, Peter used **likewise** to reflect back on the issue of humility addressed to the elders.

Then to **all** of the church members Peter directed that they **be subject one to another, and be clothed with humility**. The word **humility** is the Greek word *tapeinophrosune*, a compound of *tapeinos* (humble) and *phren* (understanding). A willingness to be submissive goes hand in hand with an attitude of **humility**. If **humility** is a hallmark of spiritual maturity—and I would argue it is the most important such hallmark—so is submissiveness. Worldly thinking belittles the thought of being submissive, but the Bible plainly teaches it. An unwillingness to be submissive reflects pride, and this is the greatest internal enemy we face to our spiritual growth and experiencing the salvation of our soul-lives.

With his exhortation to be **subject one to another** and **be clothed with humility** in mind, Peter quoted the principle from Proverbs 3:34 that **God resisteth the proud, and giveth grace to the humble**. The verb **resisteth** is the Greek *antitassomai*, a combination of the prefix *anti* (against) and the verb *tassō* (to arrange). The word means to arrange against or oppose, and can be used in a military sense of arranging troops against an enemy. The word **proud** refers to selfish ambition at its highest level. If our heart attitude is nothing but selfish ambition, we have God against us. The problem, however, is that prideful people always assume God is on their team because they are better than everyone else. In contrast to how God deals with the prideful, He gives **grace to the humble**. This is a special manifestation of His presence, and may be expressed in kindness, mercy, or a special provision for our need at the moment. We read in Hebrews 4:16: "Let us therefore come boldly unto the throne of grace, that we may obtain mercy, and find grace to help in time of need." But if we are prideful, we should not expect to receive of God's grace in our time of need.

> <u>6</u> Humble yourselves therefore under the mighty hand of God, that he may exalt you in due time: <u>7</u> Casting all your care upon him; for he careth for you.

These verses are the application of Peter's prior admonition about humility and pride. Because God resists the proud, Peter exhorted his readers to **humble yourselves therefore under the mighty hand of God, that he may exalt you in due time**. The word **exalt** is the

Greek *hupsoō* and literally means to elevate or raise up (e.g., John 3:14) but has a figurative sense of providing fame, honor, or power. We see this use in James 4:10: "Humble yourselves in the sight of the Lord, and he shall **lift you up**." We humble ourselves and God does the promoting, but prideful people are always self-promoting. Note also that the exalting occurs **in due time** or at the proper time, and that could be when we receive our inheritance. When Jesus' disciples questioned him about their forsaking all to follow him, Jesus said that they would receive authority in his Kingdom, and indeed all that have forsaken things of this world will be rewarded. (Matthew 19:27-30) And in that context, Jesus remarked: "But many that are first shall be last; and the last shall be first." (Matthew 19:30) This pictures believers in the judgment, and Jesus exalts the last and makes them first. Those disciples that served faithfully in humility and did not promote themselves will be promoted by Jesus.

In addition to humbling themselves, Peter encouraged his readers to **cast[] all your care upon him; for he careth for you**. When the trials come our way, and they will, we must **humble** ourselves before God, seeking his grace and **casting** our anxieties **upon him** because we cannot move the needle by wringing our hands in worry. Our own anxieties can keep us so wrapped up in our problems and our interests that we do not clothe ourselves with humility and serve others. Of course, there is a positive and negative to anxiety. The negative anxiety chokes the effectiveness of God's Word in our lives: "He also that received seed among the thorns is he that heareth the word; and the care of this world, and the deceitfulness of riches, choke the word, and he becometh unfruitful." (Matthew 13:22) The positive is Godly concern for the needs of others.

(1 Corinthians 12:25; Philippians 2:20) The negative kind of anxiety is a second internal enemy we must deal with. Like the nation of Israel in the days of Joshua, looking over the Jordan River to the Promise Land, we can either look at the promises of God or stay focused on the River of Impossibility. Sadly, we can waste weeks and years staring at that river and we will still be standing on the wrong side of it. Peter said we must hand our impossibilities to God and be done with it, knowing that God **careth for** us. This care is personalized and individualized. J. Vernon McGee would say, "worry about nothing and pray about everything." (see Philippians 4:6) That makes good sense because God cares.

> 8 Be sober, be vigilant; because your adversary the devil, as a roaring lion, walketh about, seeking whom he may devour: 9 Whom resist stedfast in the faith, knowing that the same afflictions are accomplished in your brethren that are in the world.

Now the third enemy, and this one is external. Peter wrote **be sober, be vigilant**. Peter previously issued the warning to be **sober** in 1:13 and 4:7, in both instances in the context of living in view of the coming return of the Lord and the salvation to be revealed at that time. The word **sober** is from the Greek verb *nephō* and is not used in the New Testament in the literal sense (i.e., not drunk), but is always used figuratively to mean prepared, alert, attentive, well-ordered or disciplined. In 1 Thessalonians 5:6, Paul used the word to indicate spiritual attentiveness: "Therefore let us not sleep, as *do* others; but let us watch and be sober." (see also 1 Thessalonians 5:8; 2 Timothy 4:5) The word **vigilant** is the Greek *gregoreuō* and means to stay awake, but is used here to mean spiritually watchful and on guard (i.e., not asleep at the wheel). The reason to **be sober** and **be vigilant** is that we have an enemy or **adversary**, namely Satan or **the devil**. We are at war!

Whole books are written on the person and strategies of Satan and so we can but scratch the surface here. But we must take seriously that he is an **adversary** or opponent to our spiritual growth, to our clothing ourselves in humility and engaging in faithful service, and to our living a life that results in a rich reward at the bema. Peter urges us to embrace our living hope and live in such a way as to appropriate our inheritance day by day. Satan is against all of that. Note that Peter wrote that Satan is prowling about **as a roaring lion...seeking whom he may devour**, which incidentally is what Satan was doing (see Job 2:2) when he challenged God concerning Job's loyalties. Satan has a great deal of experience and is ever looking for more victims. Make no mistake about it—Peter was warning Christians about the very real possibility that Satan would **devour** them. But what does that mean and what is his strategy?

We need to first understand that the spiritual warfare we are engaged in—whether we realize it or not, we are in a war—has most of its battles fought out in our minds (or hearts). Paul addressed this reality in his second epistle to the church at Corinth:

> 2 Corinthians 10:3 For though we walk in the flesh, we do not war after the flesh: 4 (For the weapons of our warfare *are* not carnal, but mighty through God to the pulling down of strong holds;) 5 Casting down imaginations, and every high thing that exalteth itself

against the knowledge of God, and bringing into captivity every thought to the obedience of Christ.

Notice that Paul acknowledged that we live or "walk in the flesh," meaning in physical bodies, but this "war" is not waged according to human standards. Instead, our weapons are not "carnal" or human weapons, but those weapons are made powerful or "mighty" by God for the purpose of tearing down "strongholds," "imaginations" or arguments, and everything raised "against the knowledge of God." Paul was talking about ideas and philosophies, and that is why he said we must make our thought-life captive so that we obey Christ. Paul similarly wrote to the church in Colossae:

> Colossians 2:8 Beware lest any man spoil you through philosophy and vain deceit, after the tradition of men, after the rudiments of the world, and not after Christ.

Paul sounded the warning with "beware" similar to Peter's warning. Why? Because someone might capture or "spoil" us with a deceitful human "philosophy" according to human traditions and not according to Jesus Christ. To be spoiled is to be taken as a spiritual captive, which is like Peter's notion of being devoured. The point is that our thinking can be train-wrecked by Satanic philosophies so that we become his pawns rather than Jesus' disciples. We can become prisoners of war as our worldview gives way to deception.

So how does Satan take us captive? He is a really good liar: "...for he is a liar, and the father of it" or the father of all lies. (John 8:44) Satan knows how to package the deception, to mix the poison with the punch, so that it is less detectable. Often this involves twisting God's Word, as in the example of the sorcerer Elymas:

> Acts 13:5 And when they were at Salamis, they preached the word of God in the synagogues of the Jews: and they had also John to *their* minister. 6 And when they had gone through the isle unto Paphos, they found a certain sorcerer, a false prophet, a Jew, whose name *was* Barjesus: 7 Which was with the deputy of the country, Sergius Paulus, a prudent man; who called for Barnabas and Saul, and desired to hear the word of God. 8 But Elymas the sorcerer (for so is his name by interpretation) withstood them, seeking to turn away the deputy from the faith. 9 Then Saul, (who also *is called* Paul,) filled with the Holy Ghost, set his eyes on him, 10 And said, **O full of all subtilty and all mischief, *thou* child of the devil, *thou* enemy of all righteousness, wilt thou not cease to pervert the right ways of the Lord?**

Note both that Satan uses human agents to spread his deceptions (here, Elymas) and that the specific means of deception is subtle, contrary to God's standards of righteousness, and a perversion of (making crooked) the "right" or straight paths "of the Lord." This is why there are so many false religions or cults that carry Bibles. It is often easier to deceive by twisting God's Word than outright denying it. Of course, the greatest antidote to this is to actually know God's Word, the very thing Peter exhorted of his audience. (1 Peter 3:15) These human agents may disguise themselves to gain our trust, for even Satan can appear (through these people) as an angel or messenger of light:

> 2 Corinthians 11:13 For such *are* false apostles, deceitful workers, transforming themselves into the apostles of Christ. 14 And no marvel; for Satan himself is transformed into an angel of light. 15 Therefore *it is* no great thing if his ministers also be transformed as the ministers of righteousness; whose end shall be according to their works.

Both Satan and his troops know how to package and deliver the deception, and again, what they deliver is primarily bad thinking, worldly philosophies, and the Bible twisted about. This is why Paul elsewhere urged Christians to "put on the whole armour of God, that ye may be able to stand against the wiles of the devil." (Ephesians 6:11)

> Ephesians 6:12 For we wrestle not against flesh and blood, but against principalities, against powers, against the rulers of the darkness of this world, against spiritual wickedness in high *places*. 13 Wherefore take unto you the whole armour of God, that ye may be able to withstand in the evil day, and having done all, to stand. 14 Stand therefore, having your loins girt about with truth, and having on the breastplate of righteousness; 15 And your feet shod with the preparation of the gospel of peace;

> **16** Above all, taking the shield of faith, wherewith ye shall be able to quench all the fiery darts of the wicked. **17** And take the helmet of salvation, and the sword of the Spirit, which is the word of God: **18** Praying always with all prayer and supplication in the Spirit, and watching thereunto with all perseverance and supplication for all saints.

Paul listed the defenses we have to the spiritual weapons of Satan. Some people have the idea of a red beast with horns and a pitchfork waiting around the next corner, but instead, Satan fires information at us all the time that leaves God out, when we turn on our radio, our televisions, open books, engage social media, and sometimes from pulpits. So Paul said first to have "your loins girt about with the truth," because there is no better way to spot deception than to know the Truth. The old saying rings true: "The best defense is a good offense."

Keep in mind that people can be devoured or captured and not know it. When this happens they proliferate the bad thinking they have. If it is a bad book they picked up at the local Christian bookstore that is contrary to the Bible, they distribute copies to their friends. In one way or another, they start scoring points for Satan, doing his bidding. This may sound extreme, but Paul was quite explicit:

> **2 Timothy 2:24** And the servant of the Lord must not strive; but be gentle unto all *men*, apt to teach, patient, **25** In meekness instructing those that oppose themselves; if God peradventure will give them

repentance to the acknowledging of the truth; 26 And *that* they may recover themselves out of the snare of the devil, who are taken captive by him at his will.

Paul affirmed that Christians can be taken captive in "the snare of the devil" like a hunted animal, and they "are taken captive by him [to do] his will," which of course, is to proliferate the kinds of thinking that leave God out or otherwise exalt itself against the knowledge of the true God. It is possible that through instruction in the truth, God may grant (and He may not) repentance to the captured Christian, meaning a change of thinking back to the truth of God's Word, i.e., "to the acknowledging of the truth."

So the truth of the Word of God matters a great deal in spiritual warfare. We are being constantly bombarded with a philosophy of life contrary to what God tells us. We must saturate our minds with God's thinking. God said in James 4:7: "Submit yourselves therefore to God. Resist the devil, and he will flee from you." But I thought I needed a spiritual warfare seminar? No, we need to submit to God, and this presumes a knowledge of His Word. When we are facing ideas and thinking that is contrary to God's Word, we need to "resist" or reject that thinking. If Satan cannot get a wedge started in our thinking, he will flee. But how does Satan get a wedge started? He knows our weak spots and manipulates our pride. To Eve, Satan (1) denied God's Word by telling her she would not die from eating of the forbidden tree (2) and accused God of withholding because eating of the tree would open her eyes and make her as a god.

Peter wrote that we must **resist** Satan **stedfast in the faith**. Understand that **the faith** is the content of apostolic doctrine and God's Word generally, which presumes knowledge of His Word. We **resist** our deceptive enemy by remaining grounded in the truth of God's Word, **knowing that the same afflictions are accomplished in your brethren that are in the world**. In other words, Peter would have us understand that our **brethren** in Christ everywhere share in our common experience of coming under the attacks of Satan, which is a form of **afflictions** or suffering. We are not alone in the war, and we can minister to one another in this regard. Certainly, we can pray for one another. (Matthew 6:13) And sometimes we may be called upon to minister the Word to another believer to help him or her see their way back to the truth. (2 Timothy 2:23-26)

We need to be men and women of the Book devoted to a knowledge and understanding of the Bible so we can weigh what we hear against what God said. Are you prepared to take a stand against the enemy? Are you prepared to help set others free?

> 10 But the God of all grace, who hath called us unto his eternal glory by Christ Jesus, after that ye have suffered a while, make you perfect, stablish, strengthen, settle *you*. 11 To him *be* glory and dominion for ever and ever. Amen.

With these two verses, Peter brought the body of his epistle to a conclusion with the idea that endurance through the suffering will lead to maturity by the **grace** of **God**. Peter wrote **after that ye have suffered a while**. As Peter maintained throughout his epistle, Christians should expect suffering to come their way, are called to suffering, and such suffering is a blessing. But in time and through the suffering, **the God of all grace....will make you perfect, stablish, strengthen, settle you**. The word **grace** is the Greek *charis* and refers to favor or blessing without regard to what we deserve. Peter referred to **all grace** because God provides **grace** even before we are justified. Indeed, God "maketh his sun to rise on the evil and on the good, and sendeth rain on the just and on the unjust." (Matthew 5:45) God provides **grace** when he justifies (saves) us from sin's penalty. (Ephesians 2:8-9) Indeed, it is by **grace** that He **called us unto his eternal glory by Christ Jesus**, which is likely a reference to having **called us** by the gospel. (1 Peter 1:12, 25; 4:6, 17) And God provides **grace** after we are justified, for as Peter said in 5:5, God "giveth grace to the humble."

Truly, He is the **God of all grace**, and in particular, by His **grace** He will **after that ye have suffered a while, make you perfect, stablish, strengthen, settle you**. The word **perfect** is the Greek *katarizō* and means according to Strong's "to complete thoroughly, i.e., repair (literally or figuratively) or adjust:--fit, frame, mend, (make) perfect(-ly join together), prepare, restore." The word **stablish** is the Greek *sterizō* and means "to set fast, i.e. (literally) to turn resolutely in a certain direction, or (figuratively) to confirm:--fix, (e-)stablish, stedfastly set, strengthen." The word **strengthen** is the Greek *sthenoō* and means "to strengthen, i.e. (figuratively) confirm (in spiritual knowledge and power):--strengthen." And **settle you** is the Greek *themelioō* and means "to lay a basis for, i.e. (literally) erect, or (figuratively) consolidate:--(lay the) found(-ation), ground, settle." As Dr. David Anderson explained this passage in a course I attended on First

Peter, if Peter had been addressing a broken bone, this sequence of verbs would indicate that God set the broken bone, put a splint on it, threw a wrap around the splint, and then gave it time to heal. This makes good sense of God's **grace** for those that have **suffered a while**.

In exuberance at the **grace** of **God** through **Christ Jesus**, Peter said, **To him**, that is, to **Jesus...be glory and dominion for ever and ever. Amen.** In this closing, as in 1 Peter 4:11, Peter thought of Jesus' exalted position and the **dominion** that is his and is to be exercised at the "end of all things." (1 Peter 4:7)

> 12 By Silvanus, a faithful brother unto you, as I suppose, I have written briefly, exhorting, and testifying that this is the true grace of God wherein ye stand. 13 The *church that is* at Babylon, elected together with *you*, saluteth you; and *so doth* Marcus my son. 14 Greet ye one another with a kiss of charity. Peace *be* with you all that are in Christ Jesus. Amen.

In what we might think of as the signature block and post-script to Peter's great epistle, he explained: **By Sylvanus, a faithful brother unto you, as I suppose, I have written briefly...** Elsewhere in the New Testament, **Sylvanus** is referred to as Silas. (e.g., Acts 15:22, 27) He was a prophet (Acts 15:32), a tremendous servant of God early in church history, and he accompanied Paul on his Second Missionary Journey (Acts 15:40). The possibilities for when **Sylvanus** accompanied Peter and thus could have assisted in the writing of the epistle are explored further in the prefatory material in chapter one of this commentary.

Peter's summary of his epistle is of a great benefit to our understanding and interpretation. The epistle was for the purpose of **exhorting, and testifying that this is the true grace of God wherein ye stand**. Peter employed the word **grace** in 1:2, 10, 13, 2:19, 2:20, 3:7, 4:10, 5:5, 10, and here. The word can mean a gift or refer to the blessing, favor or enablement of God. In 1 Peter 1:10, Peter referred to the salvation of the soul about which he wrote as "the grace that should come unto you." And just two verses later exhorted his readers to "gird up the loins of your mind, be sober, and hope to the end for the grace that is to be brought unto you at the revelation of Jesus Christ." (1 Peter 1:13) He said that men and women are "heirs together of the grace of life." (1 Peter 3:7) And later he said that believers should use their talents to minister to one another as "good stewards of the manifold grace of God." (1 Peter 4:10) Peter also called upon us to clothe ourselves in humility knowing that God "giveth grace to the humble." (1 Peter 5:5) And Peter referred to God as "the God of all grace, who hath called us unto his eternal glory by Christ Jesus" and who would through the trials of life mature, establish and strengthen us. It seems best then that we understand that everything we have in Christ Jesus, from being born again to being strengthened in our trials to receiving our inheritance at the Lord's return is of **grace**. It is not merely that we may receive such **grace**, but that we **stand** in that **grace**. And friends, but for that **grace** you could not **stand**. It is God's **grace** that props us up, and as believers our entire lives, now and beyond the grave are in **the grace of God**.

Peter wrote from **the church that is at Babylon**. As addressed in detail in the first chapter of this commentary, this may have been literal **Babylon** or a city close by, but a more likely candidate is Antioch. Peter referred to the **church** from where he wrote as **elected** or chosen **together with you**, using a compound word formed from the familiar adjective *eklektos* addressed at length in the notes on 1 Peter 1:1-2. The **church** Peter wrote from and the churches that would receive his letter were **elected**. While some teach that "election" has to do with picking individuals for salvation, the term *eklektos* is applied in the LXX to a people, animals, trees, and inanimate things, and in the New Testament to Jesus, churches and angels, with the meaning of excellence in quality or being distinguished. Peter was also accompanied at the time he wrote the epistle by John **Marcus**, who he referred to as **my son**, meaning his **son** in the faith. We know that Peter knew Mark or **Marcus** and his family, whose family home was in Jerusalem. Mark likely accompanied Peter at various points in his ministry, and many believe Peter was instrumental in the writing of Mark's Gospel.

Peter closed with a parting request that they **greet one another with a** loving **kiss** or **kiss of charity** and his blessing to them: **Peace be with you all that are in Christ Jesus. Amen**. As he had written earlier in the epistle, Peter wanted the brethren to have fervent love for one another and unity. This great salvation of the soul-life, this living hope we have, should be an enduring motivation for our lives and for how we interact with fellow believers.

## Closing

In the world of computer science, the "garbage in, garbage out" or GIGO principles means that flawed or nonsense input data will produce flawed or nonsense output. The same principal applies in formal logic. That is, an argument is only as good as its premises, and no matter how valid the logic, if any premise is false, then the entire argument is unsound. In other words, garbage in, garbage out. It is no coincidence that Satan's primary area of attack is in the area of ideologies and philosophies. If Satan can get us to accept a philosophy that dispenses with God altogether, or at least minimizes God's role in the affairs of humanity, then He can influence us away from God in our conduct as well. This is GIGO in action. But Satan is smart enough to slide the pills into a drink that masks the poison. He blends truth with lies, but just because a worldly way of thinking lines up with the Bible at a point here or there does not make it a proper Christian way of thinking.

For example, we have an entire field of study called psychology. The word itself is a combination of the Greek terms *psuche*, the familiar word for "soul" that we examined in detail in our study of First Peter, and *logia*, meaning study. But by and large, the field of psychology excludes consideration of the spirit or the immaterial aspect of man. In contrast, the Bible has a great deal to say about the immaterial aspect of man and how that immaterial aspect affects our emotions, thinking and behavior. This is not to say that psychology gets it all wrong, but at the same time, just because psychology aligns with the Bible at points does not make it Biblical. Mainstream psychology and the Bible are on many fronts at odds, and mainstream psychology has had a tremendous influence on our thinking in the United States. In my experience, many evangelical Christians accept, without much consideration, that psychology is "science" and as such trumps the Bible. And this is just one example. Darwinism (or evolution) is another philosophy widely accepted by professing Christians that explains human origins in a way that is inconsistent with the witness of the Bible and completely leaves God out.

The point is that ideas steer people more effectively than the usual weapons of war. Satan's weapons are deceptive ideas. The Bible affirms that Satan is making a play for our minds and as Christians we have to decide what we are going to fill our minds with and what we will do with worldly ideas that conflict with the Bible. Satan's goal is for our thinking to be as minimally God-dependent as possible. That is why Christians are presently being saturated with ideas attacking core issues in the Bible.

## Application Points

**MAIN PRINCIPLE:** Three principal enemies of experiencing the salvation of the soul are pride, anxiety, and Satan.

## Discussion Questions

1. What are the two primary tasks of the office of elder?

2. Can a person be both humble and strong?

3. What directives in First Peter would be difficult or impossible for a believer to comply with if that believer is not humble?

4. In practical terms, what does it mean to cast your cares and anxieties upon God? What would the opposite look like?

5. What are some specific ways Satan uses to influence believers?

6. What are some well-known philosophies that are contrary to the Bible?

# Appendix

# Excursus on the Jewish Concepts of Inheritance and Rest

The place to begin is with Paul's exhortation to the Corinthians that the historical events in the Old Testament concerning Israel are for our spiritual instruction: "Now all these things happened unto them for ensamples: and they are written for our admonition, upon whom the ends of the world are come." (1 Corinthians 10:11) We will consider some Old Testament history and how that history translates into New Testament spiritual principles. To begin with, in the Old Testament, God purposed to build a nation from whom Messiah would come, and God chose to do that through a man named Abram (later Abraham), to whom he promised "a land that I will shew thee." (Genesis 12:1-3) But it was later prophesied to Abram that this new nation would be in bondage for 400 years to another nation before being delivered to the Promised Land:

> Genesis 15:13 And he said unto Abram, Know of a surety that thy seed shall be a stranger in a land *that is* not theirs, and shall serve them; and they shall afflict them four hundred years; 14 And also that nation, whom they shall serve, will I judge: and afterward shall they come out with great substance.

And as the history in Genesis unfolded, Abraham and Sarah had a son named Isaac, who in turn had a son named Jacob (also named Israel), who in turn had sons from whom God developed the 12 tribes of Israel. By God's providence, Jacob's family was removed from Canaan to Egypt. Things started well as God used Jacob's son Joseph to save both Egypt and Jacob's family through a time of famine. The Bible says: "And Joseph died, and all his brethren, and all that generation. And the children of Israel were fruitful, and increased abundantly, and multiplied, and waxed exceeding mighty; and the land was filled with them." (Exodus 1:7) Thus, in Egypt, a family became a nation as God prospered them, but "there arose a new king [pharaoh] over Egypt, which knew not Joseph." (Exodus 1:8) This new Pharaoh, concerned there were too many Jews and that the Egyptians might be at risk, enslaved the Jews. (Exodus 1:9-11) But notwithstanding his best efforts, God continued to bless Israel and the population grew. (Exodus 1:12)

As the history continued to unfold, and as the 400 years drew to a close, God raised Moses to be a deliverer. For our purposes here, the details of Moses' early life are not critical, but what is important is that God called him from the burning bush in Exodus 3 to be God's instrument "to deliver them [the nation] out of the hand of the Egyptians, and to bring them up out of that land unto a good land and a large, unto a land flowing with milk and honey...." (Exodus 3:8) God overcame the "gods" of Egypt through a series of plagues culminating in a plague that would kill "all the firstborn in the land of Egypt." (Exodus 11:5) What occurred with regard to this plague set the foundation for the feast known as the Passover. In this feast, a lamb was sacrificed, its blood placed on the door posts to their homes (Exodus 12:7), and then as God passed through Egypt that night the firstborn were killed of both people and animals unless the blood was placed on the door posts (Exodus 12:12-13). Indeed, this feast would be celebrated even "when ye be come to the land which the LORD will give you, according as he hath promised." (Exodus 12:25) The purpose for keeping the feast thereafter was to be reminded of what occurred that first Passover in Egypt. (Exodus 12:27; Deuteronomy 16:1-3)

The plague on the firstborn resulted in God's people being freed, just as was promised Abraham centuries earlier. Moses led them through the Red Sea and into the wilderness on the way to the Promise Land. To read this history in Exodus and Numbers is to see a people that left Egypt on the basis of the blood (of the Passover lambs) and faith in God's promises. Indeed, we read in the "hall of fame of faith" found in Hebrews 11 that "by faith they passed through the Red sea as by dry land: which the Egyptians assaying to do were drowned." (Hebrews 11:29) These ancient people were believers following the "cloud" of God, having by faith left Egypt and walked through the walls of water as God split the Red Sea ("baptized unto Moses"). They even drank the living water in the wilderness, which was a type of Christ (1 Corinthians 10:4), yet the generation that left Egypt by faith ultimately failed in faith to enter the Promise Land. This particular failure is recorded in Numbers 13-14 and is the background for Hebrews 3-4, which we will reference later in these notes, and the reader is encouraged to read the entirety of Numbers 13-14. For our purposes here, we consider some excerpts below. First, God told Moses to send spies into the land of Canaan:

> <u>Numbers 13:1</u> And the LORD spake unto Moses, saying, 2 Send thou men, that they may search the land of Canaan, which I give unto the children of Israel: of every tribe of their fathers shall ye send a man, every one a ruler among them. 3 And Moses by the commandment of the LORD sent them from the wilderness of Paran: all those men were heads of the children of Israel.

Note that God referred to the land as that "which I give unto the children of Israel." This is, to use the concepts of Hebrews 11 applied to Numbers 13-14, the promise of future blessing by God that should have affected how they live in the present. Moses, of course, obeyed and sent spies into Canaan, including the faithful Caleb and Joshua. But the spies gave wildly contrasting reports. (Numbers 13:26-33) The spies confirmed that God was true when He told them the land flowed with milk and honey. But all the spies except Caleb and Joshua focused on what they saw in the land, i.e., fortified cities and strong peoples that will not leave. In contrast, Caleb said they should go take it at once. It is apparent who was living in the present based on God's promised future blessings, or in Paul's terminology, who was walking by faith and who was walking by sight. Unfortunately, the other spies prevailed upon the people and even warned of giants in the land so that the people of Israel were mere "grasshoppers" before them. The nation had God's promises on the one hand (faith) and the unfaithful spies' report on the other (sight), and they chose poorly. (Numbers 14:1-4)

So here we have the people of God, who saw the plagues fall on Egypt, who in faith placed the blood on their doorposts when the death angel passed over, who in faith left Egypt and fled Pharaoh through the sea, who ate and drank daily from God's provision in the wilderness, now ready to return to slavery in Egypt rather than remain in the care of God because they did not believe they can take the land even though God said it was a done deal. Moses asked God to forgive them and He did, but that did not mean that their rebellion would have no consequences:

> <u>Numbers 14:19</u> Pardon, I beseech thee, the iniquity of this people according unto the greatness of thy mercy, and as thou hast forgiven this people, from Egypt even until now. 20 And the LORD said, I have pardoned according to thy word: 21 But as truly as I live, all the earth shall be filled with the glory of the LORD. 22 Because all those men which have seen my glory, and my miracles, which I did in Egypt and in the wilderness, and have tempted me now these ten times, and have not hearkened to my voice; 23 Surely they shall not see the land which I sware unto their fathers,

neither shall any of them that provoked me see it: 32 But as for you, your carcases, they shall fall in this wilderness.

God forgave them of their rebellion and allowed them to live out their lives in the wilderness enjoying the benefits of His gracious provisions, but they died in the wilderness. Their disbelief resulted in their loss of the privilege of entering into the Promise Land.

To begin to point all of this back to 1 Peter, we must understand that the blessing of entering the Promise Land was frequently referred to as their promised "inheritance" and "rest":

> Deuteronomy 3:18 And I commanded you at that time, saying, The LORD your God hath given you this land to possess it: ye shall pass over armed before your brethren the children of Israel, all that are meet for the war. 19 But your wives, and your little ones, and your cattle, (for I know that ye have much cattle,) shall abide in your cities which I have given you; 20 Until the LORD have given **rest** unto your LORD, as well as unto you, and until they also possess the land which the LORD your God hath given them beyond Jordan: and then shall ye return every man unto his possession, which I have given you.

> Deuteronomy 4:21 Furthermore the LORD was angry with me for your sakes, and sware that I should not go over Jordan, and that I should not go in unto that good land,

which the LORD thy God giveth thee *for* an **inheritance**:

Deuteronomy 4:38 To drive out nations from before thee greater and mightier than thou *art*, to bring thee in, to give thee their land *for* an **inheritance**, as *it is* this day.

Deuteronomy 26:1 And it shall be, when thou *art* come in unto the land which the LORD thy God giveth thee *for* an **inheritance**, and possessest it, and dwellest therein;

Joshua 1:6 Be strong and of a good courage: for unto this people shalt thou divide for an **inheritance** the land, which I sware unto their fathers to give them.

Joshua 1:13 Remember the word which Moses the servant of the LORD commanded you, saying, The LORD your God hath given you **rest**, and hath given you this land.

The generation that was miraculously delivered from Egypt died in the wilderness wanderings, having forfeited through unbelief their inheritance and rest. Indeed, it would be the youth in the wilderness who grew up and were led by Joshua across the Jordan River to take conquest of the Promise Land city by city. Recalling that Paul said these Old Testament events serve to instruct us, we can observe that God's deliverance of His people from bondage in Egypt was made available by the blood of the lambs at that first Passover coupled with their faith in leaving under the leadership of Moses. That deliverance pictures our justification as taught in the New Testament, paid for by the blood of Jesus and appropriated by faith. Paul confirmed the fulfillment of the Passover in Jesus Christ when he wrote in 1 Corinthians 5:7: "For even Christ our passover is sacrificed for us." Similarly, John the Baptizer exclaimed when he saw Jesus: "Behold the Lamb of God, which taketh away the sin of the world." (John 1:29) And to the Romans, Paul wrote: "But God be thanked, that ye were the servants [slaves] of sin, but ye have obeyed from the heart that form of doctrine which was delivered unto you. Being then made free from sin, ye became servants of righteousness." (Romans 6:17-18)

Yet if the Passover and subsequent exodus from Egypt pictured our justification, what of the wilderness wanderings and the subsequent (partial) conquest of the Promise Land? The generation that died in the wilderness forfeited their inheritance and rest in the Promise Land, and that pictures Christians whose lives are not rich toward God and therefore forfeit their inheritance in the world to come (i.e., the Kingdom). But those that entered the Promise Land, which God gave them but they had to appropriate to themselves one city at a time, pictures Christians laboring during their lifetime toward an inheritance and rest in the coming Kingdom. By that laboring, they appropriate the inheritance reserved in heaven for them. That this is the case will become clear as we look to a key passage in Hebrews, then survey some other important New Testament passages.

With the events of Numbers 13-14 in mind, the author of Hebrews set about the task of explaining his concern that his Jewish Christian audience might, in the face of persecution and trials, return to religious Judaism and lose future kingdom blessings. He used the rebellious generation's loss of the right of entering the Promise Land (their rest and inheritance) to illustrate the spiritual truth that remains for Christians today. He began by quoting from Psalm 95.

> Hebrews 3:7 Wherefore (as the Holy Ghost saith, To day if ye will hear his voice, 8 Harden not your hearts, as in the provocation, in the day of temptation in the wilderness: 9 When your fathers tempted me, proved me, and saw my works forty years. 10 Wherefore I was grieved with that generation, and said, They do alway err in *their* heart; and they have not known my ways. 11 So I sware in my wrath, They shall not enter into my rest.)

If you look at Psalm 95 you will not see an ascription of authorship, but of course, as with all of the Bible, the one author is the **Holy Ghost** who recorded the very Words of God for us through the written Word. Psalm 95 is an intense call to worship and praise of the Creator God, and in the midst of the call to worship and acknowledgement that "we are the people of his pasture, and the sheep of his hand," the psalmist beckons the reader of his psalm to hear the voice of God: **Today if ye will hear his voice**. The call is for **today** because we cannot change yesterday and are not promised tomorrow; it is a call with urgency to **hear** God's **voice** and by implication, to respond in obedience. We **hear** the **voice** of God in His written Word (for us today, the Bible) and the Holy Spirit uses that **voice** to change us if we yield to it (e.g., Colossians 3:16, Ephesians 5:18). The psalmist issues the call to obedience **today**, which by implication of the warning that follows is coupled with the promise of a future blessing / rest. At the same time, the Holy Ghost appealed to them not to refuse to hearken to God's Word, after the example of that generation that listened to the spies' report about the giants and did not enter into the Promise Land / rest. He said, **Harden not your hearts, as in the provocation, in the day of temptation in the wilderness**. Of course, this is the sin (disbelief) from Numbers 13-14, for which God forgave that rebellious generation, but they still faced the consequence that they died in the wilderness and did not enter the rest. God said of that **generation** that **I was grieved** and **they do always err in their heart**, and as a result, **they shall not enter into my rest.**

> 12 Take heed, brethren, lest there be in any of you an evil heart of unbelief, in departing from the living God. 13 But exhort one another daily, while it is called To day; lest any of you be hardened through the deceitfulness of sin. 14 For we are made partakers of Christ, if we hold the beginning of our confidence stedfast unto the end; 15 While it is said, To day if ye will hear his voice, harden not your hearts, as in the provocation.

In view of the example in Psalm 95, based on the events of Numbers 13-14, the author warned his audience to **take heed, brethren**. Note that he spoke to them as **brethren**, that is, fellow believers, people who with the author were in the family of God. His warning to his fellow believers was that they not be like the believers in Numbers 13-14 that failed in faith and lost the blessing of entering the rest (land) God had for them. They did not enter because of unbelief, and so he said to **take heed...lest there be in any of you an evil heart of unbelief, in departing from the living God.** His concern was that in the face of the persecution and trials they face, they might turn from Christ Jesus back to Judaism, falling as grasshoppers before giants, as it were. (e.g., Hebrews 10:23-27, 13:10-14) We are reminded that he was writing to believers that were no doubt participants in local church (see also 10:25) when he encouraged them to **exhort one another daily.** Christians are not to shoot their wounded, but to build them up daily, especially in times of persecution or other trials. Just as the call to faith is urgent, so also is the call to build up one another, **while it is called today, lest any of you be hardened through the deceitfulness of sin.** The episode in Numbers 13-14 demonstrates how deceitful sin is that after all of the special revelation, provisions, and signs from God, they not only were unwilling to enter the Promise Land but were ready to return to Egypt. In the same way, the author of Hebrews was concerned that some in his audience may return to the old system of Temple worship and synagogues (their Egypt) and lose out on the future blessings God had for them (typified by the Promise Land). The **deceitfulness** is the idea that you could turn away from Jesus back to the old Judaism without dire consequences.

The author reminded his audience that they were **partakers** (mutual sharers or partners with) **of Christ, if we hold the beginning of our confidence stedfast unto the end.** Just as the generation in the wilderness lost out on the physical rest available to them in the Promise Land at that time, so also would the audience of Hebrews lose out on future blessings if they turn back in disbelief from the teachings of the new order in Jesus Christ. In Hebrews 4, the author explained more about the nature of the "rest" that remains for believers today. But here, he applied the clarion call of Psalm 95 to his audience: **Today if ye will hear his voice, harden not your hearts, as in the provocation.** In other words, **today** hear the revelation of God in His Son of the blessings of the world to come and press on / endure / labor in faith in the now of daily living. The author knew they faced genuine challenges, struggles and affliction, but they paled in comparison to the future blessings God has for them.

> 16 For some, when they had heard, did provoke: howbeit not all that came out of Egypt by Moses. 17 But with whom was he grieved forty years? *was it* not with them that had sinned, whose carcases fell in the wilderness? 18 And to whom sware he that they should not enter into his rest, but to them that believed not? 19 So we see that they could not enter in because of unbelief.

He reminded his audience that **some** in the wilderness, **when they had heard, did provoke: howbeit not all that came out of Egypt by Moses**. In Numbers 13-14, Caleb and Joshua believed God's promise that they would take the land and were ready to enter the rest. Others provoked God in disbelief. And the question was asked, **with whom was** God **grieved forty years? was it not with them that had sinned, whose carcasses fell in the wilderness?** And of course, we know that God was **grieved** with those who accepted the report of the spies that the land could not be taken and rejected not only the urging of Caleb and Joshua, but the promise of God

Himself that the land was theirs for the taking. And as a result of this sin of disbelief, that generation died in the wilderness. God did not allow them to **enter his rest** (the land) because they **believed not** His Word that they would be able to take it. These things, as Paul reminds us in 1 Corinthians 10, are an example to us. The author explained in Hebrews 4 that a rest remained for the people of God if they would labor in faith for it. The alternative for the disobedient believer, as he warned in 3:6 and 3:14, is loss of the future blessings as the partners or companions of Christ in the world to come, a loss of the rest that remains for Christians to labor to enter.

> Hebrews 4:1 Let us therefore fear, lest, a promise being left *us* of entering into his rest, any of you should seem to come short of it. 2 For unto us was the gospel preached, as well as unto them: but the word preached did not profit them, not being mixed with faith in them that heard *it*. 3 For we which have believed do enter into rest, as he said, As I have sworn in my wrath, if they shall enter into my rest: although the works were finished from the foundation of the world. 4 For he spake in a certain place of the seventh *day* on this wise, And God did rest the seventh day from all his works.

As in Hebrews 2:1, 3:1 and 3:7, the author here began with a **therefore**. As described above, the immediate context for this **therefore** was the author's example from Psalm 95 of how the generation in the wilderness lost their inheritance of the land / rest when they believed the spies that said the land could not be taken instead of the promise of God that it was theirs. The life of faith for believers is living in the present based on God's Word, including His promised future blessings. In light of the example of failed faith in Psalm 95, the author issued a warning inclusive of himself: **Let us** (the author and his audience and by implication us) **therefore fear, lest, a promise being left of us of entering into his rest, any of you should seem to come short of it**. Just as the generation in the wilderness lost the promised rest because they did not believe God's promise to give them the land, so also the present generation is at risk of losing their promised **rest**, which obviously is not the same land / rest.

The issue for the generation in the wilderness was not lack of revelation from God. They saw God bring the plagues on Egypt, God led them out of Egypt through Moses with much of Egypt's riches, then made a way for their escape through the Red Sea, led them through the wilderness with a cloud by day and fire by night, and sustained them with food and water in the wilderness. The author explained that **unto us was the gospel preached, as well as unto them**. The term **gospel** simply means "good news" and context must always determine what good news is at issue. Based on the context from chapter 3 that the author was building on, the **gospel** preached to the wilderness generation was the promise that God would lead them to the Promise Land and give them the land to dwell there in security. Of course, God revealed a great deal more to them through Moses, but the promise of future blessing in the land is what was at issue in this context, which is why the author explained that **the word preached did not profit them, not being mixed with faith in them that heard it**. Again, based on chapter 3 and the reliance by the author there on Psalm

95, the good news from God that was not believed and thus **did not profit them** was God's promise that they could take the land. And again, the author drew the parallel to his audience, to whom was also **the gospel preached**. Just as justification (salvation from sin's penalty) was not at issue in the example, it is not under consideration for the current generation, for whom the author already explained were "holy brethren, partakers of the heavenly calling."

This "good news" God delivered in Jesus His Son is that a future rest is promised to Christians as they participate as "partners" (companions or partakers) with Christ (Hebrews 1:9, 3:14). Thus, the author wrote that in contrast to the generation in the wilderness who lost out on the promised rest, **we which have believed do enter into rest**. The verb tense for **have believed** is Greek perfect, indicating past action with continuing consequences (here, the point is they still believe), and it is having believed the fuller orb of the good news revealed in the Son, including the kingdom promises, that is in view. And by continuing to believe those promises, the author did not mean head knowledge or acquiescence but obedience and steadfast endurance (see Hebrews 11). Those who do that will **enter into rest**.

At this point, he began to explain how it is a new rest in view and not the land, by again quoting from Psalm 95: **As I have sworn in my wrath, if they shall enter into my rest**. Note here that the KJV translation is of the same Greek language as in 3:11 but takes a very literal sense ("if they shall enter into my rest") instead of the idiomatic understanding ("They shall not enter into my rest") in reliance on Psalm 95. We need to understand that author was quoting Psalm 95 and the sense is, **they shall not enter into my rest**. Thus, the consequences faced by that unfaithful generation in the wilderness foreshadowed (was a type of the) consequences for his first century audience of what they might lose if they continue down the road of disobedience rather than living in steadfast endurance.

The author then added to this warning, **although the works were finished from the foundation of the world**. Remember that Genesis 1 records six literal days of creation (the description of each day ends with "and the evening and the morning were the... day") and then a seventh day when God ceased his creative activities. This seventh day does not contain the familiar statement that "the evening and the morning were the [seventh] day" because the "day" of rest from creating would not end. Thus, the author quoted from Genesis 2:2, **And God did rest the seventh day from all his works**. His point was that while the "rest" available to that generation of Israel in the wilderness was obviously not available to believers now (we are not being told to enter a physical Promise Land), there was still a "rest" available that partakes in the seventh day rest of God.

> 5 And in this *place* again, If they shall enter into my rest. 6 Seeing therefore it remaineth that some must enter therein, and they to whom it was first preached entered not in because of unbelief: 7 Again, he limiteth a certain day, saying in David, To day, after so long a time; as it is said, To day if ye will hear his voice, harden not your hearts. 8 For if Jesus had given them rest, then would he

not afterward have spoken of another day. 9 There remaineth therefore a rest to the people of God. 10 For he that is entered into his rest, he also hath ceased from his own works, as God *did* from his. 11 Let us labour therefore to enter into that rest, lest any man fall after the same example of unbelief.

The author continued to build on the concept of another type of rest that remains, returning again to Psalm 95 with the phrase, **If they shall enter into my rest**, and again the idiomatic sense from Psalm 95 is, **They shall not enter into my rest**. Since the Psalmist warned his audience of the danger of not entering into **my rest** centuries after the events of Numbers 13-14, the author of Hebrews concluded that a different rest must remain for believers, **seeing therefore it remaineth that some must enter therein**. Concerning the events of Numbers 13-14, **they to whom it was first preached entered not in** the rest **because of unbelief**, namely that generation did not believe God's message that the land was theirs to take. Yet after these events, God **limiteth** or fixed **a certain day, saying in David** (this may mean David wrote Psalm 95 or may simply being referencing the Psalter as **in David** since he wrote so much of the Psalter), **To day**, after so long a time. Again, the point was that the call to hear the voice of God **To day** came centuries after the events of Numbers 13-14, meaning that the call to God's rest remains. Thus, the psalmist made the call to enter God's rest to people who could not possibly enter in the same way as those of Numbers 13-14 (i.e., entering the Promised Land physically since they were already there), indicating that a different rest remains, **To day if you will** hear his voice, harden not your hearts. The author made the point that if Joshua (note that **Jesus** is the Greek equivalent of the Hebrew name Joshua, and contextually here Joshua is indicated) **had given them** the **rest** that remained in view in Psalm 95 when he led the people into the Promise Land centuries earlier, **then** the psalmist in Psalm 95 **would... not afterward have spoken of another day**. And the necessary conclusion is that **there remaineth therefore a rest to the people of God**, and that rest remained available to the audience of Hebrews, and by application, to us **today**.

The message to the Hebrews and to us is that **he that is entered into his** (God's seventh day) **rest...hath ceased from his own works, as God did from his**. With this, the author tied the instruction on **rest** to the larger argument that is the thrust of the entire book of Hebrews, namely a call to believers who are experiencing adversity and trials to continue in steadfast obedience with a view to a future when the trials are past and blessings come. Nowhere in the Bible are Christians promised an easy life, nor is it taught that sufficient faith guarantees material or physical blessings during our earthly sojourn. Rather, the Bible presents the reality that the Christian life will have trials (e.g., James 1:2-4; Romans 5:3-5, 8:18; 2 Corinthians 1:5-7) and the faith / life God calls us to is maintaining steadfast endurance and obedience now in view of the reality (or confident hope) of God's promised future blessings (e.g., Hebrews 3:6, 14). Or in the language at hand in this passage, we are to **work** now (steadfast endurance and obedience) so that we can enjoy God's seventh day **rest** (blessings) later. The seventh day rest lost to humanity in the Fall is made available again in Christ. Thus, he exhorted them, **Let us labour** (work) now **therefore to enter into that rest** that remains.

If salvation from sin's penalty (justification) were in view, then the instruction would be to earn your justification by works. When we read verses like this it is critical that we read in view of the immediate and larger context of Hebrews, a message to believers facing adversity who are tempted to fall back into Judaism. Justification is not in view here, but instead, the author stressed the relationship between living in steadfast endurance and obedience now and their enjoyment (or forfeiture) of future blessings. And thus the admonition to these believers was to **labour** (endure in obedience in this life) **lest any man fail** or forfeit their rest **after the same example of unbelief** as the generation of Israel in Numbers 13-14. That generation of believers was forgiven and sustained by God throughout their lives but forfeited the physical rest of the Promise Land God offered. So we may summarize, "God promises that if you live a life of steadfast endurance and obedience you will inherit future blessings (rest), but if you do not steadfastly endure you will forfeit the future blessings." The wandering in the wilderness pictures forfeited rest (inheritance), while the generation that entered the Promise Land pictures an inheritance obtained.

# About the Author

HUTSON SMELLEY resides in Houston, Texas with his wife and children. He holds advanced degrees in mathematics, law and Biblical studies, and is an adjunct professor at the College of Biblical Studies. He can be contacted at: proclaimtheword@mac.com

www.proclaimtheword.me

www.ingramcontent.com/pod-product-compliance
Lightning Source LLC
LaVergne TN
LVHW051726080426
835511LV00018B/2907